£1.99

EQUITY
AND TRUSTS

D1826291

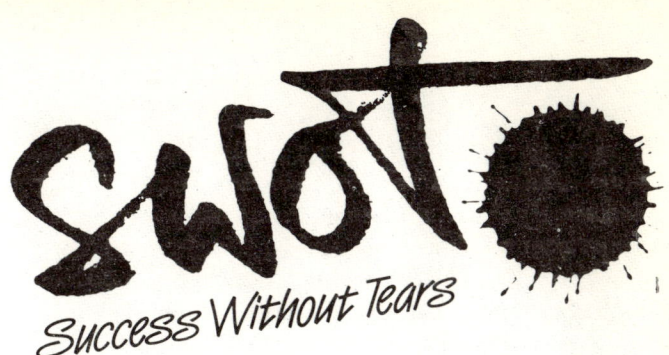

SWOT

Success Without Tears

EQUITY AND TRUSTS

THIRD EDITION

PAUL TODD, MA, BCL
Cardiff Law School, University of Wales

Series Editor C.J. CARR, MA, BCL

BLACKSTONE
PRESS LIMITED

This edition published in Great Britain 1991 by Blackstone Press Limited, 9–15 Aldine Street, London W12 8AW

Previously published by Financial Training Publications Limited

© Paul Todd, 1986
First edition, 1986
Second edition, 1989
Third edition, 1991

ISBN: 1 85431 151 4

British Cataloguing in Publication Data
A CIP catalogue record for this book is available from the British Library

Typeset by Kerrypress Ltd, Luton
Printed by Loader Jackson Printers, Arlesey, Beds

Cartoons drawn by Anne Lee

CONTENTS

Contents

PREFACE

This is not intended to be another introductory trusts textbook. If you want a conventional textbook on the subject there are plenty to choose from, in varying degrees of clarity and detail (and price). In common with other books in the series its purpose rather is to help students who have already embarked on a study of the law of trusts (or equity and trusts) to succeed as well as possible in examinations in the subject, at degree or equivalent level.

Unlike normal textbooks, therefore, this book concentrates primarily on the exam process itself, and though the substance of the subject is by no means relegated to second place, you will not find here an overview of equity and trusts in the didactic style that textbooks usually adopt.

It does not follow that this book is aimed at the weak student. Far from it. Under-performance in exams is just as likely to pull a student down from an upper to a lower second as it is to pull a weaker student down from a pass to a fail.

Concentration on assessment is easier with trusts than with most other subjects, first because it is nearly always assessed entirely by three-hour unseen examination, with no element of course work assessment, and secondly because there is relatively little variation in trusts courses taken in universities, polytechnics and colleges throughout the country.

Whether or not you approve of this is neither here nor there. Success at exams depends on understanding and beating a system, and whether or not it is a good system is of no consequence whatever. Nevertheless, it must be understood that the exam process is the way it is for a reason, and you have to understand that reason before you can succeed to the best of your ability.

Nobody would suggest that you can succeed at exams without a sound grasp of the subject. But every university teacher is familiar with students who apparently under-perform disastrously in exams. Such students work hard and attend classes diligently, only to produce an examination performance which fails to do justice to their effort or ability. Indeed, I believe that the *majority* of students under-perform, at least to some extent.

This may seem surprising given that trusts is rarely if ever a first-year subject, and is probably most frequently studied in the third year. Students of trusts therefore already have considerable experience of university or polytechnic exams, in addition to O and A levels for home students, and whatever the equivalent is for overseas students. Yet it is by no means uncommon for people who have succeeded admirably in all exams up to their third year at university or polytechnic, for some reason to get their final exams hugely out of proportion, and forget all the exam techniques earlier learned.

The reason for poor achievement is usually rooted in failure to appreciate the purpose of exams, without which appreciation it is impossible to acquire the skills necessary for a creditable performance. This book seeks to remedy that, and the first chapter is directed to an examination of the exam process itself. Only once you have understood the system can you hope to beat it, and chapter 2 is about working during the course to achieve that aim. The rest of the book deals with the substance of the subject, the emphasis again being directed towards success at exams.

How then in detail does this book differ from a conventional textbook? There are three main ways. First, it is assumed that you are already a student of trusts (or equity and trusts), and so there is no need for material which is purely introductory, or setting the scene. Secondly, not all subjects are covered, but rather the material is selective. Thirdly, each substantive chapter is directed primarily towards the type of question you might get in an exam (including some real exam questions). There is no attempt at model answers as such, because individual styles can legitimately differ widely, but instead each section considers what an examiner might be looking for. Exam questions (if well set) are drafted with a specific purpose in mind, and if you are to succeed you must appreciate what that purpose is.

I have said that the book is selective, and indeed, the more arcane aspects of the subject are not covered in this book at all. All the really central areas *are* covered, however (i.e., the areas which will almost certainly appear in any exam). Also, because examiners tend to concentrate on areas where there have been important new developments, I have included these as well. This is the justification, for example, for chapter 10 (which is new to this edition).

On the other hand, because no attempt has been made to cover the whole of the law of equity and trusts, it has been possible to go into considerably more detail than would be possible in a conventional textbook of this length: this is not intended to be merely an introductory textbook.

I should like to thank my wife, Dr Pauline Todd, for the very substantial assistance she has given me in writing this book. Virtually everything that appears in this book I have discussed at length with her, and though she by no means agrees with everything I have written, two minds on any academic matter really are much better than one. Indeed, if you can find anyone as long-suffering with whom to discuss your work, I would strongly advise it.

Paul Todd
University of Wales College of Cardiff

ONE

PREPARING FOR EXAMS

A myth frequently perpetuated is that some people just cannot do exams. This is simply untrue, though undoubtedly many students under-perform, simply because they fail to appreciate the purpose of examinations, and therefore do not prepare themselves properly for them.

For example, the number of people who revise for exams without studying and working through sample questions, and past papers, never fails to astonish me. Perhaps they think they have too little time. They prefer instead to bury themselves in the same old notes day in day out, without giving a moment's thought to what is actually the aim of the exercise. You have to work towards the specific goal, or study becomes aimless and inefficient. If instead you choose, as many students do, to revise in a vacuum, without considering in detail the final purpose of that revision, much of the work will be wasted.

'buried in notes'

The most depressing feature of all for university and polytechnic teachers is how stringently so many students resist all advice about preparing for and sitting exams, preferring to play 'safe' and bury themselves in their well-worn notes instead. In fact playing 'safe' is usually the worst possible course, virtually guaranteeing failure to perform to the full extent of one's ability.

Let us consider, then, what exams are for, and what examiners are testing for. Only then will it be possible to study effectively towards them.

Why exams, in equity and trusts in particular?

This is not the place to argue over the merits of the various different methods of assessment, but it is noteworthy that, unlike many other subjects, equity and trusts is almost invariably assessed by traditional three-hour unseen exam. Coursework assessments, or assessed essays, rarely if ever play any part. This is not accidental. There are some skills which can only really be assessed by unseen exam, and once you have appreciated what they are then you will have gone a long way towards appreciating also what examiners in equity and trusts are looking for.

An obvious difference between exams and the other methods of assessment is that memory plays at least a small part in exam success. Yet contrary to general belief, exams at degree or equivalent level are not primarily a memory test, especially where higher marks (e.g., upper second and first class marks) are at stake. At that level at any rate, their *primary* purpose is to test your understanding of the main principles of the subject, and your ability to apply them to a given situation. Even at lower levels, for example at the third class and pass degree levels, exams still serve this purpose, although obviously a lower level of understanding only needs to be demonstrated, whereas conversely, memory probably plays a greater proportionate role.

Especially at the higher levels, then, it is not enough merely to memorise the main principles of the subject, something which, at any rate in equity and trusts, is relatively easy to do: not only are the principles old and well-established, but some have been codified into the 12 equitable maxims, and even those that have not (e.g., 'equity will not allow a statute to be used as a cloak for fraud'), have been reduced into a form that is similar to that of the 12 established maxims. What is being tested is your understanding of these principles, and your ability to apply them to real-life situations. That is, of course, the rationale of any problem question, but even a well-drafted essay question ought to be capable of testing the same skills.

This of course requires you not only to remember but also to analyse the main principles of the subject, to ascertain their exact meaning and extent, and how far they apply. You are also being tested on your ability to advance legal arguments, and master those advanced by others. Thus your technique in distinguishing cases, recognising *rationes* and *dicta*,

assessing the weight of an authority, and applying the principles stated
in the cases, are all subject to assessment.

Where will you find the material to enable you to do this? The answer
is, primarily in the cases themselves (after all, that is where the main principles
of the subject are in fact analysed, and applied to a real-life situation).
I have often been surprised, during nearly 15 years of teaching, how reluctant
students are to read cases. If I suggest to a student that a case should
really be read, the student will almost invariably respond by asking me
to summarise it, or to repeat what I said about it in my lectures, or where
he or she can find it in a textbook, or whether it is acceptable merely
to read the headnote. Almost anything, it seems, is preferable to reading
the case itself. And these are not first-year students, since trusts at Cardiff
is almost exclusively taught as a final-year subject. Yet once you know
what you are looking for, cases are no more difficult to read than lecture
notes or textbooks (and they are usually far more interesting). And the
plain fact is, that in order to do really well in trusts exams, you need
to read the *judgments* of the most important cases (and there are not that
many really important cases), and think hard about them.

This important aspect of preparing for exams is too often overlooked
by students, many of whom instead concentrate on learning textbook-style
general statements. No doubt it is possible to *pass* the exam on that basis,
and even (possibly) to obtain a lower second-class degree, but if you are
aiming for a higher mark than about 55% you need to show more than
the ability merely to memorise textbooks. (I am assuming, by the way
that 55% is in the middle of the lower-second class. It is at Cardiff, and
in most other universities and polytechnics, but I believe that Oxford, for
example, still adopts a letter-based system of marking. 55% would probably
translate to around β– at Oxford.) To obtain more than about 55% (which
is about the average mark for most university courses), you obviously need
to demonstrate that your level of understanding is greater than that of
the majority of your colleagues. Remember that what is being tested is
an understanding of legal reasoning, rather than legal knowledge *simpliciter*.
In trusts, which is not to any great degree a statute-based subject, this
means the ability to analyse the primary source materials, which means
the main cases.

I hope to show in this book that learning and revising through the cases
is not particulary difficult, and is more interesting than concentrating instead
on textbooks and lecture notes. Of course it is possible to gear one's revision
around textbooks and lecture notes, and if you choose to do that, and
also look at past papers so that you have some idea what will be coming
up, you may well get by perfectly adequately, since only at the upper levels
of achievement is a more detailed understanding required. Remember,

though, that if you adopt this approach exclusively, as apparently many students do, you are almost certainly *limiting* your maximum mark to around 55% (or β– at Oxford). In addition, revising will be very boring, and there is a good chance that you will substantially under-achieve.

Assuming, though, that you are prepared to abandon the rote learning approach in favour of something more interesting (and rewarding), how do you go about it? Let us be clear about this. There is no need to know about every case that is remotely relevant to an area, and in any case time constraints will certainly prevent this. Rather, you should aim to know the most important cases (and there are no more than about half a dozen in each area) really well, even if less important authorities escape you. If a case stands for a major point, you ought to know in which court it was decided, what view has been taken of it in later cases (has the principle been limited or extended?), and whether there were dissenting judgments. Even if the result was unanimous, the reasoning (if more than one judge) may not be.

A good example is the unanimous Court of Appeal decision in *Binions* v *Evans* [1972] Ch 359, considered in chapter 6. Lord Denning MR's reasoning is quite different from that of the other two judges. Change the facts of *Binions* v *Evans* a little and he would reach a different result from them. A really good exam problem will aim to test whether you can apply the different reasoning, say, of Lord Denning MR and Megaw LJ. The least able students, however many revision notes they have learned up, will fail *even to see the main point of the problem*, for which nearly all the marks above about 55% will probably be given. They will have spent too much time on their revision notes, and too little time in reading this most important case in the detail it deserves.

Another good example is *Re Baden's Deed Trusts (No. 2)* [1973] Ch 9, another important and unanimous Court of Appeal decision (considered in chapter 4), where all three judges reasoned by totally different routes. The problem question considered in that chapter makes clear why it is important to have read all three.

There are a number of cases, then, where it really is necessary to read, *and think about*, the entire case. Cases of this nature, which develop important points of principle, are not all that numerous, and it is not necessary to adopt the same approach to every single case on the course. Remember always that the aim is to demonstrate a good grasp of principle, and not, for example, that you have a voracious memory.

It does not matter unduly, for example, if details like the name of a minor case, or section of a statute, are forgotten, so long as the mistakes are not so serious as to show a misunderstanding of principle. Some mistakes, apparently of memory, it is true, do make examiners suspicious, but they are not really mistakes of memory at all. It is not unreasonable to assume that '*Bordman* v *Fips*' suggests that the case has never been read at all, or that anything has ever been read about it. '*Re Vickery* (1919)' also suggests a major misunderstanding, because the decision in that case depends upon legislation which was enacted in 1925.

Conversely, no amount of memorising detail will compensate for the inability to see the point of a rule, or to apply it to answer the question set. Understanding, then, is the foundation of examination success. This is the primary ability (especially at the higher levels) which an examination sets out to test, in conditions where the student has only his or her own resources to draw upon.

If memory is relatively unimportant, then, why assess by unseen exam rather than, for example, a series of essays written at leisure? Unfortunately, it is not at all easy to assess understanding of a subject by essays. Often essays have to be submitted during the course, before all the principles of the course have been grasped. Even if that problem is overcome, so many essays are heavily reliant on source materials and reveal little of the student's true ability. Further, it is impossible without a *viva voce* examination to be certain that the work submitted is really the student's own. I am not suggesting deliberate cheating, but a line of reasoning may appear, for example, without the writer necessarily understanding all the stages, or even the meaning of all the words used. *Viva voce* exams can pick this up, by the device of asking the student to explain the reasoning, but they are both subjective and labour intensive.

The main justification for exams, then, has nothing to do with memory, but is simply that they are the most efficient method of assessing whether you have a genuine grasp of the principles of the subject, and are able to apply those principles to the given fact situation in a problem type of question. That is what you must show, therefore, to attain the highest marks.

A second justification for testing understanding rather than memory is that the exams are only the first step in (hopefully) a long professional career, and the skills required, whether in the legal or any other profession, are not unlike skills required to succeed at exams. In your professional career, you will be very lucky indeed if your clients are so obliging as to arrange their problems to match perfectly the details of the cases which you so laboriously memorised as a student. An understanding of principle, and an ability to reason by analogy, will be essential when you give professional advice. Time and again you will be faced with demands for concise and logical opinions on points of law, often in an embarrassingly short time, and you will be expected to deliver the goods, headache that particular afternoon or not. People who succeed at exams can do all of these things. It is perhaps not surprising, then, that the professional bodies regard with suspicion attempts to replace exams with alternative forms of assessment.

Now that the true purpose of exams has been revealed, and is no longer shrouded in mystery, it is possible to direct more positive efforts towards preparation for them. Remember that they are not primarily a memory test, but that to succeed you must have a sound grasp of the principles of the subject, and you must be sufficiently flexible to be able to apply your understanding, under pressure of time, to a wide range of situations.

Sitting the exams

By your second or third year of study it should not be necessary to remind you to ensure that you are thoroughly familiar with the times and places of your exams well before they occur, though it is surprising how often students even in their third year fail to turn up to exams because they have mistaken the day or the place.

It is important to examine the rubric. Make special note of how many questions you are required to answer, and whether there is any restriction on choice (e.g., 'at least two of which must be from section B'). Never make assumptions based on past papers. This paper may be unique, and the consequences of getting it wrong are too serious to take any risks.

Exam boards vary in the way they deal with candidates who answer too many questions, or questions from the wrong sections. It is quite possible for questions answered from the wrong section to be scored at zero, which is nearly always disastrous, though sometimes a more lenient approach is adopted, the question being marked subject to a penalty (e.g., being dropped a class). If you answer (say) five questions instead of four, your best four may count, but it is probably more common to count only the first four, and ignore the fifth. But whether a lenient approach is adopted or not, some penalty is inevitable, quite apart from the tactical disadvantage of giving the examiner the idea that you may be stupid!

Answering less than the required number of questions is even more risky, in fact normally disastrous, but surprisingly common. It is worth remembering that a typical system of marking gives each question 70%+ for a first, 60–9 for a higher second, 50–9 for a lower second, 45–9 for a third, with a pass mark of 40. Usually the mark for the paper is based upon the average of the marks for each question. It may not actually end up as the average, since the examiner may be allowed, or even required, to assess the paper as a whole, but the average will almost certainly be the starting point for this assessment, and it is unlikely that the final mark will differ significantly from the average of the marks for each question.

I should perhaps point out that no marking system is universally adopted, but this one, or minor variations of it, is probably the most common.

It is quite easy to score a pass mark on a question, but very difficult to score a first, and virtually impossible to score above about 75%. It therefore follows that the first 40 marks are much easier to obtain than the next 30, and indeed marks become progressively more difficult to obtain as you go higher up the scale (especially, as already explained, above about 55%). So if you have written three decent answers and are stuck for a fourth, it is much more sensible to have a shot at the fourth, even if you are really short of time, than to spend time in trying to improve the answers you have already written. It would be difficult to raise their quality by (say) an extra 30% (that is 10% or a whole class on each question), but relatively easy to coax the examiner into awarding you 30% on the fourth question, even if you are really stuck, especially as he or she will probably sympathise if your other answers are good.

On the other hand, by answering (say) three questions where four are required you will reduce your overall mark by a quarter which, because of the relatively high pass mark, is substantial. Suppose that your three score 60% each (i.e., respectable higher-second answers). Your mark for the paper is 180/4, or a miserable 45% (a bare third). If your marks on the three questions were 50% each (still a decent mark), your average will actually fail you overall (37.5%). Yet I have seen this happen over and over again, presumably because students are unaware of the importance (in all but exceptional cases) of the average mark, and do not appreciate how much more difficult marks are to obtain towards the top of the scale. You should appreciate these points, and never answer less than the required number of questions.

Suppose you have run yourself short of time towards the end. One of the skills for which you are being tested is your ability to argue in English prose, and indeed it is difficult to advance legal arguments fully in any other form, but as a last resort note form is better than nothing. So long as you do this only towards the end of the final question you will probably not lose too many marks (but avoid at all costs the temptation to write 'short of time' in the second question and to carry on in note form from there on).

On the answers themselves, remember that understanding rather than memory is being tested. Therefore the organisation of the answer is more important than the total amount of material contained in it. The most important attribute is the ability to reason logically, and above all clearly. It is a good idea, therefore, to structure your answer in rough before you start, making a note of important points and cases in case you forget them later. Make full use of short paragraphs (perhaps three to a page), each of which make a distinct point, and make it clear where each paragraph begins and ends, even to the extent of leaving a line between paragraphs. Shoulder headings and diagrams can also be useful, but some examiners do not like these, so try to find out what your examiner's prejudices are if you can.

Of course a first-class script will include a great deal of material (none of it repetitive) in addition to being well organised. A surprising number of good-second scripts, however, are quite short, relying on clarity of presentation and cogency of argument. Conversely, huge quantities of repetitive and unconnected waffle will be penalised. Once you have a sound structure you can build on it, but the structure itself must take top priority.

Problem questions will usually contain more points than any candidate will spot, and indeed even the examiner may not have appreciated all the ramifications, so do not despair simply because you think you may have overlooked something. A far more serious (but very common) mistake with this type of question is where a candidate sees the central point of the problem but avoids it. Commonly this will be a murky area of law, where there is quite simply no clear answer. The candidate writes something like 'The law in this area is very confused', and then moves on.

I still find it difficult to believe that so many people commit this error year after year. Often the candidate is one whom I know to be intelligent and to be aware of the issues involved, but who cannot have given any thought to what the exam is all about. A typical problem is set with a handful of important cases in mind, where though the decisions themselves may be clear enough, the extent to which the reasoning applies is not. The facts of the problem will be deliberately chosen so that no authority clearly applies, though the reasoning of a number might. Favoured cases for this treatment typically contain a number of judgments, all different (like *Binions* v *Evans* or *Re Baden's Deed Trusts (No. 2)*, mentioned in the previous section), the application of each of which to the particular problem would lead to a different result.

The *whole point* of such a problem is to test your ability to handle legal arguments, and application of principles and authorities, where the law itself is uncertain. The conclusion you reach is far less important than the quality of the argument. After all, there *is* no correct answer, though you should generally express a preference. A great number of marks will be allocated to this particular test, so you *must* have a go at it. The student who avoids the issue in the way described above is throwing marks away, and the most frustrating part about it is that often he or she knows of the authorities in question.

This is a classic example of the pitfalls of burying yourself in notes rather than gearing yourself up for the exam itself. Further, your notes will not usually provide the material and ideas necessary to deal with this type of question, which is probably why so many people avoid the issue.

Now some small points. Never waste time by rewriting the question. Not only will this not score any marks (it will almost certainly be simply crossed out), but it is quite likely to annoy the examiner, because it looks like bluff. And never joke — it is very difficult to amuse an examiner!

When the paper is over avoid at all costs the pointless exercise of the post-mortem. It is almost invariably depressing, and in any event your mind should be turning towards the next exam. You can do something about the exams to come, but nothing at all about the exams you have finished. Further, any other candidate who tries to involve you in this exercise should be scrupulously avoided. Indeed, if your circle of friends includes people outside your own course seek them out after the exam, and shun those who are on your course.

There is only one excuse for a post-mortem, and that is when you think it likely that a *viva voce* exam may be required. Even here, though, wait until the other exams are over, since the *viva* will usually not take place until considerably later.

Your performance in the exam may have been adversely affected by illness or some domestic difficulty. Exam boards vary as to the extent these are taken into account, but many boards take a sympathetic view, at least if you are on a borderline. But no board can act in the absence of knowledge, so if you are ill get a medical certificate, and if there are other difficulties make sure the faculty or department office (or whoever is the appropriate person) is informed, so that they can be taken into account as appropriate.

Revising

One of the saddest, but apparently inevitable aspects of the examination run-up is the almost universal practice of students to revise in the manner least likely to lead to examination success. Every year the majority of students guarantee that they will perform at less than their full capability. Every year sensible advice on how to revise effectively is steadfastly ignored. It is the playing-safe mentality coming to the fore again, which is in fact the most dangerous way to play.

Consider what happens. Several weeks before the exam it suddenly becomes possible to find seats in the library again. The university empties, candidates shutting themselves away in their residences, or at home. They have 'finished' the course, and need use the library no more. All the information they now need is contained in their notes, possibly combined with the main textbook recommended for the course. All that is necessary,

surely, is to rewrite the notes in a more comprehensible form, and learn
them up for the examination.

Also, as the exams loom closer stress builds up, more hours are spent
beavering away in this manner. Balanced life-styles are thrown into turmoil
as recreations, and even meals, are cut out. Weekends vanish. Eight hours
a night of sleep are condensed at both ends. Worse still, pep pills or other
evil and noxious substances are taken to boost performance on the great
day.

Not only does this show a fundamental misunderstanding of what exams
are all about, and what examiners are looking for, but it also ensures that
the revision itself is done in the most boring, and therefore least efficient,
manner possible.

In fact, many candidates during this time seem to forget that they are
working towards an exam at all. Revision becomes an abstract exercise.
'These notes must be learnt. No time to worry why.' Few even look back
over the past papers, and gear their learning towards the particular types
of question that are likely to arise. Of course, in some subjects past papers
can be of little use, if, for example, the syllabus or examiner has changed
recently, but this is unlikely to be the case in trusts, where variations between
courses and types of exam are not usually great.

Always work towards the exam. That is the entire purpose of revision.
Immerse yourself thoroughly in past papers, perhaps even to the extent
of practising answering some of them under simulated exam conditions.
Whether or not this is worthwhile depends on the time available, as it
is a time-consuming exercise, but at the very least consider how you would
structure an answer on the types of question you think most likely to arise,
or on the areas in which you are most interested. Consider also what the
examiner is looking for in the question, especially in problem questions.

Should you try to spot questions? There are pros and cons. The advantage
is that by reducing breadth of coverage (assuming there will be a reasonable
choice of questions) you can increase depth of coverage, and develop real
expertise on some parts of the course.

The disadvantage of question spotting is obvious, that there is an element
of risk involved. The predicted questions may not come up. Also, questions
often contain issues from more than one area. For example, take the
following question:

'Equity will not permit a statute to be used as a cloak for fraud.' Discuss.

This question does not confine itself conveniently to any self-contained
area of the course, and shows up well the penalties of concentrating too
narrowly during exam revision. This question encompasses a number of

separate areas, certainly at least secret trusts (chapter 7), part performance (chapter 5) and some of the material considered in chapter 6, so it would be unwise to attempt it unless you are reasonably confident about a substantial proportion of the syllabus.

Alternatively, you may be faced with a question involving an imaginary will containing various dispositions, all of which may be invalid, but for a variety of reasons. One disposition may infringe the rule against perpetuities, another may attempt to create a charitable trust which for some reason fails, another may attempt to create a private purpose trust, or make a gift to an uncertain class of objects, and so on.

A number of examples of problems which cover a number of areas can be found at the beginning of chapter 8, and questions of this type may possibly defeat the question spotter. On the other hand, some areas pretty well always appear, and some areas are more likely to go together in the same question than others. For example, a question primarily on private purpose trusts often also involves points on unincorporated associations, charities, or certainty of objects, but would be unlikely to include anything on trustees' duties to invest, or accumulation of income. So a limited degree of question spotting is probably advisable, but with caution.

Suppose you have to answer four questions out of 10. It would be very foolish to pick on only four areas, but probably quite sensible to concentrate your efforts on a little over half the course. At least that way you should be able to achieve one or two really good answers. But concentration on one half should never be to the total exclusion of the other half. In the first place, you should have a sufficient smattering of the entire course to be able to spot if an area you have neglected arises as part of a question. Then it might be advisable to avoid that question (e.g., if a perpetuity point arises incidentally, and you have largely neglected that area). Secondly, if your predictions have gone awry, and you are unable to pick four questions on your expert areas, at least you have a fall-back position. It would be surprising if this did not occur in at least one exam at finals, but you would be unlucky if you had to compromise on more than one question.

Remember also three other points about the exams. First, they are, as has been explained, not primarily a memory test, but a test of understanding. Secondly, they will require a good deal of thought actually during the exam itself, so it is important to be fresh actually on the day. Thirdly, at any rate for the problems, a thorough knowledge of the most important cases is required. This must include both the decision itself and the reasoning, and such criticisms as there may be of that reasoning.

This brings us on to the revision process itself. The commonest factors preventing learning are boredom and fatigue. Yet the revision techniques adopted by the majority of students seem deliberately designed to maximise these factors. Such is the foolishness of playing 'safe'.

The first pitfall of revision is to believe that there is some natural cut-off point beyond which it is impossible for you to take further knowledge on board. The course is after all 'finished'. Hence the emptying of the library in the weeks preceding the exams. In fact the belief is simply not true, and indeed it is often the case that learning something new helps to clarify and consolidate what you have already learned. This is especially so if you read recent cases and articles, because they will always review what has gone before. But this is precisely the material that students never seem to read at this stage; rather, the end of formal teaching is followed by an exodus back to their homes, armed with little more than a lecture file and their textbooks.

I will term this the 'hermit approach'. There may be advantages in cutting oneself off from the distractions of university life, but they are far outweighed by the disadvantages.

The hermit approach prevents you learning anything new, and reading the materials (the most important cases and articles) which are most useful for the exam. Its other disadvantage is that it prevents inquiry, and because of that is very boring. Revision is the time for reflection and inquiry, which for reasons of pressure of time you have probably had to neglect during the formal part of the course. The best friend of memory is curiosity. If you are really interested in finding out the answer to something you will probably remember what you discover. If you learn by rote, as a boring chore, or simply ask your tutor for an 'authoritative view', you probably will not.

You should therefore develop an inquisitive approach. Ask questions. Past exam papers are a good source. So are the two main casebooks (see chapter 2). Another good approach is to consider why two apparently similar cases were decided in different ways, or why some apparently relevant arguments were not relied upon. Or vary the facts of a case slightly — would the result be the same? Then try to find the answers, or if there are none which are clear-cut then at least a range of possible solutions. More questions will inevitably arise, and the process is self-perpetuating.

But if you are at home armed only with your notes you cannot make any inquiries. For that you have to be in the library (which has the additional advantage of being almost empty at this time of year) close to the law reports. No set of lecture notes, or even textbook, however clear, explores every avenue (if you really must go home at this stage, casebooks are much more useful, because after all by this stage you *know* the basic material). If you are at home you will simply come up against a brick wall, and remain confused.

Another point to remember is that exams require freshness on the day. You will certainly under-perform if you are exhausted. So do not wear yourself out in the run-up. If you are working really effectively, and not merely fooling yourself that you are working by, for example, transcribing notes (an intensely useless exercise), you will find six hours a day is pretty well the absolute maximum. If you try to do more you will end up taking in less, and will become tired and confused into the bargain. And even for a fairly short period, a five-day week (or at most six for very short bursts) is the maximum desirable.

So do not suddenly change your life-style for the revision period. If you need plenty of sleep and good meals, your performance will suffer if you do not get them. If you need plenty of exercise the same applies. You should also aim to relax completely at least towards the end of every evening, and do something unrelated to study. This should ideally be social, but even reading a novel or watching the television is better than nothing. Not only will you be fresher the next day, but also you are less likely to suffer from insomnia, which for some people is a real problem.

On the other hand, do try to work at the same rate through the Christmas and Easter vacations, except for a short holiday period, retaining access to a law library if possible. Work at a steady pace can be kept up for many weeks or months, and there is no advantage in wasting the considerable period covered by these vacations.

Most important of all, this is not a good time to begin experimenting with evil pills in the hope that they will increase your alertness. They are unlikely to increase your concentration even in the short term (if anything you will find it more difficult to settle to anything), and in the longer term you could find yourself awake all night and asleep all day, by no means the ideal situation. I have known people pep themselves up for revision the night before exams, only to enter the exam the next day totally exhausted, and in no state to work through complex problem questions. However good the night's revision, the performance has been disastrous.

TWO

WORKING DURING THE COURSE

Since I would recommend that you regard revision as a continuation of coursework rather than as a wholly separate enterprise, it follows that such considerations as apply to revision also apply in general to your coursework. In particular, you should always work towards the exam, and the greatest enemy is probably boredom. Also, given that lectures and tutorials are not only time-consuming themselves, but also force you to work at a particular rate, you will need to organise your work so as to use your time as efficiently as possible. This final consideration should dictate especially the order in which you study materials, and this is considered later in the chapter.

How much work?

Getting the most out of your course need not mean working yourself like a horse. If you cast your eye around your fellow students, it will probably

'plenty of lower class degrees can be attributed to the real sloggers'

strike you that the real sloggers, the people who are always in the library when you arrive in the morning and are still there when you leave later in the day, rarely come out at the top of the class. It is true that they rarely fail or do very badly either, but given the hours of dedicated study they put in, they generally perform less well than might be expected. Plenty of lower-second-class degrees can be attributed to the real sloggers, but few higher seconds or firsts.

The sloggers would do better by working less hard, but more effectively. Effective work requires thought, not just transcription, or photocopying reams of material, or learning by rote. Quality of work counts more than quantity. Mere acquisition of knowledge is no substitute for real thought.

Thinking is very interesting, but also extremely hard work. Indeed, it is one of the hardest forms of work there is. No doubt there are plenty of people who will scoff at this. It is fashionable to hold intellect in contempt these days. A moment's reflection will confirm the truth of this statement, however.

Consider, for example, how many people (even 'successful' people) hold prejudices which are indefensible in the face of rational argument. Consider how many (even intelligent people) are deliberately innumerate, and proud of it. How many are terrified of, and feel threatened by, ideas which are different from their own? Probably the majority, *even among students and academics themselves*. Indeed, the overwhelming majority of people seem to organise their lives specifically in order to have to think as little as possible. This is by no means irrational, because thinking is very hard work.

In fact you cannot work effectively more than a few hours each day, and if you try to do so, you will end up achieving less, not more. On the other hand, effective work in short bursts not only achieves more, but makes the subject much more interesting. It is not a question of diminishing returns. The returns after a point actually become negative.

How much work should you do, then? It is important to begin by emphasising that the only work that really counts involves being actively inquisitive, asking the sort of questions that were discussed at the end of the last chapter. This is the only sort of work that really achieves anything. Transcribing notes, looking for a place or books in the library, or photocopying may be time-consuming, but they do not constitute real work. All these, especially the last, are in fact substitutes for work. All actively prevent thought. All (though necessary of course up to a point) should therefore be minimised as much as possible.

Photocopying in particular ought to be carried out sparingly. So should copying out headnotes. Both are often used not to assist the reading and understanding of a case, but as a substitute for it. I suspect that a great deal of photocopied material is never read, and if so, since there is no direct connection between the photocopying machine and the brain, a lot of time and money have been wasted. That is not to say that photocopying can never be justified. It can, for example, if the library is about to close and you need materials to be able to continue working elsewhere.

Having defined what should be regarded as work, I would have thought that four hours a day for a six-day week or five hours a day over a five-day week is about the limit, and you may find that even less obtains better results. A 25-hour week may not sound much, but do not forget that study at this level is much more intensive than most other forms of work. Working lunches, hanging around waiting for things to happen (a large part of many people's working lives), committee meetings and afternoons on the golf-course may all be vital activities, but they are by no means as intensive as learning any subject to a good degree standard. There is a limit to how much intensive work can be done, and if you try to extend the working day you will simply burn yourself out.

There are two other reasons for not attempting to extend your working day beyond a reasonable limit. First, your mind must remain active, and it is important not to become stale. Secondly, opportunities to gain many of the experiences available at university will not recur in later life. Do not work so hard that you waste them.

So never be ashamed of your working day, or be tempted to extend it beyond the limits with which you can cope. If you are taking nothing in there is no point in continuing, and you will only tire yourself unnecessarily for the following day. If there are mundane tasks like photocopying to be done (or domestic chores, or letter writing) they can be left to the end of the working day, but really effective study will simply not be possible once you are too tired.

But this should by no means be taken as a justification for laziness. Do not try to get away with very much less than the four or five hours a day suggested above. One of the advantages of working at a steady, rather than insane pace, is that it can be continued over many months. So do not waste the Christmas or Easter vacations. Of course you should take a short break over those periods, but four weeks for each is ridiculous. Sustained work over many weeks is better than trying to go at an insane pace until you are burned out, and certainly better than having to sprint in the few weeks immediately preceding the exam.

There are usually each year, it is true, a small proportion of candidates who appear to do very little during the year, but by getting things together a few weeks before the exam, obtain apparently respectable results (perhaps a good lower or even poor upper second). They are nearly always highly intelligent (otherwise they would fail), and undoubtedly it is possible for some people to do reasonably well on very little work. But in reality these candidates are letting themselves down badly. Had they worked steadily throughout the year, their intelligence would have reaped far greater rewards. In effect, candidates who are capable of obtaining high seconds or even firsts settle for a much lower class of degree.

Laziness can also lead you into what I might call the 'boredom trap'. A lot of law courses are not at first sight very interesting, and trusts does not, on first acquaintance, arouse great enthusiasm among undergraduate students. It is very conceptual, and abstract concepts tend to be uninteresting at first glance. Even on a factual level, since much of the subject (but by no means all) is about how to hang on to your wealth, it can be rather boring to students who rarely have much wealth to worry about. Nor is everybody intrinsically interested about law which has developed around Victorian family arrangements.

On the other hand, it becomes both easier and more interesting as one progresses through it. Once you have a reasonable grasp of the whole subject everything seems to fall into place. Also, you begin to appreciate how concepts, though developed from Victorian family arrangements, are also utilised in today's commercial world, and that many aspects of the subject have relevance for ordinary transactions, such as buying a house. Students who were thoroughly disillusioned with the subject initially can end up finding it quite interesting.

In other words, there is a boredom threshold, and a minimum level of attainment is required before the subject becomes interesting. Thereafter, however, it becomes more interesting as one goes on. A lot of students, both in trusts and other subjects, never seem to do enough work to get over the boredom threshold. Therefore they remain bored throughout their whole period of study. Hence the term 'boredom trap'. A bored student can never study effectively, and cannot therefore do himself or herself justice in the examinations.

Though it may be true that only very gifted people can expect to obtain the very best results in a trusts exam, everybody who is capable of getting a polytechnic or university place ought to be capable of attaining a good second-class standard, so long as he or she works effectively.

Lectures

Since you are almost certainly in your second or third year of study before embarking on equity and trusts it should not be necessary to advise you on how to take effective notes etc., and in any case this is likely to depend on the sort of lecture you are attending, the speed of delivery, the extent of the hand-outs and so on.

On most courses today lectures are voluntary, and although most students seem to be fairly regular attenders this is by no means necessary, and it is perfectly possible to succeed without attending any lectures at all. It is probably best not to adopt an inflexible policy, but to judge on the basis of each lecture course whether the time spent attending the lecture could be more profitably spent in the library, or elsewhere.

Two types of lecture course are nearly always worthwhile. The first is where the lecturer really is an expert, who is perhaps preparing material which will eventually be published. You will not be able to find the content of these lectures anywhere else, so you really should attend. The second is the revision or updating lecture near the end of the course. These will nearly always contain new and original material, on which little will yet have been published, and will pull together various strands of the course.

So far as general course lectures are concerned, some will probably be more useful than others. Where there is a good introductory textbook you may be better off spending your time reading that, but there is not in all subjects, and a clear set of introductory lectures may be a real bonus. There may also be tactical reasons for attending. For example, if the lecturer is also examiner in the subject, you may decide to attend partly in order to discover his or her special interests. Or it may be difficult to remain in contact with the course without attending the lectures. Materials may be handed out in lectures, or announcements made (though if you really do not wish to attend it should be possible to persuade the lecturer to use the notice-board for announcements instead).

If none of the above reasons applies, or if the lectures are simply bad, then there is very little point in attending, and you could almost certainly spend your time better elsewhere. Some students, however, appear to be captivated by the 'talking head' syndrome, and only feel confident that they know a topic when they have had the reassurance of hearing someone in authority actually telling them about it. This is not a good reason for attending a set of lectures which is otherwise bad, or which you have decided not to attend for some other reason.

In deciding whether a course of lectures is worth attending, remember that the first lecture is rarely representative. Often it will include little more than handing out materials and recommending books. Even the second lecture will often be only introductory. The third or fourth is likely to be more representative, however, and this is probably the stage at which to judge how good the lecture course as a whole is likely to be. And of course, if you can discover which topics are likely to be covered when, you may decide to attend only for particular areas, rather than the entire course.

Tutorials and seminars

A lot of students think these are a waste of time, and in many cases they are probably right. On the other hand they are usually compulsory, and given that you have to go you may as well make the best of them. If you do so, they will probably be worthwhile anyway.

You have to do the assigned work, and be prepared to ask questions, to get anything out of tutorials. Ideally, a tutorial should involve a degree of input from every student present, so that at the end of the class you all go away with the benefit of each other's research and ideas. In reality, students all too often refuse to participate, and the tutorial degenerates into what is in effect a mini-lecture. This is a waste of time, because even if the lecture is worth giving in the first place, it is very inefficient to lecture to a small group. There is not much the tutor can do to force people to participate, however, so it really is up to you to provide the input. There is no need to be embarrassed by this. In any case all lawyers will have to perform publicly to some extent during their careers.

Probably if you take the initiative others in the group will follow, and the tutorial will become much more lively and valuable. If not, and it remains deadly dull, you would be well advised to change to a different group if you can. In summary, then, tutorials can be useful, but too many are not. Whether or not they are depends to a great extent on your own personal effort.

It may be difficult at first to think up questions to ask in tutorials. Past exam papers are not usually much use until well into the course, because they are rarely on self-contained areas. The tutor of course may direct the work towards specific questions, and the casebooks are quite useful. Another good starting-point is to look at the more important cases, as was suggested in chapter 1 for the revision process. Consider how far the facts would have to change before the decision itself would be reversed. This forces you to consider exactly what the case stands for, and where there is more than one judgment, forces you to compare them. Remember also that no case ever reaches a higher court unless both sides have a plausible argument, and another possibility is to consider how you would have argued for the opposite result had you been counsel in the case. Casenotes and articles can assist you in this regard.

You will find, however, that as you go further into the subject questions will occur to you naturally, and study will become more interesting in the process.

In any case discussion should not end with the tutorials. You should try and get to know the other students in your tutorial group and continue the discussion after the tutorial has ended, perhaps over coffee. This should not be frowned upon as not being 'real work'. In fact, informal discussion is one of the best methods of working there is. Almost certainly it will give you ideas to explore during your private study, and will make the study more interesting. It is sadly neglected among many students. It may even be worth actively seeking out people who are prepared to argue over points arising from work on the course.

Written work

Most universities and polytechnics require periodic submission of written work, to which students sometimes object on the grounds that they could spend their time more usefully on other types of work. Nevertheless, essay-writing is useful, because you need to do far more than merely reproduce material. You need also to collect your ideas, work out a line of reasoning that is both coherent and logically consistent, assess contradictory views, and work out a logical order to which to present the material. This is not only time-consuming but also involves a great deal of hard thinking, which no doubt accounts in part for its unpopularity, but for precisely those reasons you are far more likely to remember the area covered.

It is interesting to observe that many lecturers keep only the most basic lecture notes (often far less extensive than the notes the students take away from the lecture), but because they go through an exercise of organisation, which is essentially similar to essay-writing the first time they give a series of lectures, they need no more than trigger notes to enable them to remember the subject for lectures in future years.

In reality, of course, the processes required to produce a good essay are essentially the same as those required to attain a genuine understanding of the subject. At the risk of repeating what I have already said in chapter 1, you are being examined primarily on your understanding of the subject, and not merely on your recollection. For this reason, a good essay can be far more valuable than any other form of notes when it comes to revising for the exams, and it may well be a mistake to skimp on essay-writing.

How to work

A lot of this has already been covered, because there should be no great difference in emphasis between working on the course and revision for exams, considered in chapter 1.

Try if you can to arrange your days so that your most active study can be accomplished in the part of the day when you are at your freshest, and banish the mundane tasks (e.g., note-taking or photocopying) to some other time. You do not, after all, need to be fresh for the mundane tasks.

There is another factor to bear in mind, which is that your time will certainly be limited, and you may not be able to read everything you wish. I would therefore suggest that the following order of reading materials has the advantage that even if you do not get time to cover them all, you will at least achieve a good basic coverage. This should not be regarded as a rigid order. If questions occur to you as you go along, you may wish to go straight to, e.g., the law reports to answer them, and in that case you should satisfy your curiosity before moving on.

(a)   The relevant chapter of the textbook. Remember that this is only the first stage, and that textbooks only really cover the basic groundwork, though they can also be useful as triggers when you revise. I believe this to be true even of the very comprehensive textbooks, such as Pettit, *Equity and the Law of Trusts*, or Hanbury and Maudsley, *Modern Equity*. No student should rely on *any* textbook, however detailed, except to provide a starting-point for further study. Though textbooks are often quite good for answering essay-type questions, they are not well-suited to problems, where the examiner is probably looking for a close reading of the cases. Another disadvantage is that they are never right up to date except immediately after publication, and examiners often ask about the most recent developments.

(b)   Casenotes and articles. Read the most recent first because they will discuss the earlier authorities and articles. Read them before reading the cases, because then you will get some idea of the points you should look for at that next stage. In effect, this is a form of introductory reading, which can enable you to take short cuts when you get to the next stage (i.e., the cases themselves). Also, if you run out of time you will have covered more ground by doing this first.

A number of such recent articles are discussed in the substantive chapters of the book. For example, the article by P.J. Millett on *Quistclose* trusts (1985) 101 LQR 269, mentioned in chapter 10, can give you a good idea what to look for when reading the cases themselves, as can the article by Brian Green (1984) 47 MLR 385, on the formalities cases discussed in chapter 5. Though neither of these articles is particularly easy, reading them at this stage is likely to save you considerable time at the next stage, whereas reading, e.g., the *Vandervell* litigation (chapter 5) without introduction is likely to be confusing in the extreme.

(c)   The cases themselves. Again, read the most recent first, because the earlier authorities will be discussed there. Examples of cases which constitute excellent reviews of earlier authorities are *Re Gonin* [1979] Ch 16 (chapters 3 and 5), *Lloyd's Bank plc* v *Rosset* [1990] 1 All ER 1111 (chapter 6) and *Ashburn Anstalt* v *Arnold* [1988] 2 All ER 147 (also in chapter 6). Reading the earlier cases first would have been a lot less efficient in terms of information gained per minute of study.

It is at this stage that the real work begins, and you can ask yourself the sort of questions mentioned above. You might also at this stage consider whether the authorities actually bear out the views of the article and textbook writers, and indeed the lecturer (assuming you have attended any lectures). Frequently different writers have different views (see, for example, the discussion of *Re Denley's Trust Deed* [1969] 1 Ch 373 in chapter 4). You should now be in a position to decide whose views you prefer (at least provisionally), and why.

It is quite common for students in tutorials to claim that they could not read a case in time because too many other students were also trying to get hold of it, and the report was always out. This should rarely be a problem, though. Remember that nearly all cases are reported in several different reports (e.g., QB, All ER and WLR), so if you cannot find (say) the QB reference then *do* check through the indexes of the other reports, rather than leave it altogether.

There are other useful sources which should be mentioned. First, students of this subject are lucky in that there are two excellent casebooks: Hayton & Marshall, *Cases and Commentary on the Law of Trusts*, and Maudsley & Burn, *Trusts and Trustees Cases and Materials*. Their coverage and style are slightly different, but it is not easy to choose between them. They are useful in three main ways. First, they can be used as introductory reading at stage (b), before reading the cases themselves (indeed, some cases are so well covered that you may not need to read the full report at all). Secondly, they contain questions you can usefully work through. Thirdly, at times when access to the library is difficult (e.g., late at night or during vacations) you can still pursue your studies quite effectively.

You should not expect *never* to need the full reports, and casebooks suffer the same deficiency as textbooks in that they can never cover the most recent material. This is most likely to catch you out if a case has been appealed after publication of the casebook. Nevertheless, a good casebook can save a great deal of time. In fact, given the limited income of students relying on grants, there is a good argument that a cheap introductory textbook used in conjunction with one of the casebooks is better value than a single expensive textbook.

Further useful sources, given that examiners sometimes like to concentrate on the most recent material, are the casenotes on the subject in the general journals (e.g., *Law Quarterly Review, Modern Law Review, New Law Journal*) and in *The Conveyancer and Property Lawyer*. Though this last is primarily concerned with land law there is also quite a significant coverage of equity

and trusts. Reading these from time to time will allow you to keep abreast
of developments in the subject, and the exercise is especially valuable towards
the end of the course. Only read the notes which are actually relevant
to equity and trusts, of course! There may not be very many. Also towards
the end of the course it may be worth checking through the most recent
index of the *All England Law Reports* or *Weekly Law Reports*, to see if
there are new developments (and if there are then reading the cases
themselves, of course).

THREE

CONSTITUTION OF TRUSTS AND COVENANTS TO SETTLE

In many trusts courses, this is the first really tricky area that you are likely to encounter. Some syllabuses confuse you further by calling the topic 'incompletely constituted trusts', which gives the idea that you are dealing with some peculiar specialised variety of trust. However, there is in fact no such entity as an 'incompletely constituted trust'. Either a trust is completely constituted, which means that all the elements which have to be present before equity will enforce the trust are in fact present, or else there is no trust at all.

What this topic is really about is the question of whether, if for some reason a settlor has failed to do everything necessary to create a fully valid trust, the people who had hoped to benefit from the settlement can do anything to secure those benefits, notwithstanding the failure to create a valid trust in their favour. It is a ripe area for examination problems, for although real-life cases which raise these issues are very unlikely to arise today, the topic calls for a good grasp of basic principles and an ability to apply them logically.

Most questions will combine constitution of trusts and covenants to settle, but it is necessary to consider constitution in general terms before we look in detail at a problem.

Constitution of a trust, and attendant consequences

In order for a valid private trust to come into existence, these two elements are both necessary and sufficient:

(a) There must be a manifest intention on the part of the settlor to create a trust (and not to effect some other kind of transaction, such as making an outright gift or loan). As a corollary to this proposition, we might add that the intention must be expressed in a way which complies with the certainty requirements (see chapter 4).

(b) A trust involves a division of the ownership of property. The trustees become owners at common law, and are given control of the property.

The beneficiaries become owners in equity, and in effect it is they who may enjoy the property. The property must therefore be properly vested in trustees who hold it in that capacity on behalf of the beneficiaries.

Usually, the property will be transferred to third parties as trustees. This is also the stage at which problems may arise in exam problems, e.g., if the settlor fails to observe the proper formalities of the transfer or if, as in the problem considered in the next section, having agreed to transfer the property, he omits to do so.

It is not necessary that the property be transferred in the manner that the settlor intended. If it is conveyed to trustees in any manner, even accidentally, this is sufficient to constitute the trust. This occurred in *Re Ralli's Will Trusts* [1964] Ch 288, considered later in the chapter.

Generally speaking, the legal title has actually to be transferred to the trustees, but there is an apparent exception where the settlor has done all that is within his power to constitute the trust by transferring the property to a trustee, but has been thwarted by formalities which are outside his control. Equity regards the trust as constituted by the last act of the settlor. An example is *Re Rose* [1952] Ch 499, CA, where the settlor intended to transfer shares, but where the directors of the company had an effective veto over any transfer. The Court of Appeal held that the date of constitution of the trust was when the settlor had done all he could, not when the directors consented to and registered the transfer. The precise date was important for the purposes of assessing estate duty.

Evershed MR noted 'In this case, as I understand it, the testator had done everything in his power to divest himself of the shares in question . . . ', and it is clear that the case turns on this. In *Re Fry* [1946] 1 Ch 312, by contrast, more may have been required from the testator effectively to transfer legal title to the shares. The reason in this case that the shares could not be registered was because Treasury consent had not been obtained, as required by the Defence (Finance) Regulations 1939. Although all the requisite forms had been filled in by the donor, the required Treasury consent had not been obtained before he died.

This may appear. at first sight, to be a similar to *Rose*, but as Romer J explained (at p.317):

Now I should have thought it was difficult to say that the testator had done everything that was required to be done by him at the time of his death, for it was necessary for him to obtain permission from the Treasury for the assignment and he had not obtained it. Moreover, the Treasury might in any case have required further information of the kind referred to in the questionnaire submitted to him, or answers supplemental to those which had had given in reply to it; and, if so approached, he might have refused to concern himself with the matter further, in which case I do not know how anyone else could have compelled him to do so.

In this case, therefore, the testator may not have done all that was required, so the principles later elaborated in *Re Rose* could not apply.

Declaration of self as trustee

Another possibility is for the settlor to declare himself trustee of the trust property, in which case no transfer of the legal title is necessary.

The courts are not keen, however, except in the clearest cases, to infer on the part of a settlor an intention to declare himself trustee, because of the onerous nature of trusteeship. An intention must be shown to create a trust, rather than some other transaction (e.g., an outright gift). Conversely, an intention to make an outright gift will more easily be inferred.

Thus in *Jones* v *Lock* (1865) LR 1 Ch App 25, the father of a baby boy handed a cheque to his nine-month-old son, uttering words which made it clear that he meant the child to have the sum represented by the cheque, although he immediately removed the cheque from the baby for safe-keeping. He died some days later, without having endorsed the cheque, which would have been necessary to pass title in it to the child. The court refused to construe his actions as amounting to a declaration of trust, with himself as trustee, in favour of the child.

Lord Cranworth LC did not think that an irrevocable intention to part with the property had been manifested. There was an intention to make an outright gift, but no gift had actually been made. It was not therefore a declaration of trust.

One of the few cases where a declaration of trust was inferred was *Paul* v *Constance* [1977] 1 WLR 527. Constance was injured at work, and obtained £950 in damages, which he put into a bank account in name alone. The evidence suggested, however, that the money was intended for himself and Mrs Paul, with whom he was living, but he was not married to Mrs Paul, and the reason for not opening a joint account was to save her embarrassment.

Subsequent additions were made to the account, in particular from bingo winnings which Constance and Paul played as a joint venture. One withdrawal of £150 was also made, which was divided equally between them.

Constance died, and the question at issue was whether Mrs Paul could claim any share of the fund. If the money in the account had belonged solely to Constance, then his wife, Mrs Constance, from whom he had parted, would be entitled to it on his death.

The Court of Appeal held that Constance held the money on trust for Mrs Paul. No words of trust were used, but regard was had to the unsophisticated character of Constance, and the nature of his relationship with Mrs Paul. However, Scarman LJ made clear this was a borderline case, and in general it must be assumed that, in the absence of express words of declaration, the courts will be reluctant to infer that an owner of property intends to become trustee of it for another.

Effect of validly constituted trust

If both of these elements are present, there is a valid, enforceable trust, and the following consequences always follow:

(a)   Once constituted, the trust is irreversible (unless the settlor has specifically granted himself or someone else a power to revoke the settlement) and the settlor can no more reclaim his property than you could reclaim a birthday present that you have given to a friend.

(b)   The beneficiaries have enforceable rights even though they may have given no consideration in return for their benefits under the trust. Yet is is they, and not the settlor, who can enforce the trust, because the settlor retains no interest in the property (assuming he is not also a trustee or beneficiary).

The creation of a trust, therefore, is a method whereby third parties to arrangements can obtain directly enforceable rights, whereas if there is no trust the privity of contract doctrine prevents this.

So whereas, for example, a contract made by A and B for C's benefit can be varied at any time by A and B, C having no enforceable rights, if A conveys property to B on trust for C, C has an enforceable right and neither A nor B can later vary the arrangement (unless C consents).

Of course, if the trustee is acting by virtue of a contract with the settlor, for example, if he is acting as his solicitor or banker, then the settlor can enforce this contract. Further discussion of contract actions follow below.

(c)   The beneficiaries obtain an equitable interest in the property which forms the subject-matter of the trust. A comparison between trusts and loans illustrates the importance of the property interest. It has also given rise to important recent litigation, so may well therefore be a ripe area for exam questions.

Usually, when A loans money to B, B becomes a debtor, not a trustee, and A becomes a creditor, not a beneficiary. Since A has retained no property in the loaned money, if the debtor goes bankrupt, he is merely one among many unsecured creditors, and is unlikely to see the return of much, if any, of his money.

A loan can also constitute a trust, however, so if A can retain a beneficial interest in the money loaned, this protects him in the event of B's bankruptcy. This is explained more fully in chapter 10.

Sub-trusts

A further point to note is that the property settled can include an equitable interest. In other words, a beneficiary under a trust may constitute a further trust of his equitable interest, thereby creating a sub-trust. Sub-trusts are common in tax-avoiding settlements. The beneficiary under the sub-trust can himself repeat the process, creating a further sub-trust, and there is no limit to the number of times this process may be repeated.

Equity will not perfect an imperfect gift

Conversely, if the elements outlined in the last section are missing, then there is no trust. Thus, for example, no trust is created, whatever intention the settlor has manifested, unless legal title is vested in trustees. This is absolutely fundamental. If the trust property is not transferred to trustees, 'equity will not perfect an imperfect gift', and no valid trust is constituted. *Milroy* v *Lord* (1862) 4 De G F & J 264 is the leading authority.

The settlor had executed a voluntary deed, purporting to transfer shares to a trustee on trust for the plaintiffs. The voluntary deed was incapable of transferring legal title, however, since that could only be achieved by registering the name of the transferee in the books of the bank.

The Court of Appeal in Chancery held that no trust had been constituted, Turner LJ stating the law as follows:

in order to render a voluntary settlement valid and effectual, the settlor must have done everything which, according to the nature of the property comprised in the settlement, was necessary to be done in order to transfer the property and render the settlement binding upon him. He may of course do this by actually transferring the property to the persons for whom he intends to provide, and the provision will then be effectual, and it will be equally effectual if he transfers the property to a trustee for the purposes of the settlement, or declares that he himself holds it on trust for those purposes; . . . but, in order to render the settlement binding, one or other of these modes must . . . be resorted to, for there is no equity in this Court to perfect an imperfect gift. The cases I think go further to this extent, that if the settlement is intended to be effectuated by one of the modes to which I have referred, the Court will not give effect to it by applying another of those modes. If it is intended to take effect by transfer, the Court will not hold the intended transfer to operate as a declaration of trust, for then every imperfect instrument would be made effectual by being converted into a perfect trust.

In this passage, which must be one of the most frequently cited in the law of trusts, Turner LJ does not require the settlor necessarily to transfer the property, but only that the settlor must have done everything which was necessary to be done in order to transfer the property. *Re Rose*, considered above, is not inconsistent with *Milroy* v *Lord*, therefore, and indeed, this passage was accepted in *Re Rose* as being an accurate statement of the law.

Turner LJ also allows for the settlor to declare himself trustee, but goes on the say that if he has neither done all that is necessary to vest the property in trustees, nor declared himself trustee, equity will not complete the imperfect transaction for him. Nor will a court infer a declaration of trust from an incomplete gift.

We have already seen an example of this last principle in *Jones* v *Lock* (1865) LR 1 Ch App 25. One rationale for the principle is that the obligations of a trustee are extremely onerous, whereas a donor's responsibilities end from the time date of the gift. There is no reason, therefore, to infer from a failed gift that the intended donor is prepared to accept the onerous obligations of trusteeship.

Another example is *Richards* v *Delbridge* (1874) LR 18 Eq 11. Delbridge wished to give his infant grandson, Richards, the lease he had on his place of business as a bone manure merchant. He indorsed on the lease: 'This deed and all thereto belonging I give to Edward Benetto Richards from this time forth, with all the stock-in-trade'. He gave the lease to Richards' mother to hold for Richards, but died before the lease was actually delivered to Richards himself. It was held that there had been no transfer of the lease to Richards, nor declaration of trust in his favour. Sir George Jessel MR refused to infer a declaration of trust from the failed gift:

the legal owner of the property may . . . declare that he will hold it from that time forward on trust for the other person. It is true that he need not use the words, 'I declare myself a trustee', but he must do something which is equivalent to it, and use expressions which have that meaning . . . for a man to make himself trustee there must be an expression of intention to become a trustee, whereas words of present gift shew an intention to give over property to another, and not to retain it in the donor's own hands for any purpose, fiduciary or otherwise.

This passage emphasises the difference between gift and trust, that the donor retains no interest after the property has been transferred, whereas a trustee's fiduciary obligations continue. It is no surprise, therefore, that the courts will not infer a declaration of trusteeship from a failed gift.

Nearly all the difficulties which arise in this area are caused by attempts to avoid the fundamental principle that property must be properly vested to constitute the trust.

Covenants to settle property

Factual situations in which the cases arise

As already explained, this topic is really about what those people who hoped to benefit can do if the settlor has failed properly to constitute the trust. Nearly all the cases are of essentially the same type, and it is worth briefly examining the factual nature of the situation in order to explain the issues which have arisen.

Nearly all the cases have concerned marriage settlements, and the agreements to settle are therefore usually made in consideration of marriage. The parties may also enter into a deed of covenant, to which trustees, or intended trustees, may also be a party. A typical arrangement might be where the husband-to-be agrees to settle not only the property he owns now, but also *property yet to be acquired* (for example, an expected inheritance yet to be received), on the terms of the settlement. Under the terms of the settlement, the beneficiaries will usually include the issue of the marriage, and in default of such issue, the next of kin of the wife.

The first point to note is that the settlement usually covers not only existing, but also after-acquired property. The courts have held, e.g., in *Re Ellenborough* [1903] 1 Ch 697, that future property, or expectancies, cannot form the subject matter of a trust, because there is insufficient certainty of subject matter. There is not usually, therefore, a failure by the settlor properly to constitute the trust: the trust *cannot* be properly constituted since the trust property does not yet exist.

The second point to note is that the agreement is made, not in consideration of money or money's worth, as with most contracts, but in consideration of marriage. The relevance of marriage consideration (which means that the marriage must actually constitute consideration, and must therefore be a future marriage) is that it enables not only the parties to the contract to sue on it, but any issue *of that marriage* can also sue. This is usually regarded today as a narrow and anomalous exception to the rule that equity will not assist a volunteer. Historically, it appears to have been a device to impose upon the conscience of the husband (forcing him to settle the property he had agreed to settle) at a time (before the Married Women's Property Act 1882) when the wife herself had no economic independence (and could not sue in her own right).

It is clear, however, that only the issue of the marriage can sue, and not, for example, in the event of failure of issue, the next-of-kin of the wife, who will typically be the intended beneficiaries in that event (see *Re Plumptre's Marriage Settlement* [1910] 1 Ch 609, below). Furthermore, the policy behind marriage consideration would probably not go beyond providing an action against the husband, and indeed there is no authority on whether the issue of the marriage, who though parties to the marriage consideration are otherwise volunteers, can sue anyone *apart* from the husband.

It is sometimes argued that others, apart from the issue of the marriage, can sue on the marriage consideration, for example step-children, but Buckley J made it clear that it is indeed limited to the issue of the marriage in *Re Cook's Settlement Trusts* [1965] 1 Ch 902.

The third point to note is that the parties may also have entered into a deed of covenant, to which, indeed, the intended trustees may also be party. At common law, parties to a deed can sue on it even in the absence of consideration, but they are limited to common-law remedies (i.e., damages), and cannot obtain specific performance of the covenant. It is in any case very unlikely that the intended *beneficiaries* will be party to the covenant, at any rate if they are the issue of the marriage, since at the time of the covenant they will not have been born. For an unusual example, where a beneficiary *was* party, see *Cannon* v *Hartley* [1949] Ch 213, below.

The final point to note is that although the cases usually arise because a trust has not been constituted, the intended trustees under the settlement are often actually trustees of other family property. Another possibility is that trusts of the settlement *have* been constituted, but not of the particular property in dispute. It is likely that although no trusts had been constituted of the property in dispute, the decisions in *Kay* and *Pryce*, below, may well have been influenced by the fact that the intended trustees of the settlement were actually trustees of other property.

A problem question

Occasionally examiners will raise the issue in the form of an essay question, but as the same rules apply, and since a problem question will provide a convenient illustration of the difficulties, let us begin with one of those. There is, of course, no reason why examiners should base their problem questions, even remotely, on fact situations similar to those which have been considered in the cases themselves:

Alpha, a successful racing driver, decides that in view of the risks of her profession she ought to make proper provision for Romeo, her secretary and companion, so one evening in 1986 in her hotel room in London, she tells her cousin Mercutio that she intends to make provision for Romeo, and requests him to act as trustee. Mercutio agrees, and he and Alpha enter into a deed of covenant whereby Alpha agrees to settle the following property on Romeo:

(a)   A large block of shares which she owns in Juliet Engineering.
(b)   £10,000 which she expects to receive under the will of her elderly Uncle Montague.
(c)   One quarter of any prize money she may win during the 1987 season.

The next day, however, Alpha flies to Monza for the Italian Grand Prix without taking any steps to transfer the legal title to Mercutio. While they are in Monza, Romeo quarrels with Alpha and leaves, and is soon making a handsome living by selling to the press her highly coloured tales of life with a woman racing driver. Alpha now refuses to transfer the shares to Mercutio.

During 1987 Alpha is highly successful, and wins £100,000 in prize money. Uncle Montague dies in the same year, and leaves £10,000 to Alpha in his will. Alpha refuses to transfer any of this property to Romeo.

Romeo seeks your advice.

Would your answer be different in any of the following ALTERNATIVE situations (ANSWER ALL PARTS):

(a)   Romeo is also a party to the deed of covenant.
(b)   Mercutio is a good friend of Romeo, and had in fact persuaded Alpha to enter the deed of covenant by agreeing in return to arrange sponsorship for Alpha for the 1987 season. Mercutio kept to his side of the bargain, and Alpha was only able to race during 1987 because of the sponsorship arranged by Mercutio.
(c)   Mercutio is an executor under Uncle Montague's will.

This problem is based, rather loosely, on one in a university exam paper. It is not exactly the same, because the real exam problem contained an additional formalities point, and I should prefer to postpone discussion of formalities until chapter 5. The fact that both areas occurred in the same question in the real exam illustrates again, however, the dangers of trying to be too clever over question spotting.

The common factor to each of these situations is that there is no trust. The missing element, as is typical in problems of this type, is the actual vesting of the property in the trustee. Alpha, having agreed to transfer property, omits to do so. The problem therefore breaks down into a very simple issue. Alpha (the would-be settlor — WS for short) has made a covenant (a contract, in other words) with Mercutio, the would-be trustee (WT) to confer a benefit upon Romeo, the would-be beneficiary (WB).

If you get a problem of this type in your exam paper, there is a lot to be said for drawing a diagram using these symbols, making clear what role each of these parties is playing, and the relationship between them. Examples can be found in *Equity and Trusts; Text, Cases and Materials*, at p. 40.

The question in effect is whether, as between these three people — WS, WT and WB — there exists any relationship which the courts will enforce. You will need to consider both contract and trust possibilities.

In addition to tackling the problem itself, the following discussion will be interspersed with the basic principles relevant to the topic. It is important to note, though, that not only is there no need to do this in an examination, but many examiners actively dislike answers which are, in effect, an essay on the topic, with a mere paragraph or so actually directed at the problem tacked on at the end. The general propositions in the following discussion may be useful for your revision, or if the topic comes up in the form of a general essay, but if you get a problem then on no account attempt to answer it by writing down all you know about the topic. A problem is intended to test your ability to sort out the relevant from the irrelevant, and to apply your knowledge of an area to a particular fact situation. It is not simply a memory test.

Covenants to settle in general

'Incompletely constituted trusts' are situations where WS, having undertaken to transfer property to trustees, does not do so. There is thus no trust, and for that reason it is misleading to continue to speak of 'settlors', 'trustees' and 'beneficiaries' as though a trust actually existed. Indeed, this practice is probably the major cause of the difficulties people have with this area.

In this book, therefore, I prefer to use 'would-be settlor' (WS), 'would-be trustee' (WT), and 'would-be beneficiary' (WB). It sounds horrible and clumsy, but once we start to use these terms any difficulties caused by textbooks, and even judges, speaking of the parties as though there was a fully constituted trust, disappear.

The whole point at issue, of course, is whether any of the parties can compel the would-be settlor to carry out his promise, and actually to constitute the trust. Let us consider the parties in turn, still in general terms.

Can WB compel WS to transfer the property to WT?

The answer to this depends upon whether there is an enforceable contract between WB and WS. No one has the right to demand that someone should gratuitously create a trust in his favour (although the courts have statutory powers to compel the creation of a trust in certain cases, e.g., under s. 25 of the Matrimonial Causes Act 1973 — see chapter 6), but if WS has bound himself by a contract enforceable at the instance of WB, then the court may compel him to carry it out.

A contract between WB and WS, made for conventional consideration in the form of money or money's worth, would be rather unusual, though not of course impossible. People sometimes 'buy' a benefit in this way, for example, in certain types of commercial transactions, and if WB has indeed provided consideration, then there is no difficulty in the way of his obtaining a remedy. At common law, he can simply sue on the contract and obtain compensation for his lost benefit by way of damages. Alternatively, he may be able to obtain an order of specific performance to compel the settlor actually to carry out the terms of his promise. Since specific performance is an equitable remedy its award is discretionary, rather than as of right, and certain conditions have to be satisfied before the court will grant it, but the court may award damages under the Chancery Amendment Act 1858.

There are two complications concerning this type of contract. The first is that the common law recognises contracts made under seal, such as a deed of covenant, as enforceable even though no consideration moves from the promisee. Equity does not, however. So, if WB is a party to the deed executed by WS, but otherwise gives no consideration for the promised benefit, he will be unable to obtain the equitable remedy of specific performance, though he can still get common law damages, which may be perfectly adequate.

As has already been explained, it would be unusual under the conventional form of marriage settlement for the intended beneficiaries to be party to the deed, but an unusual case, where an intended beneficiary was party, was *Cannon* v *Hartley* [1949] Ch 213, where on the breakdown of a marriage, a father (WS) covenanted to make provision for a daughter (WB) by settling on her property expected later to be acquired under the will of his parents. When he received the property he refused to settle it on the agreed terms.

The daughter was not of course within the marriage consideration, as the covenant itself was not made prior to or in consideration of marriage. But as a party to the deed, she could enforce the contract at common law, and obtain substantial damages.

The second complication is that marriage consideration is recognised only by equity, and where the beneficiary relies on this form of consideration, he must seek an equitable remedy: specific performance or damages in lieu. As stated above these remedies are discretionary, though this causes no difficulty in a straightforward case.

Thus in *Pullan* v *Koe* [1913] 1 Ch 9 the children of WS, being within the marriage consideration, could obtain specific performance. More remote kin, however, not being within the consideration, would be volunteers in the eyes of equity unless they had provided other consideration of value.

If on the other hand WB is neither a party to the covenant nor within any marriage consideration, and has given no other consideration, then there is no remedy, by virtue of the maxim that 'Equity will not assist a volunteer'.

Authority for this proposition can be found in *Re Plumptre's Marriage Settlement* [1910] 1 Ch 609, where the WBs were the next of kin of the wife, this being a settlement of the conventional type and there having been a failure of issue, and so not within the marriage consideration. The only way they could benefit from the covenant would be if there were beneficiaries who were not volunteers, such as the children of the marriage, on whose behalf the trustees could enforce, as in *Pullan* v *Koe*, or if they were themselves parties to the covenant.

Let us return to the particular problem.

Can WB (Romeo) compel WS (Alpha) to transfer the property to WT?

In the main part of the problem WB is neither a party to the covenant nor within any marriage consideration, and has given no other consideration. This is similar to *Re Plumptre's Marriage Settlement*. Our conclusion on this part of our problem will therefore be that Romeo has no right either at law or in equity to compel Alpha to perfect the trust in her favour.

In the alternative fact situation (a) Romeo is party to the deed, so this is like *Cannon* v *Hartley*. Romeo can sue for damages, which should be substantial, but not for specific performance (in other words she cannot claim the actual property).

We now have to consider whether Mercutio, WT, may have a remedy for Alpha's failure to transfer the shares and other property as promised.

Can WT enforce WS's promise?

If he can obtain specific performance of their agreement, he will of course hold the shares on the terms of the trust, and thus in a roundabout way, he could compel Alpha to perfect the trust in Romeo's favour. Romeo herself cannot compel Mercutio to take any steps on her behalf, because unless and until the shares are transferred to him, there is no trust of which Mercutio could be a trustee, or Romeo a beneficiary. The initiative lies with Mercutio.

Supposing he were to sue, what remedy might he obtain? As a party to Alpha's covenant, he can of course claim damages at common law for breach of that covenant. Such damages are unlikely to be more than nominal, however, since damages are intended to compensate the plaintiff for the damage which he has personally suffered, and cannot take into account any loss to a third party. Mercutio himself has lost nothing by Alpha's change of heart, and indeed has avoided being saddled with an onerous office, so it would hardly pay him to sue.

From Romeo's viewpoint, the most desirable remedy which Mercutio might claim is of course specific performance, but in the main part of the problem the bar to this is the fact that Mercutio has provided no consideration recognised by equity: a bare promise, even when supported by a seal, will not do.

Part (b) of the problem is probably quite unusual, however, in that WT actually provides substantial consideration. Thus specific performance may now be at least theoretically possible.

In *Beswick* v *Beswick* [1968] AC 58, a case you may recall from contract days, old Mr Beswick transferred his coal business to his nephew in return for the nephew's promise to pay Mr Beswick a consultant's fee during his life, and a small annuity to his widow after his death. When Mr Beswick died, the nephew refused to make payments to Mrs Beswick.

Though this is not a covenant to settle, the nephew can be regarded as equivalent to WS, old Mr Beswick to WT and Mrs Beswick as WB.

As a mere third party to the agreement, Mrs Beswick as WB could claim no remedy on her own account, but as the personal representative of Mr Beswick she could maintain an action on behalf of his estate (in her other capacity, as WT). Since Mr Beswick himself suffered no loss, one would expect any damages in such an action to be nominal, the very real benefit to Mrs Beswick being quite irrelevant in calculating those damages.

Partly because damages would be an inadequate remedy, the House of Lords granted specific performance to Mr Beswick's estate (WT). This reasoning has been criticised, for the basis of equitable remedies is the inadequacy of the common law remedy, and from the standpoint of

Mr Beswick, the legal remedy was quite adequate. Nonetheless, it would seem that where a WT has provided consideration, he may be able to obtain specific performance as against a recalcitrant WS, provided always that the other conditions for the grant of this remedy are satisfied.

It should be noted that the remedy depends in general upon the mutuality requirement being satisfied, that is to say that the same contract would also have been specifically enforceable by WS against WT. The mutuality requirement was satisfied in *Beswick* v *Beswick*, because old Mr Beswick had promised to transfer the goodwill of a business, but it will by no means always be so. In particular, the mutuality requirement is unlikely to be satisfied where the consideration moving from WT is money alone. Nor is it satisfied in the problem, because Mercutio's obligations would have required supervision, and would not therefore have been specifically enforceable.

For the sake of completeness, even if WT cannot obtain specific performance, if WS does not perform the bargain at all, then WT can get back any consideration provided by him (if he has transferred property or money to WS) on the ground of a total failure of consideration by WS. But this is of no direct benefit to WB. Nor is this remedy possible in the problem, because of the nature of the consideration provided by Mercutio.

But — and here we arrive at the core of our problem — the courts appear to have laid down a principle that even if WT has a useful remedy, he may not sue in this situation. Students are apt to take this as an absolute rule (so are some academic writers), but for a good answer, you ought to explore the issue further.

The chief stumbling-block to the WT is *Re Kay's Settlement* [1939] Ch 329, where the WTs (though they were actually trustees of other property) were parties to a covenant under seal to settle after-acquired property. Note that the 'would-be' terminology is continued even though there was a properly constituted trust of other property, because no issue arose regarding that other property. No consideration moved from the WTs, however. The WBs were not party to the covenant, nor were they within the marriage consideration, so were therefore volunteers. On a request for directions as to whether the WTs could sue to enforce the covenant or recover damages, Simonds J, following Eve J in *Re Pryce* [1917] 1 Ch 234 said:

[I]t appears to me that . . . I must direct the trustees not to take any steps either to compel performance of the covenant or to recover damages through [the settlor's] failure to implement it.

This dictum was followed by Buckley J in *Re Cook's ST* [1965] Ch 902, a case in which, as part of a resettlement of family capital, a son covenanted with his father, who provided consideration, and with WTs (who were also actual trustees of other property) who did not, to settle the proceeds of sale of some paintings which he owned absolutely. One painting, which he had given to one of his numerous wives, was eventually sold by her after her divorce from him, and the issue arose as to whether the WTs were obliged to take steps to enforce the covenant. Buckley J thought not, which on the facts is perhaps not surprising, on the basis that the *Re Pryce* and *Re Kay's Settlement* line of authority was a bar to an action by the WTs. The case is not a particularly strong authority on this point, however. It did not decide that the trustees had no remedy, or that they should not themselves enforce the covenant, but only that they could not be compelled to do so by the WBs.

In the actual problem Mercutio's remedy does not seem very useful in any event, because it seems unlikely even in fact situation (b) that he can obtain specific performance. But you might get a problem where the WT has provided consideration in the form of, e.g., a conveyance of land. In that case he may have a worthwhile remedy, if only he could find a way round the inconvenient *Re Pryce* and *Re Kay's Settlement* decisions.

On the face of it, the dictum of Simonds J in *Re Kay's Settlement* seems extraordinary, and deserves close scrutiny. It appears to deprive a plaintiff of an otherwise perfectly valid personal right to sue on a contract, for which very good reasons would have to be found. One wonders whether the answer might have been different if the facts of the case had been closer to our own problem (varied so that Mercutio had a useful remedy), however.

In *Re Pryce* and *Re Kay's Settlement* (and *Re Cook's ST*) the personal nature of the WT's right was in fact obscured. The facts were that a WS refused to add, to an already constituted trust, further property which was yet to be acquired. The WTs were therefore already trustees of a perfect trust (of other property), and the question seems to have been regarded as one in which they were contemplating taking steps to get in property which is owed to a trust, as of course they should. The court appeared to regard them as acting on behalf of the trust, thereby obscuring the status of their personal rights as parties to the covenant. If, as in our own problem, there is as yet no trust at all, those rights are thrown into clearer relief.

There is also the point that the cases were in the form of a summons for directions. Had the WTs been told to go ahead and sue, the cost of the suit would presumably have fallen on the trust fund (this is one reason why trustees seek directions before suing in the first place: if they obey the court, they are not personally liable for costs in an action which goes against the trust). With the outcome so uncertain, it would have been arguably inapposite for a court to direct trustees to engage in speculative litigation. But if Mercutio wants to spend his own money in an attempt to perfect the trust on Romeo's behalf, there seems no good reason in principle to stop him.

Perhaps, then, Simonds J did not decide that a WT is prohibited from bringing an action, but only that the court would not direct them to sue, and force upon them the onerous burdens of trusteeship, in favour of volunteers. Professor Elliott (1960) 76 LQR 100 has argued that the WTs should have been directed that they need not sue, not that they ought not to sue. It would indeed be perfectly proper for the court to leave the decision as to whether to exercise one's rights to the private individual, just as in any other case where a person has a right of action.

On the other hand, this apparently gives trustees a discretion as to whether or not to enforce the trust, and it is arguable that this is inconsistent with the mandatory nature of a trust. Since the court will not force the WTs to act in favour of a volunteer, it can only prohibit them from suing. Though this argument has a superficial plausibility, remember that they are not yet trustees, so objections based on giving them discretion should not be relevant. The choice given to a WT is not whether to carry out his or her duties under a trust — there is no trust — but whether or not to become a trustee at all. This is a perfectly proper choice which anyone faced with a request to become a trustee is entitled to make.

Whether or not you find this argument convincing, it serves to illustrate that nothing in law should be accepted without contention, especially where, as here, you are confronted with a line of decisions at first instance only.

Returning to the problem, even where Mercutio has provided consideration he may not be permitted to bring an action, and even if he can, he may be unable to obtain a remedy which is of any value to Romeo. But that is not entirely the end of the matter, for there is one more possible line of argument. This is pretty unpromising on our set of facts, but again it is fully reviewed here in case you get a problem with more promising facts.

A trust of the promise?

There is no reason in principle why a covenant to settle property should not of itself form the subject matter of a trust. Such a covenant, giving the other party a right to sue on it, is itself a form of property: a chose in action. If a settlor so wishes, he can settle (i.e., create a fully constituted trust) of that chose in action in just the same way as he could settle land, shares or the proceeds of betting on a fast greyhound. All he has to do is to transfer that property — the benefit of the covenant — to the intended trustees. This will perfect the trust, and the beneficiaries can now enforce that trust just as if the subject-matter were land or cash.

Nevertheless, transferring the benefit of a covenant is not the most obvious option open to would-be settlors, and the courts are reluctant to place this interpretation on a transaction. One such case, however, was *Fletcher* v *Fletcher* (1844) 4 Hare 67. Ellis Fletcher covenanted by deed to pay £60,000 to his trustees, on trust for his illegitimate sons, who were outside the marriage consideration, and were thus volunteers. The surviving son, Jacob, was able to compel the trustees (note that the term is here correctly used) to enforce the covenant on his behalf. Though the *money* was never settled, Wigram V-C held that the *covenant* was held on a fully constituted trust for Jacob. Thus Jacob could enforce it in his own right, despite being a volunteer. Substantial damages were recoverable, amounting to the promised £60,000.

This was in spite of the fact that the trustees knew nothing of the covenant until the death of the settlor, Ellis Fletcher, and even then were most reluctant to sue upon it. However, the ignorance of the trustees, or their unwillingness to accept the trust, should not be a bar to a finding that Fletcher meant to give his trustees a chose in action rather than the money itself, so creating a valid trust. The relevant intention is that of the settlor, not of the trustees. Reluctant trustees can always be replaced by the court (see Feltham (1982) 98 LQR 17).

Nevertheless, the later case of *Re Schebsman* [1944] Ch 83 suggests that the courts today would demand much more conclusive evidence before construing that the settlor really did intend to settle the benefit of the covenant, and it seems likely that were the same facts as in *Fletcher* v *Fletcher* to arise today, no such intention would be construed. Without some strong evidence that Alpha intended to create a settlement of the promise, in lieu of transferring the shares themselves, Romeo's claim will almost certainly fail.

A note on after-acquired property

In *Fletcher* v *Fletcher* itself, the £60,000 was real, existing property, and the trustees were able to recover substantial damages for the failure to transfer it to them, even though they had personally suffered no loss. This is probably because they were regarded not as suing in their personal capacity, but as trustees of the promise for the estate. Effectively, therefore, a promise held in trust for the estate may be regarded as ha.ing been made with the estate (rather than with the trustees personally), and the trustees were suing only as the estate's representatives. The same principle probably applies to covenants to settle existing property other than money, presently owned by the settlor, and authority can be found in the judgment of Younger J in *Re Cavendish Browne's ST* [1916] WN 341. There seems no reason not to apply it also to property to which I have a contractual right, but have not yet received, such as the royalties I may hope to receive from a book.

In our problem, Alpha already owns the shares in Juliet Engineering, but she neither owns nor even has any contractual entitlement to the other property mentioned. It has been held (in *Re Ellenborough* [1903] 1 Ch 697) that such future property cannot form the subject-matter of a trust, and there is also doubt about whether a covenant to settle such property can itself form the subject-matter of a trust. Buckley J thought that it could not in *Re Cook's ST* [1965] Ch 905, already referred to. If so then *Fletcher*-style arguments would not work at all with this type of property.

On the other hand, if Alpha actually transfers her prize money as promised, she cannot later reclaim it, because the act of transfer will have created a perfect trust of the money. In *Re Ellenborough*, the court would not compel Miss Emily Towry Law to pay over the legacy when it arrived, but there was no argument in favour of allowing her to reclaim earlier payments which she had made in fulfilment of the same covenant which she now declined to perform.

Nor, it would seem on the basis of *Re Ralli's WT* [1964] Ch 288, would it prevent the trust from becoming fully constituted if the property came into the trustee's hands in some other capacity than that of trustee. This brings us to fact situation (c) in the problem. If the property bequeathed to Alpha comes into Mercutio's hands in his capacity as executor, that is sufficient to perfect the trust, and Mercutio will hold the property for Romeo.

Quite how far this principle can be extended is not certain. What if Mercutio comes by his legal title to Uncle Montague's property, not as his executor, but as his trustee in bankruptcy? Or as a judgment creditor? Or suppose that Uncle Montague has mortgaged his villa to Mercutio before leaving it to Alpha in his will, and Mercutio forecloses? For that matter, must the trustee acquire title to the property, or is it enough that he or she obtains physical possession? The possibilities are endless, and have not been fully worked out, so you have plenty of scope for reflection on this case.

'Exceptions' to the principle that equity will not assist a volunteer

This section covers *donatio martis causa*, and the rule in *Strong* v *Bird*. Whether these are true exceptions to the above principle or merely additional methods by which a trust can be fully constituted is not really important. They operate as if they were exceptions to the general rule.

Although these areas might be thought to be moribund and obscure, their inclusion is, surprisingly enough, justified by recent case law, including a recent decision of the Court of Appeal, where a *donatio mortis causa* of land was actually argued *successfully*.

However, no settlor would deliberately invoke either of the exceptions considered here. Problems in this area, in so far that they occur at all in practice, arise *ex post facto* because of competing claims to a deceased person's property.

Donatio mortis causa

A *donatio mortis causa* is a gift made in contemplation of, and conditional upon, the death of the donor. It is different from an ordinary, immediate gift, for the donee's title does not come into existence until the death occurs: until such time, the donor may revoke. Nor is it a testamentary gift taking effect under the terms of a properly attested will.

To return to the scenario of the problem, let us suppose that Alpha is superstitious, and that when, on the day before the Italian Grand Prix, she reads in her horoscope that she must beware of serious accidents, she takes this sufficiently seriously to hand over her jewellery to Romeo, telling her that if she (Alpha) should die, she wants Romeo to keep it. This is a *donatio mortis causa*, and if Alpha dies Romeo will keep the jewels, but although Romeo has custody of the jewels she will not own them unless and until Alpha is killed in the race.

If that happens, equity regards Romeo's title as perfected, and she may claim the jewellery in preference to anyone to whom Alpha may have chosen to bequeath it in her will. So if Alpha has already made a will in which all her personal property, which would otherwise include the jewellery, is left to her cousin Capulet, Romeo has a better claim by virtue of the conditional gift.

To permit the making of a disposition which is neither an immediate perfect gift nor a formal testamentary disposition is to invite fraudulent claims intended to defeat the expectations of legatees, and it is therefore not surprising that equity hedges a *donatio mortis causa* with stringent conditions. The necessary conditions for a *donatio mortis causa* were set out by Farwell J in *Re Craven's Estate* [1937] Ch 423:

(a) The transfer must be with the intention of giving, and not simply of securing the goods. There is no *donatio mortis causa* if Alpha simply wants Romeo to look after her jewellery while she is out on the track.

(b) It must be clear that the property was handed over in contemplation of a real possiblity of death, and some specific focus upon the possibility of death must be shown. The donor must anticipate some hazard to life. This is usually a serious illness, but extreme hazard (such as motor racing) is probably covered, but not everyday risks, e.g., air travel.

The gift must be conditional upon death occurring, and otherwise revocable, i.e., Alpha must intend to keep the for jewellery herself if she survives. This looks a little odd, since she could have made a valid immediate gift if she chose, and the requirement is therefore superfluous where the property is a chattel which could be transferred by simple delivery. It becomes relevant where some further formal step is required, however, to perfect the title, as for example, in the case of land, below.

(c) The donor must have effectively parted with dominion over the subject matter of the gift, i.e., the property must have been handed over, or the means of access to it transferred, e.g., giving Romeo the key to the bank deposit box where the jewels are lodged, without keeping a duplicate key. The test is whether the donor has put it out of his power between the dates of gift and death to alter the subject matter of the gift and substitute other property for it: see also *Re Lillingston* [1952] 2 All ER 184, at p.191.

It is also possible to transfer property which is not capable of physical delivery, e.g., by handing over *indicia* of title, such as a savings bank book, or (presumably) a bill of lading covering a consignment of cargo aboard a ship. The test is whether handing over the document 'amounted to a transfer', in which case possession or production of the document would entitle the possessor to the money in the account.

Donatio mortis causa and land   Long after most students of the law of trusts must have thought that *donatio mortis causa* cases were ancient history, a *donatio mortis causa* was successfully argued before the Court of Appeal in *Sen v Headley* [1991] 2 All ER 636. It had long been thought that it was impossible to have a *donatio mortis causa* of land, because the third of Farwell J's conditions cannot be satisfied, even by delivery of the title deeds, but on the assumption that *Sen v Headley* is correct, this view must now be regarded as wrong.

Mr Hewett, who was at the age of 86, on his death-bed, gave the plaintiff, Mrs Sen, the keys to a steel box with the title deeds to his house inside, saying to her: 'The house is yours, Margaret. You have the keys. They are in your bag. The deeds are in the steel box.'

It appeared that Mr Hewett and Mrs Sen had previously lived together as if married.

Clearly, the transfer of title deeds could not amount to a transfer of the land itself during Hewett's lifetime, since no deed was executed, and a declaration of trust would require writing. This is because it would have to be a declaration of trust of land (see chapter 5). Here there was no documentation at all, and Margaret could at most acquire a 'mere *spes*' (hope or expectation) of obtaining the property.

After Hewett's death, the gift was challenged by his next-of-kin. At first instance, [1990] Ch 728, Mummery J analysed Farwell J's criteria, set out above, and held although there were no problems over the first two requirements, there were over the third: Hewett had not parted with dominion over the house. On the question whether there could be a *donatio mortis causa* of land, he said that:

(a)   Judicial caution should be exercised, particularly at first instance, before extending the *donatio mortis causa* doctrine.

(b)   The policy of the law required formality for dispositions of land and interests in land.

(c)   Accordingly, the *donatio mortis causa* doctrine would not allow an attempt at disposition on death which avoided the Will Act formalities (on which, see chapter 7), or the perfection of an imperfect *inter vivos* gift.

The clear inference from Mummery J's judgment was that *donatio mortis causa* could *never* apply to land. This view, at any rate, was in line with the orthodox views that had been long-held.

Mummery J was reversed in the Court of Appeal, however, on analogy with extensions of the doctrine in previous cases. In *Snellgrove* v *Bailey* (1744) 3 Atk 213, the doctrine had been applied to a gift of money secured by a bond, by delivery of the bond; in *Duffield* v *Elwes* (1827) 1 Bli (NS) 497, the House of Lords had applied the doctrine to a gift of money secured by a mortgage of land, by delivery of the mortgage deed. In each case, transfer of *indicia* of title was all that was required.

No doubt the doctrine was anomalous, but in the view of Nourse LJ, that did not justify creating anomalous exceptions to the admittedly anomalous doctrine. The only reason why, with unregistered land, transfer of the title deeds did not transfer title to the property was because of a formality statute. All *donationes mortis causa* avoid formality provisions, usually the Wills Act (on which, see further, chapter 7). There was no reason why the formality provisions relating to land should be regarded as presenting any greater obstacle than any other formality provisions, and no reason why this case should be treated differently from the cases mentioned in the previous paragraph.

It does not necessarily follow that shares in private companies, which cannot be physically transferred, can also be the subject of a *donatio mortis causa*, since registration of a new owner may be refused. They are therefore not directly analogous to land.

Death sooner than expected It seems on the basis of *Wilkes* v *Allington* [1931] 2 Ch 104 that the gift is valid even if Alpha dies sooner than expected and even from a different cause. The donor was suffering from an incurable disease, and made a gift knowing that he had not long to live. In fact he died even earlier than expected of pneumonia, but the gift was held to be valid. So a *donatio mortis causa* should still work if Alpha is killed while flying to the race-track in her private helicopter. Whether the same principle would apply even if the death were completely different from Alpha's expectation is less clear (e.g., she dies of food poisoning).

Death later than expected What if Alpha is killed just after the race, say on the winner's rostrum by a bottle flung by an outraged fan of another competitor? Was the gift to Romeo revoked as soon as Alpha's survival of the race itself became assured (when she took the chequered flag), or is it possible to argue that the whole enterprise of the day's racing comes within the area of risk contemplated by the gift? If the death can be said to be an inherent risk of participation in the race, then perhaps Romeo should keep the jewels.

The rule in Strong v Bird (1874) LR 18 Eq 315

The other exception to the principle that equity will not assist a volunteer is the rule in *Strong* v *Bird* (1874) LR 18 Eq 315, and it could arise in some such fashion as this. Alpha hands Romeo her share certificates but fails to procure the transfer and registration of Romeo as owner. She then dies in the race, leaving a will which appoints Romeo as her executor but makes Capulet the legatee of all her personal property. Again, equity treats the gift as perfected, this time by the vesting of Alpha's property in Romeo in her capacity as executor, and the claims of the beneficiaries under the will are overridden.

The same principle operates if Romeo owes Alpha money, but Alpha makes no effort to collect her debt and appoints Romeo her executor: these were the facts of *Strong* v *Bird* itself. The appointment is, as it were, a conclusive release of the debt. But it must be clear that there was an intention to make the gift or release the debt, and that this intention continued until death.

One might have thought that the logic of the rule in *Strong* v *Bird* requires that Romeo be *voluntarily* appointed executor by A, but there is some authority that the rule operates if Romeo becomes Alpha's administrator, instead of her executor. This was the view of Farwell J in *Re James* [1935] Ch 449, where a housekeeper had herself appointed one of two administratrices of testator's estate.

In *Re Gonin*, however, a case considered in another context in chapter 5, Walton J cast doubt on *Re James*. In *Re Gonin*, the plaintiff alleged that, in return for her returning home after being called away during the Second World War, and going to live with and look after her parents, her parents had orally agreed that the parental home and its contents should become hers on their deaths. The plaintiff's father died in 1957, leaving no estate. After the death of the plaintiff's mother in 1968, the plaintiff took out letters of administration to her estate, and began an action to determine whether she was entitled, as administratrix, to vest the freehold in the property in herself.

She claimed both land and contents (furniture) under the rule in *Strong* v *Bird*, on the basis that the plaintiff's mother intended to give the plaintiff the house on her death, and by the plaintiff taking out letters of administration, the gift was perfected.

Walton J took the view that the appointment of an administrator was quite different to the appointment of an executor, since it was not a voluntary act of the deceased, but of the law. It was also often a matter of pure chance which of many persons entitled to a grant of letters of administration actually took them out:

> Why, then, should any special tenderness be shown to a person so selected by law and not the will of the testator, and often indifferently selected among many with an equal claim? It would seem an astonishing doctrine of equity that if the person who wishes to take the benefit of the rule in *Strong* v *Bird* manages to be the person to obtain a grant then he will be able to do so, but if a person equally entitled manages to obtain a prior grant, then he will not be able to do so.

Walton J did not need actually to decide whether the earlier authority was correct, however, since he also held that even if the rule in *Strong* v *Bird* applied to administrators, the evidence did not point to a continuing intention on the part of the plaintiff's mother to give the house to the plaintiff.

The plaintiff also advanced an argument based on the part performance doctrine, which is considered in chapter 5.

FOUR

CERTAINTY OF OBJECT, PRIVATE PURPOSE TRUSTS AND UNINCORPORATED ASSOCIATIONS

Certainty of object, private purpose trusts and unincorporated associations may appear at first sight to be a motley collection of unrelated subjects, but in fact they are all interrelated, and it is by no means unlikely that a single exam question will include elements of more than one of these areas. They are also central to the law of trusts, so it would be a very odd paper that did not cover any of them.

If question spotting, you should also bear in mind that any question about whether a trust is charitable will, in all probability, invite you to consider the alternative possibility of a valid private purpose trust. These two areas should also be considered together, therefore. Charities are dealt with in chapter 8.

The connection between the areas discussed in this chapter is (in general terms) as follows. Certainty of object problems are (at least in part) about identifying the human beings who, as possible beneficiaries (who are also referred to as 'objects'), can enforce a trust (or power). If they cannot be identified in accordance with the test to be applied, the trust (or power) will fail.

One of the problems presented by private purpose trusts is precisely that they usually fall foul of certainty of object requirements. They may not be for the benefit of human beings at all (for example animal trusts), and even if they are there may be no human beneficiaries in the full sense (i.e., having a full beneficial interest). There are also sometimes perpetuity difficulties with purpose trusts.

Unincorporated associations usually exist to further a purpose, so the problems of private purpose trusts would also apply to them, except that it is usually possible to construe gifts to them so as to avoid the problems of a trusts analysis altogether.

If a purpose trust is charitable, or if an unincorporated association exists to further a charitable purpose, the above problems do not apply. Because the Attorney-General can always enforce a charitable trust they are exempt from certainty of object requirements, and they are also exempt from the perpetuity rules.

Certainty of object

The most difficult part of certainty of object probably lies in the actual method of application of the *McPhail* v *Doulton* test, discussed later in this section, especially in the light of the decision of the Court of Appeal in *Re Baden's Deed Trusts (No. 2)* [1973] Ch 9. A problem question will be discussed later in the chapter, which will examine this particular difficulty, but first it is necessary to consider certainty of object in general terms.

What are the rules for?

Certainty of object rules apply to both trusts and powers, and serve two main functions. The certainty tests have been developed to further (to a greater or lesser extent) these two functions, and virtually all the discussion that follows can be related to them. So it is of the utmost importance that you know what they are.

First, if a trustee, or donee of a power fails to carry out his duties, or exercises such discretion as he may have, in an improper manner, it is important to be able to ascertain who has *locus standi* to come to court to remedy the situation. Note that throughout this chapter 'he' includes 'she'.

You may think at first sight that the settlor would be the appropriate person, but in fact he drops out of the picture once a settlement has been made, and ceases to have any interest in the property. The settlor, therefore, cannot enforce the trust, and indeed, in the common case of a settlement by will, he will naturally be unable to have any further personal say.

It is true that if the trustee has agreed to act for consideration, the settlor, or if he is dead his personal representatives, can sue in contract. It is less likely that the trustee is appointed under a contract in an ordinary family settlement, however, and in any case a contract action is not a satisfactory solution, because of the remedies difficulty (see chapter 3).

Therefore the courts have always been very concerned that someone who benefits in equity (i.e., an object) is able to enforce the trust or power. People with a full beneficial interest certainly have sufficient interest to enforce it (whether the same can be said of people with lesser interests is considered in the discussion of purpose trusts, below). The certainty requirements must allow these people to be identified. If certainty of object tests are not satisfied the property will be held on resulting trust for the settlor, because otherwise there would be nothing to stop the trustees keeping it for themselves.

The stringency of the test required depends on how the courts ultimately enforce the trust or power. This varies depending on whether they are faced with a fixed trust, discretionary trust or power, and so will be discussed separately for each variety of disposition. The minimum requirement, applicable to any disposition, is first that there must be human beneficiaries capable of enforcing the trust (or power), and secondly, that if one of them comes to court it must be possible to show that he has *locus standi*. This minimum requirement is satisfied by the individual ascertainability test, discussed in detail below. Note that it is enough to show of any individual that he is or is not an object: it is unnecessary to be able to draw up a list of all the objects.

The second reason for certainty rules is to enable trusts or powers to be administered. A trustee, or donee of a power, may have to be able to ascertain who the objects are in order to be able to exercise any discretion he may have in a proper manner. Again the precise requirement will vary depending on the nature of the disposition, but often a stricter test is required for the second function than for the first. For example, if a trustee or donee of a power has to get an impression of the size or composition of the entire class of objects in order to carry out his duties, it may be necessary to draw up a list of all or at any rate most of the objects, in effect to ascertain the entire class, or most of it. This requirement is satisfied by the class ascertainability test, discussed below.

The rules themselves

Powers   Whereas trustees under a discretionary trust must distribute the trust property, albeit that they have a discretion as to how, the donees of a power have a discretion not only as to *how* to distribute the property, but also as to *whether* to distribute it. They are under no obligation to appoint at all. In other words, whereas a trust is imperative, because the trustees have to appoint, a power is discretionary, because the donees of a power need not appoint at all — the choice is theirs.

If there is a gift over in default of appointment, the disposition must take effect as a power, not a trust, since the existence of the gift over is obviously inconsistent with an imperative duty to appoint. The absence of a gift over in default is not necessarily indicative of a trust, however, since the alternative construction, of a power with a resulting trust in favour of the settlor in the absence of appointment, is also possible. It will all depend on the words used in the instrument.

In the case of mere powers, the donee's discretion seems to be unfettered except in so far that he must not dispose of the property otherwise than in accordance with the terms of the power. The objects can come to court to enforce the power, therefore, only to the limited extent that the court will restrain disposal of the property otherwise than in accordance with the terms of the power.

This limited negative duty can be carried out and enforced so long as 'it can be said with certainty that any given individual is or is no a member of the class'. No more stringent test of certainty than the individual ascertainability test is required.

It is probably more common for powers of appointment to be given to trustees, in which case the donees of the power will not enjoy an unfettered discretion. Sir Robert Megarry V-C took the view in *Re Hay's ST* [1982] 1 WLR 1202, that the extent of the duty to consider both whether or not a power should be exercised, and how it should be exercised, is stronger when the power is given to someone who is also a trustee, than when a mere power is exercised. For example, it is not sufficient simply to appoint to the objects who happen to be at hand, whereas the donee of a mere power can do this. It seems that it is necessary periodically to consider whether or not to exercise the power, and at least to appreciate the width of the field of objects, even if it is not possible to compile a list of all the objects, or ascertain accurately their number. Also, individual appointments need to be considered on their merits:

> The trustee must not simply proceed to exercise the power in favour of such of the objects as happen to be at hand or claim his attention. He must first consider what person or classes of persons are objects of the power within the definition in the settlement or will. In doing this, there is no need to compile a complete list of the objects, or even to make an accurate assessment of the number of them: what is needed is an appreciation of the width of the field, and thus whether a selection is to be made merely from a dozen, or instead, from thousands or millions . . .

Nevertheless, if at the end of the day the donees of the power refuse to exercise it, that is a choice that they are entitled to make, and there is no reason why the courts should be required to distribute on their behalf. It is still necessary to be able to ascertain of any given individual whether or not he or she is an object of the power, since only objects of the power will have *locus standi* to enforce it, even to the limited extent of preventing the donees acting otherwise than in accordance with its terms. It is also necessary for the objects to be defined so that the donees can, as required by Sir Robert Megarry V-C above, get a feel for the width of the class.

Despite this, the duty to consider is not so stringent as to require the donees, in order to carry it out, to draw up a list of the entire class of potential beneficiaries, and there is therefore no reason in principle to apply the class ascertainability test to powers.

In *Re Gestetner's Settlement* [1953] 1 Ch 672, Harman J had to consider the validity of a power given to trustees to distribute among a very wide class, including directors and employees or former employees of a large number of companies, with a gift over in default. Since membership of the class constantly fluctuated, it was impossible to draw up a list of the entire class at any one time. He held that it was not necessary to know all the objects in order to appoint, and that it was not fatal that the entire class could not be ascertained.

In *Re Gulbenkian's Settlements* [1970] AC 508, trustees were given a power to apply income from the trust fund to maintain, among others, any person in whose house or in whose company or in whose care Gulbenkian may from time to time be residing, and there was a gift over in default of appointment. In upholding the power, the House of Lords held that the individual ascertainability test was the applicable test for powers: a power would be valid if it could be said with certainty whether any given individual was *or was not* a member of the class, and would not fail simply because it was impossible to ascertain every member of the class.

There are two points specifically to note about the *Gulbenkian* test. First, the italicised words, *or was not*, are important. Secondly, the House of Lords expressly rejected Lord Denning MR's test in the Court of Appeal in *Gulbenkian* [1968] Ch 126, at pp. 132–4. On the basis that a power would be held void for uncertainty only if it was impossible to carry it out, he had taken the view that it should be necessary only to be able to identify one single beneficiary as being clearly within the class. The House of Lords disagreed, primarily because this test took no account of the trustee's duty to carry out the power in a fiduciary manner. The Denning test would only really be appropriate were the trustees at liberty to distribute to the first person who came to hand, and as we have seen that is not the case.

The importance of these two points will become apparent later in the chapter.

Discretionary trusts   Whereas a court will never be called upon ultimately to enforce a power, if the donees refuse to distribute, if no distribution is made by trustees under a discretionary trust, the court may, as a last resort, be called upon to effect a distribution itself. The certainty test for discretionary trusts has largely depended on the nature of their ultimate enforcement, and the courts' view of this has changed recently. At one time they took the view that the court could not exercise any discretion on behalf of recalcitrant trustees (see, e.g., the view of Jenkins LJ in *Inland Revenue Commissioners* v *Broadway Cottages Trust* [1955] Ch 678). It could remove the trustees and appoint others in their place, but in theory it could be impossible to find any other trustees prepared to execute the trust. It followed that, however unlikely this eventuality may be, at the end of the day a court had to be prepared to carry out the trust itself. Since it refused to exercise any discretion it could only divide the property equally among all the objects.

Though there is a logic to this conclusion, given the premises, equality of distribution will often not implement the intentions of the settlor, and indeed is quite likely to frustrate them. It seems that the equality principle originated in 19th-century family settlements (e.g., *Burrough* v *Philcox* (1840) 5 My & Cr 72), where it may have been the most reliable method of carrying out the settlor's intention. It is much less likely to be appropriate, however, in modern settlements, for example, dividing proceeds among employees of a company.

Nevertheless, equality of distribution was the rule, and of course it could only be done if it was possible to draw up a list of all the objects. For this reason, *Inland Revenue Commissioners* v *Broadway Cottages Trust* applied the class ascertainability test to discretionary trusts.

The class in *Broadway* was undoubtedly extremely wide, consisting mostly of remote issue, as well as a number of charities. Two charities (Broadway Cottages Trust and Sunnylands Trust) had received income under the settlement, and claimed an income tax exemption on it, but in order to do so they had to show that the settlement was valid. The class was never held to be unascertainable, since the charities conceded the point (perhaps unwisely, since it was conceptually certain, and only evidential difficulties prevented drawing up an entire list of objects: see further, the discussion on fixed trusts, below). The Crown for its part conceded that the individual ascertainability test was satisfied. On the basis of these concessions, the Court of Appeal held that the trust failed: *Gestetner* did not apply, since here there was no gift over, there was an obligation to distribute, and the whole range of objects had to be ascertainable.

Jenkins LJ took the view that if the court was called upon to enforce the trust: 'It could not mend the invalidity of the trust by imposing an arbitrary distribution amongst some only of the whole unascertainable class.' The court could only effect a distribution to all the objects equally. The irony of this is that, given that some of the objects were charities and others people, equality of distribution was probably the last thing the settlor would have wanted.

One result of this case was that the test for certainty was much more stringent for discretionary trusts than for powers (on which, see above). This had two main consequences: first, many perfectly reasonable trusts failed; secondly, the courts were at pains to construe doubtful dispositions as powers, rather than discretionary trusts.

In *McPhail* v *Doulton* [1971] AC 424, however, the House of Lords decisively rejected the principle of equality of distribution, in a case where equal distribution would have made a nonsense of the settlor's intention. The House accepted that even in the final analysis, assuming in other words that no trustee could be found who was prepared to execute the trust, it could exercise the necessary discretion itself. Therefore, at least so far as ultimate enforcement is concerned a less rigid certainty test should be sufficient. All that is required is for it to be possible to tell, with certainty, whether any individual coming to court to enforce a trust or power has sufficient interest to do so: in other words whether or not he is within the class of objects. This requirement is of course satisfied by the individual ascertainability test.

The *ratio* of *McPhail* v *Doulton* is that the test for certainty for discretionary trusts is essentially the same as that for powers, the individual ascertainability test, not the class ascertainability test. *Inland Revenue Commissioners* v *Broadway Cottages Trust* was overruled.

Lord Wilberforce also made the point that in applying the test the courts are concerned only with conceptual uncertainty. A trust will not fail merely because there are evidential difficulties in ascertaining whether or not someone is within the class, as the court is never defeated by evidential uncertainty, and can deal with problems of proof when an application for enforcement arises:

> I desire to emphasise the distinction clearly made . . . between linguistic or semantic uncertainty which, if unresolved by the court, renders the gift void, and the difficulty of ascertaining the existence or whereabouts of members of the class, a matter with which the court can appropriately deal on an application for directions.

Thus, a discretionary trust in favour of the first 20 people who crossed Clifton suspension bridge in 1991 should be enforceable: the class is conceptually certain even though proof may be difficult. A trust in favour of 'all my friends' is different, however. It is conceptually uncertain, because 'all my friends' is not a phrase capable of precise definition. Such a trust ought therefore to fail even on the *McPhail* v *Doulton* test.

A major problem is that the change in *McPhail* v *Doulton* was consequential on the court changing its views about ultimate enforcement. Unfortunately, the relaxation may lead to difficulties over administration. Unlike donees of mere powers (see last section), the trustees' discretion is not absolute. In considering its exercise, they must, according to Lord Wilberforce in *McPhail* v *Doulton* itself, make a survey of the entire field of objects, and consider each individual case responsibly, on its merits. This ought to require a more rigorous certainty test than individual ascertainability. For example, the Clifton suspension bridge example should fail (assuming no central record is kept of people walking over Clifton bridge), because the trustees could not possibly survey the entire field.

Since under the new test trustees may be unable to discover the identities of all the possible beneficiaries, they will sometimes be unable to carry out their duties. Some discretionary trusts could be very difficult to administer were the trustees unable to survey the entire field of possible beneficiaries. An example might be a discretionary trust to distribute property 'according to the age and ability of the potential beneficiaries'.

Lord Wilberforce himself suggested a way out of the difficulty. He thought that dispositions might fail if the class is so widely drawn as to be administratively unworkable, even if they otherwise satisfy the new test. An example he gave was a gift to 'all the residents of Greater London', but the acceptable width of the class presumably depends on the exact nature of the trustees' duties, and whether they must actually survey the entire field.

Another possible solution is that if the terms of a trust negative any sensible intention on the part of the settlor, it may fail on the grounds of capriciousness. This was suggested *obiter* by Templeman J in *Re Manisty's Settlement* [1974] Ch 17. The same applies, incidentally, to powers, and indeed *Re Manisty's Settlement* actually concerned a valid power.

Perhaps these qualifications are sufficient to give the trustees the protection they require, though at the expense of the vagueness inherent in tests of this nature. Further discussion of this problem follows in consideration of the problem, below.

Another problem with the new certainty test is how, if at all, the doctrine in *Saunders* v *Vautier* (1841) 4 Beav 115 applies. Under this doctrine, all the beneficiaries, collectively entitled, can (so long as they are adult and *sui juris*) terminate the trust and distribute or resettle the trust property. It is difficult to see how this doctrine can operate if the entire class of beneficiaries cannot be ascertained.

One possible answer is that *Saunders* v *Vautier* applies only to fixed trusts, on the grounds that the objects of a discretionary trust do not have full beneficial interests unless and until the trustees' discretion is exercised in their favour, but Lord Upjohn in *Gulbenkian* suggests otherwise. The other possible answer is that the courts would use a device similar to the *Benjamin* order discussed below (in the section on fixed trusts).

The settlement in *McPhail* v *Doulton* was further litigated as to the application of the new test in *Re Baden's Deed Trusts (No.2)* [1973] Ch 9. This is a very difficult case, and will be considered in detail in discussing the problem, below.

Fixed trusts It is usually argued that, since it is the essence of a fixed trust that the property is to be divided among all the beneficiaries in fixed proportions (e.g., in equal shares), it can only be workable if the entire class of beneficiaries is known; the conventional view, therefore, is that the test of certainty is the class ascertainability test.

This was certainly the view of Jenkins LJ in *Broadway* (at p. 29): 'There can be no division in equal shares amongst a class of persons unless all the members of the class are known.' In other words, a complete list of objects must be able to be drawn up. From the fact that, in *McPhail* v *Doulton*, the House of Lords was concerned only to assimilate discretionary trusts and powers, the implication usually drawn is that the reasoning was not intended also to apply to fixed trusts.

However, there are fairly convincing contrary arguments (see, e.g., *Matthews* [1984] Conv 22). The orthodox view presupposes that *Broadway* still stands in so far that later cases have not directly detracted from it, but it is arguable that even when it was decided, *Broadway* was wholly out of line with other authorities, in which case there is no reason for it still to be regarded as authority for anything at all.

The central issue, I would suggest, is the basis upon which the trust property is distributed by the trustees, or if the issue becomes one of ultimate enforcement, by the courts. It is often assumed that distribution is impossible unless the entire class can be ascertained, but this need not be the case, and even if it is, application of the class ascertainability test may not necessarily resolve the difficulty.

Suppose, for example, that in 1986 Michael settled property upon trustees with directions in 1991 that the property was to be sold, and that the proceeds of sale were to be distributed equally, in favour of those of his three sons, Paul, Quentin and Richard, who are still then living. Assuming that in 1986 all three of the settlor's sons were known to be alive, it is obvious that this is a fixed trust, and that it satisfies the class ascertainability test.

Suppose now that at some time after 1986 Richard went on an Antarctic expedition, from which by 1991 he has not returned. He is thought (but not known definitely) to have perished on the expedition. The trustees sell the property, and wish to distribute it in accordance with their directions. Despite the fact that the class ascertainability test was clearly satisfied, and that the trust did not fail for want of certainty, it is obvious that they have a problem.

If at this point the trustees asked for directions, it is likely that the court would resolve the difficulty by making a *Benjamin* order (based on *Re Benjamin* [1902] 1 Ch 723). The trustees would be directed to distribute on the basis that Richard was dead. If Richard later turned up alive, he would still have an interest in the proceeds of sale, which he would be able to claim from Paul and Quentin if it were still traceable, and assuming that his claim was not barred by limitation. The trustees personally would be protected from any action, however.

It is clear, then, that evidential difficulties, even in the distribution of fixed trusts, can be resolved by the courts. Is there any reason of logic or principle why the position should be any different if by the time of the settlement in 1986, Richard had already embarked upon the expedition, and it was not know even then whether he was alive or dead? In those circumstances it would not after all, be possible at the date of the settlement, to draw up a list of all the objects, since it would not be possible to say with certainty whether Richard should be included or not. The question is one upon which you must form your own views, but a strong argument can be made that there is no need to apply the class ascertainability test, even to fixed trusts.

As we saw in the last section, in applying the individual ascertainability test, Lord Wilberforce distinguished between evidential and conceptual uncertainty, on the ground that the courts are never defeated by evidential uncertainty. Another interesting question is whether, if the class ascertainability test does still apply to fixed trusts, the same distinction also applies. If it does, it leads to some interesting consequences.

It may be remembered that in *Broadway*, although the class was very large, it was not conceptually uncertain. There was no problem over defining the class conceptually, and *it was conceded* in *Broadway*, rather than concluded from rational agrument, that the class could not be ascertained. Perhaps the concession was wrongly made, and that in reality, even in *Broadway* itself, the class ascertainability test was satisfied. *Broadway* was indeed criticised in *Gulbenkian* (in particular, by Lords Reid and Upjohn), and by Lord Wilberforce in *McPhail* v *Doulton*, on the grounds that the Court of Appeal had confused conceptual and evidential uncertainty.

If, however, the distinction between conceptual and evidential uncertainty applies equally to the class as to the individual ascertainability test, it is difficult to see any difference between the two tests. If it can be said of any individual that he or she falls outside the class, then there can be no conceptual difficulty in defining the class as a whole. Indeed, there is no *conceptual* difficulty in defining the class in the above example, merely an evidential difficulty in ascertaining whether Richard is a member. In principle, however, evidential difficulties, as in *Broadway* and the example, are capable of resolution by the courts.

There are, I would suggest, two possible answers to the rather startling conclusion that the individual and class ascertainability tests are in reality the same. One is that the class ascertainability test has always been an evidential test, and that the distinction between conceptual and evidential uncertainty applies only to the individual ascertainability test. The other is that, even if that is wrong, trusts can also be struck down on the grounds of administrative unworkability, and it does not follow that merely because a discretionary trust is administratively workable with a given class of objects, a trust with the same class of objects will necessarily be so, if the trustees' discretion is removed.

Administrative unworkability is considered in greater detail in the discussion of the problem question.

Note that I have provided no answers in this section, merely, I hope, food for thought.

Problem question

In recognition of the merger of University College, Cardiff, with its sister institution, UWIST, in September 1988, Jones, a former student made a will in which he left his residuary estate to University of Wales, College of Cardiff on trust to apply the money as the officers of the College in their absolute discretion see fit for the benefit of the descendants of those ex-students of University College, living at his death, who appeared in the official College photograph of 1910. Jones has now died, and his next of kin wish to challenge the bequest. Discuss.

This question concerns the detailed application of the *McPhail* v *Doulton* test. Though it looks easy it is a lot more difficult than appears at first sight, and you will need to have a sound knowledge of the post *McPhail* v *Doulton* cases. It is a likely area for a problem question in an exam.

It looks at first sight like a valid discretionary trust, which satisfies the individual ascertainability test, because any given object should be able to show whether he is within the class. No conceptual uncertainty arises in applying the test. It was Sachs LJ in *Re Baden's Deed Trusts (No. 2)* [1973] Ch 9 who elaborated on the distinction between conceptual and evidential uncertainty. He gave 'someone under a moral obligation' as an example of conceptual uncertainty, and 'first cousins', 'members of the X trade union' and 'those who have served in the Royal Navy' as examples of conceptual certainty where proof might be difficult. This problem falls into the latter category because whether or not you are a descendant of one of a number of people can be answered yes or no. It is not a matter of degree, on which opinions may differ, like for example 'fat middle-aged men'. That would be conceptually uncertain.

So here apparently is a very easy question about a trust which is obviously valid. Not so by any means. Difficulties begin to emerge when one considers the detailed application of the certainty test. This is what the examiner is really looking for, and where the majority of marks will go. There are at least two arguments that this disposition is invalid.

First, it is arguable that the class is so widely drawn as to be administratively unworkable, as in 'all the residents of Greater London' (discussed above), in which case on Lord Wilberforce's own view the disposition should fail.

On the other hand, the trustees are ostensibly given 'absolute discretion', so arguably may not need to survey the entire class to administer the trust. But even 'absolute discretion' must be exercised on equitable principles, so the trustees would be in breach were they to appoint the first objects who happened to be at hand. Indeed, the trustees were ostensibly given 'absolute discretion' in *McPhail* v *Doulton* itself, yet Lord Wilberforce thought that they would need 'to know what is the permissible area of selection and then consider responsibly'.

The question of administrative unworkability was considered in *Re Manisty's Settlement* [1974] Ch 17, where a power given to trustees was upheld where they were able to appoint anyone in the world apart from a small excepted class (a power where the objects are defined only by reference to an *excepted* class is called an intermediate or hybrid power). A similar decision was reached in *Re Hay's ST* [1982] 1 WLR 1202. These decisions suggest that very rarely will a power fail on grounds of administrative unworkability, simply because of the width of the class.

The courts are not concerned with questions of ultimate enforcement with a power, however, and it is arguable that the decisions in *Hay* and *Manisty* ought not to apply directly where, as here, the instrument is drafted as a trust. Indeed, in *Re Hay's ST* [1982] 1 WLR 1202 itself, Sir Robert Megarry V-C noted that: 'The words of Lord Wilberforce [about adminstrative unworkability] . . . are directed towards trusts, not powers.'

The problem arose directly in the Divisional Court in *R* v *District Auditor, ex parte West Yorkshire Metropolitan County Council* [1986] RVR 24. Prior to the abolition of the Metropolitan County Councils, they were prohibited from incurring expenditure under Local Government Act 1972, s. 137(1), 'which in their opinion is in the interests of their area or any part of it or some or all of its inhabitants,' after 1 April 1985.

When West Yorkshire Metropolitan County Council realised that they were going to have a large surplus on 1 April 1985, they sought to find ways of ensuring that this money could still be spent after the 1 April deadline. In their attempt to achieve this aim, they purported to set up a discretionary trust of £400,000, having a duration of 11 months, 'for the benefit of any or all or some of the inhabitants of the County of West Yorkshire'. The trust also directed the trustees to use the fund specifically:

(a) To assist economic development in the county in order to relieve unemployment and poverty.

(b) To assist bodies concerned with youth and community problems.

(c) To assist and encourage ethnic and other minority groups.

(d) To inform all interested persons of the consequences of the proposed abolition of the Council (and the other Metropolitan County Councils) and of other programmes affecting local government in the county.

This was held to be administratively unworkable. The inhabitants of the County of West Yorkshire numbered about two and a half million. The range of objects was held to be so hopelessly wide as to be incapable of forming anything like a class.

There are clear statements in the case that trusts may be treated differently from powers in this regard, since a court may be called upon ultimately to execute a trust, whereas it will not, of course, be required to execute a power.

The second argument that can be advanced is that the terms of the trust negative any sensible intention on the part of the settlor, in which case the disposition should fail on another principle discussed in *Re Manisty's Settlement*. The argument is quite plausible here, and indeed Templeman J thought this was the real problem over 'residents of Greater London':

> The settlor neither gives the trustees an unlimited power which they can exercise sensibly, nor a power limited to what may be described as a 'sensible' class, but a power limited to a class, membership of which is accidental and irrelevant to any settled purpose or to any method of limiting or selecting beneficiaries.

In addressing these issues the width of the class is not the only factor, since other factors may make clear what the intention of the settlor was. For example, in *Re Hay's ST* [1982] 1 WLR 1202, Sir Robert Megarry V-C said of this passage:

> In *Re Manisty's Settlement* [1974] Ch 17 at 27 Templeman J appears to be suggesting that a power to benefit 'residents in Greater London' is void as being capricious 'because the terms of the power negative any sensible intention of the part of the settlor'. In saying that, I do not think that the judge had in mind a case in which the settlor was, for instance, a former chairman of the Greater London Council, as subsequent words of his on that page indicate.

Alternatively, suppose that trustees were directed to use the fund, in their discretion, to provide library facilities for the residents of Greater London.

It might also be perfectly possible to infer a sensible intention on the part of the settlor. On the other hand, fairly precise guidelines were laid down in *R* v *District Auditor, ex parte West Yorkshire Metropolitan County Council*, but this was still insufficient to save the trust. In any case, in the problem question itself, no guidance is given to the officers of the college, so the trust may fail on this ground.

Even if the disposition does not fall foul of either of the above arguments, there are further difficulties to be resolved in the actual application of the test. It should not be forgotten that the disposition in *McPhail* v *Doulton* was remitted to the Chancery Division so that the House of Lords test could be applied. Eventually it came again to the Court of Appeal, where differing opinions were given: *Re Baden's Deed Trusts (No. 2)* [1973] Ch 9. By this time some 12 years had passed since Mr Baden's death, the fund was still sterilised by litigation, and a considerable proportion had been dissipated in legal costs. Sachs LJ observed that the situation 'lacks attraction'.

Re Baden's Deed Trusts (No. 2) is a very important case, and must be studied in detail. The disposition was 'to or for the benefit of any of the officers and employees or ex-officers or ex-employees of the company or to any relatives or dependants of any such persons'. It was argued by John Vinelott QC, who was challenging the disposition on behalf of the executors, that it could not be shown that any person definitely is or *is not* within the class (as required by the *Gulbenkian* test). Had this ingenious argument been accepted it would have meant virtually returning to the rejected class-ascertainability test, as Megaw LJ observed. In the disposition in the problem, for example, it would have been necessary to draw up a list of all the objects to show that any given applicant was *not* among them, and the disposition would fail. The Court of Appeal rejected the argument, but not on identical grounds.

Sachs LJ avoided the difficulty by emphasising that the court was concerned only with conceptual certainty, so that it should not be fatal that there might be *evidential* difficulties in drawing up John Vinelott QC's list. This effectively destroys the Vinelott argument, which was addressed primarily towards *evidential* difficulties in drawing up the class. Sachs LJ also took the view that the courts would place the burden of proof, in effect, on someone claiming to be within the class. This seems acceptable if ultimate enforcement is the issue, and the test is of the *locus standi* of the claimant, but it does not help the administration of the trust. If the test is correct the disposition in the problem satisfies it.

Megaw LJ adopted a different solution, however, requiring that as regards a substantial number of objects, it can be shown with certainty that they fall within the class. This is rather a vague test — clearly it is not enough to be able to show that *one* person is certainly within the class, as this test was rejected in *Gulbenkian* (see the discussion of powers, above). Presumably, the test requires evidential, as well as conceptual, certainty. Maybe Megaw LJ adopted it simply because he could find no other way of rejecting Mr Vinelott's argument without returning either to the rejected *Broadway* test, or to the test which had been rejected in *Gulbenkian*. Indeed, none of the judges in the Court of Appeal was able to find a satisfactory solution to this difficulty. The test may have the merit, however, of ensuring that the trustees will be able to get a feel for the width of the class, which they need properly to be able to exercise their discretion.

Whether the disposition in the problem satisfies Megaw LJ's test is largely a question of fact, depending on how difficult the descendants of these particular students are to ascertain.

Stamp LJ's test is probably the strictest of the three, and he seemed to be quite impressed by the Vinelott argument. He emphasised that it must be possible for the trustees to make a comprehensive survey of the range of objects, but he did not think it would be fatal if, at the end of the survey, it was impossible to draw up a list of every single beneficiary. He would have taken the view that the trust failed, had he not felt compelled to follow an early House of Lords authority, which had held that a discretionary trust for 'relations' was valid, 'relations' being defined narrowly, as 'next of kin'. If Stamp LJ's view is correct, it is very unlikely that the disposition in this problem is valid.

This problem illustrates then what many others also illustrate. First, there are not very many relevant cases, but you have to know them well (all three judgments in *Re Baden's Deed Trusts (No. 2)*). Secondly, you must be fresh *on the day* because you will have to think *in the exam itself* to apply the cases to the particular facts before you. You might also consider whether there is any substance to Mr Vinelott's argument in *Re Baden's Deed Trusts (No. 2)*, and if not how you would have dealt with it had you been sitting in the Court of Appeal.

Private purpose trusts

Examiners also like questions on private purpose trusts, and though these are often combined with charities issues (e.g., the problem question alluded to at the beginning of chapter 8), they need not be. A possible essay question might be:

How, if at all, does the beneficiary principle affect the validity of private purpose trusts?

A lack of ascertainable beneficiaries is also a reason why private (non-charitable) purpose trusts are usually struck down, because for that reason they are not enforceable by anyone (trusts for a charitable purpose are valid, but they are enforced by the Attorney-General).

Sometimes humans are not intended to benefit at all, in which case no one can enforce the trust. Dispositions of this nature are generally void. A classic example is *Re Astor's ST* [1952] Ch 534, where trustees were instructed to hold a fund upon various trusts including 'the maintenance of good relations between nations [and] . . . the preservation of the independence of newspapers'. The purposes were not charitable, but the settlement was drafted expressly so as to be valid under the perpetuity rules. The trust was held by Roxburgh J to be void, because there were no human beneficiaries capable of enforcing it. Further examples are *Re Shaw* [1957] 1 WLR 729, where Harman J held void on the same principle a trust to research the development of a 40-letter alphabet, and *Re Endacott* [1960] Ch 232, where a gift 'to North Tawton Devon Parish Council for the purpose of providing some useful memorial to myself' was held void by the Court of Appeal.

On the other hand, trusts to erect or maintain tombs and monuments have been upheld, as have trusts for the maintenance of specific animals (e.g., *Re Dean* (1889) 41 ChD 522) and even, in *Re Thompson* [1934] Ch 342, a trust for the promotion and furtherance of fox-hunting. It is difficult to reconcile these with the general principle; on the other hand too much reliance has been placed upon them for them now to be regarded as wrong (except perhaps *Re Thompson*), and they are usually regarded as exceptions (e.g., in *Re Astor's ST*).

Sometimes, on the other hand, humans are intended to benefit, but the gift is nevertheless limited to use for a particular purpose. Here the problem is different. There are people (who must be ascertainable within the certainty tests discussed above) with an interest in enforcing the trust, but none is entitled to a full beneficial interest, because of the limitation to the particular purpose.

It is arguable that these dispositions are also void, on similar principles to those considered above. In *Leahy v Attorney-General for New South Wales* [1959] AC 457, property was to be held on trust for 'such order of nuns of the Catholic Church or the Christian Brothers as my executors and trustees shall select'. The trust was not charitable, and Viscount Simonds in the Privy Council thought that it failed as a private trust on the grounds that though the individual members had an interest in enforcing the trust, they were not granted a full beneficial interest. Since this is invariably the case with purpose trusts of this nature, the reasoning leads to the conclusion that such trusts are never valid.

Leahy v *Attorney-General for New South Wales* is not an especially strong authority, however, because it is explicable on other grounds. The gift ought also to have failed for perpetuity, except that in any case it was validated by the New South Wales Conveyancing Act, so Viscount Simonds's views are technically *obiter*.

Goff J took what may have been a different view in *Re Denley's Trust Deed* [1969] 1 Ch 373. He thought that the principles of *Re Astor's ST* and *Re Endacott* invalidated only 'abstract or impersonal' purpose trusts. He went on to say that:

> Where, then, the trust, though expressed as a purpose, is directly or indirectly for the benefit of an individual or individuals, it seems to me that it is in general outside the mischief of the beneficiary principle.

This quotation is unfortunately not very clear. One view is that the test is not whether a full beneficial interest is granted, but whether individuals who are ascertainable have *locus standi* to sue. They will have so long as the benefit is not too indirect or intangible. The trust (which was upheld by Goff J) was 'for the purpose of a recreation or sports ground primarily for the benefit of the employees of the company . . .', with a gift over at the end of the perpetuity period.

Another view of *Re Denley's Trust Deed*, however, which is easier to reconcile with Viscount Simonds's views in *Leahy* v *Attorney-General for New South Wales* is that Goff J construed it as a trust for individuals, and not as a purpose trust at all. If this view is correct then the case breaks no new ground, and all private purpose trusts remain void, apart from the anomalous exceptions discussed above. This view was advanced by (among others) Vinelott J in *Re Grant's WT* (considered in the next section) and P.J. Millet QC (1985) 101 LQR 269, 280–2, as part of an analysis of the *Quistclose* and other similar trusts (see chapter 10). He was concerned to reject the view that *Barclays Bank Ltd* v *Quistclose Investments Ltd* [1970] AC 567 concerned a resulting trust arising on the failure of the primary trust (to enable dividends to be paid), that primary trust being a variety of a *Denley*-style purpose trust. I would reiterate what I say in that chapter, that the article is well worth reading.

Given that the trust was enforceable in *Denley*, and that similar trusts will continue to be enforceable, does it matter how the case is analysed? Well, it might. Consider the question of enforcement. If the trustees decided to use the fund to install a kidney machine for the benefit of the patients, then that can be relatively easily prevented by injunction. Suppose, however, the trustees do nothing, and no trustees can be found to build and/or maintain the sports ground. Specific performance cannot be awarded, as constant supervision would be required, and an injunction is clearly of no use.

At the end of the day, it is difficult to see what solution can be adopted, apart from distribution of the income from the fund directly to the employees of the company (not the capital, because of the gift over). That puts them into exactly the same position as a beneficiary under an ordinary discretionary (or is it fixed?) trust.

The issue could also arise if the objects of the trust wanted to terminate it on the basis of *Saunders* v *Vautier* (see the discussion of discretionary trusts, above). Presumably, only beneficiaries in the conventional sense can invoke this doctrine, and if the objects of a *Denley*-style purpose have a lesser interest, they will be unable to do so.

Unincorporated associations

Consider the following essay question:

Analyse the possible legal bases for a gift to a non-charitable unincorporated association. What difficulties, if any, are posed by the trust solution (or solutions) to this problem, and how are they avoided by a contractual solution?

This question, in effect, asks you to compare contractual and trust solutions to the problem of making a gift to a non-charitable unincorporated association, which is incapable itself of owning property.

On the conventional view, it might be thought that a *Denley*-style purpose trust might be a good method of allowing property to be conveyed to a non-charitable unincorporated association. Such an association (e.g., club or society) would be unable to hold the property itself, and would exist to use the property for a particular purpose.

On this view the property would be held in trust for the members of the association, for the purposes of the association, and it would be necessary only that the identity of those members was sufficiently certain. Unfortunately, however, a gift to members for the time being (i.e., present and future, assuming a fluctuating membership) will usually infringe the perpetuity rules (another difficulty in *Leahy* v *Attorney-General for New South Wales* [1959] AC 457), so the purpose trust solution is not generally appropriate.

It should be noted that in *Re Denley's Trust Deed* [1969] 1 Ch 373 itself the grant was only effective until 21 years from the death of the last survivor of a number of specified persons, so no perpetuity difficulty arose. There are also, of course, no perpetuity difficulties where the association is charitable.

Undoubtedly it is possible for any association, by clever drafting of its rules, also to avoid the perpetuity problem (see, e.g., Warburton [1985] Conv 318, 321), but most existing associations have not in fact drafted their rules so as to allow a purpose trust solution which avoids these difficulties.

The purpose trust solution also depends upon it being generally possible to make gifts for non-charitable purposes, so long only as there exist persons with *locus standi* to enforce the trust, even where they do not have a full beneficial interest. As has already been noted in the previous section, this is by no means certain.

Perpetuity difficulties can be avoided by construing the gift to present members only. The problem is that, if it is construed simply as a gift to them as joint tenants, then a retiring member is perfectly at liberty to sever and sell his or her share. New members could obtain any benefit from association property only by acquiring shares (or part shares) from existing members. No doubt it would be theoretically possible to run an unincorporated association on that basis, but it would be very inconvenient.

For this reason gifts to non-charitable unincorporated associations are usually construed as being to the existing members only, but subject to their contractual duties as members of the society or club. These will be determined by the rules of the association, but usually a member will be prevented from severing his share, and it will accrue to other members on death or resignation. Thus, although present and future members of a fluctuating body will benefit *de facto*, because the gift is construed as one to existing members alone, there is no perpetuity problem.

This was Cross J's analysis in *Neville Estates* v *Madden* [1962] Ch 832, and a similar approach was taken by Brightman J in *Re Recher's WT* [1972] Ch 526. Both views are technically *obiter*, in *Neville Estates* v *Madden* because the property was in the event held on charitable trusts, and in *Re Recher's WT* because the society (the London and Provincial Anti-Vivisection Society) had been dissolved at the date of the gift. It had in fact been amalgamated with the National Anti-Vivisection Society, and the gift failed in the end because it could not be construed as a gift to the larger combined society. Thus in neither case was the analysis of unincorporated associations a necessary part of the decision.

The issue arose directly in *Re Lipinski's WT* [1977] Ch 235, however, where Oliver J adopted the same analysis, and in *Re Grant's WT* [1980] 1 WLR 360 a gift failed precisely because it could not be fitted into this analysis. The testator attempted to make a grant to Chertsey and Walton Constituency Labour Party, but it could not be construed as a gift to the members of the CLP; they did not have exclusive control over the CLP rules, because those rules were also subject to the control of the National Labour Party.

In *Conservative & Unionist Central Office v Burrell* [1982] 1 WLR 522, the Court of Appeal held that the Conservative Central Office was not an unincorporated association (and therefore did not come within a statutory tax provision). The problem was not the same as in *Re Grant's WT*, however. Here there were no enforceable mutual understandings between the members, and the court held that members of unincorporated associations must be subject to mutually enforceable obligations. It was assumed (though not clearly held) that these would usually be contractual.

Contract theories lead to a different distribution of property when a club or society is wound up. Since on resignation from a club or society the retiring member gives up any contractual claim on the property of the association, it follows that only existing members have a right to claim any part of the fund.

If the rules provide for the contingency of dissolution of the fund, division will be according to the rules. Often the rules do not so provide, however, and in this event the courts are left to imply terms into the contract of membership.

In accordance with normal contractual doctrine, implication of terms is on the basis of inferred intention, and since this is largely a question of fact, no rigid rules of law can be stated. Nevertheless, generally in the case of members' clubs, the inference is that division is equally among existing members. In mutual benefit or friendly society cases, the prima facie rule also appears to be equal division, though there have also been cases where division has been proportional to total contributions. This is appropriate where the benefit contracted for while the fund subsists is also proportional to total contributions.

As we saw above it is possible in theory (though rare in practice) for club or society funds to be held on the basis of a trust, so long as perpetuity difficulties are overcome. If such a club or society is dissolved, the property will be held on resulting trust for the contributors. The main difference is that *all* contributors, including those who have ceased to contribute (e.g., past members), will be entitled to a share, and division will be in proportion to the *total amount* they have contributed. Thus, assuming everyone pays subscriptions at the same rate, a person who has contributed for 10 years is entitled to twice the share of the proceeds as someone who has contributed for only five.

Such was the basis of division in *Re Hobourn Aero Components Ltd's Air Raid Distress Fund* [1946] Ch 86, affirmed on other grounds [1946] Ch 194. It seems that this fund was limited to known and existing employees of a company who were on war service, to compensate for air raid damage in the Second World War. Since the contributors to the fund fluctuated, it is difficult to see how a trust analysis avoids perpetuity difficulties, although the fund was wound up after only four years, and may have been intended from the start to be of short-term duration. It has been suggested that Cohen J's analysis does not form part of the *ratio* of the case, the inference being that it may be wrong. Whether or not this is so, the case is clearly not of general application, since the duration of most funds is, in principle, unlimited, and fluctuations in contributors are assumed.

FIVE

FORMALITIES

Dealing with intricate subjects

Of all areas of the law of trusts which are likely to be examined, with the possible exception of perpetuities, formalities is perhaps the most intricate. It is the nearest you are likely to get to learning a detailed set of rules.

It may seem, therefore, that memory plays a more important part in this area than in those already considered, but it does not necessarily follow that an intricate subject should be approached differently from one less intricate. In the first place, it is unlikely that an examination question will invite you simply to narrate the rules, since that would not test any particularly valuable skill. It is far more likely that you will be required to concentrate on an area where the law is still developing, or is in some regard uncertain. In that case the technique of legal analysis will be essentially similar to that required for any other area of study: it makes no difference that you are being asked, in effect, to interpret a few words of a statute. The skills required are the same, whether you are dealing with a general principle, for example, that a trustee should not put himself into a position where his duties and interests may conflict (see chapter 9), or with the application to a particular set of facts of an intricate rule.

Policy behind section 53

Alternatively, you might get a question of the following nature:

> What, in your view, is the policy behind s. 53 of the Law of Property Act 1925? Explain, with the aid of reported decisions, the meaning of 'disposition' for the purposes of s. 53(1)(c). How far do the cases accord with the policy of the legislation?

It may well be that you have not thought much about the policy behind s. 53, or even assumed that there is no coherent policy. By examining what it might be, however, and criticising the cases in terms of that policy, it becomes a great deal easier to remember the details of the subject.

Remembering details in a vacuum is difficult, whereas if a structure can be found the task becomes a whole lot easier.

Let us therefore consider what the policy might be, and look in detail at the three main House of Lords cases, which are the only really important cases in the area, and must be mastered. The whole area was reviewed in an article by Brian Green (1984) 47 MLR 385, which is well worth reading.

Though the bulk of the question concerns s. 53(1)(c) of the Law of Property Act 1925, we are asked to consider the question of policy for the entire section, so s. 53(1)(b) should not be forgotten. It relates specifically to land:

[A] declaration of trust respecting any land or any interest therein must be manifested and proved by some writing signed by some person who is able to declare such trust or by his will.

Land differs from personalty in that even declarations of trust require writing, whereas as far as personalty is concerned, a settlor may create a trust merely by manifesting an intention to create it, and no special formalities are required (except in the case of wills). Only dispositions of equitable interests are caught in the case of personalty.

Presumably one reason why land is subject to special rules is because of its value, but that cannot be the only reason because even personalty of great value may be settled without formality. Another likely reason is that transactions involving land are sufficiently complex for it to be undesirable for them to be taken lightly.

But why require formality for dispositions of equitable interests in other property? There are two main reasons. Remember that we are dealing specifically with transactions involving *equitable* interests, which are intangible, so that it may be difficult to trace their movement unless that movement is evidenced by written documents. So, bearing in mind these evidential problems, the primary purpose of a writing requirement is to prevent fraud, to prevent people claiming interests to which they are not entitled. Indeed, the precursor to the 1925 Act was the Statute of Frauds 1677. The secondary purpose is to enable the trustees to ascertain where the equitable interests lie, to enable them to carry out the trusts.

The litigation has borne little relation to these primary and secondary purposes, however, but nearly always results from settlors avoiding taxation, and particularly stamp duty, the *ad valorem* part of which (now abolished on *inter vivos* gifts) was imposed only upon the written instrument by which property was transferred. If writing was not required, *ad valorem* duty was not payable.

It could be argued, then, that the courts should take into account taxation policy in addition to the policy referred to above, and perhaps they do. But in principle I would argue the courts should construe the formalities legislation on its own account, without regard to tax legislation which is parasitic upon it. If the Inland Revenue wishes to close a potential loophole there should be fresh taxation legislation for the purpose.

In my opinion, therefore, it would be wrong to interpret formalities legislation, the main purpose of which is quite unrelated to taxation, in such a way as to ensure a consistent tax position, if to do so would be at the expense of that purpose.

Let us now look at the law in the light of the relevant policy. The question relates specifically to s. 53(1)(c), on dispositions of equitable interests, so a general review of all formalities requirements is not required.

Dispositions of equitable interests

Section 53(1)(c) of the Law of Property Act 1925 provides:

> [A] disposition of an equitable interest or trust subsisting at the time of the disposition, must be in writing signed by the person disposing of the same, or by his agent thereunto lawfully authorised in writing or by will.

This provision covers both land and personalty, and even in the case of land it is much more stringent than s. 53(1)(b). The disposition must *itself* be in writing, not merely manifested and proved by writing, and failure to comply probably renders the disposition void, not merely unenforceable.

If the law were to accord with the policy discussed above, dispositions would be defined to include dealings with the beneficial interest which can be kept secret from the trustees, but to exclude other dealings. After all, the whole reason for treating dispositions of equitable interests differently from other dispositions is precisely because of the difficulties which would ensue were the trustees to be kept unaware of them. The precursor to this section, s. 9 of the Statute of Frauds 1677, caught 'grants and assignments', clearly reflecting this policy, but the term 'disposition' is at least theoretically wider.

Nevertheless, generally speaking the law defines 'dispositions' in accord with the policy described. The creation of a trust, by declaration, is outside the scope of the section. So, in general, is its extinguishment (by merger with the legal interest). If the purpose of formality rules is to prevent hidden transactions which prevent trustees from ascertaining who the beneficiaries are, there is no reason ever to require them where the legal and equitable interests merge. The same ought also to apply to the extinguishment of sub-equitable interests.

The position is not clear for a surrender of an equitable interest. A surrender cannot, of course, be kept secret from the trustees, and on the principles discussed above surrender should probably not be a disposition. The Court of Appeal held in *Re Paradise Motor Co. Ltd* [1968] 1 WLR 1125 that a *disclaimer* of an equitable interest is not a disposition. Danckwerts LJ commented that 'a disclaimer operates by way of avoidance and not be way of disposition'. A surrender, however, differs from a disclaimer in that surrender requires a transfer of equitable interest, whereas with a disclaimer there is never any movement of the beneficial interest at all. I would suggest that a surrender may well be a disposition, even though this does not accord with the policy described above.

Transfers or assignments of existing equitable interests, on the other hand, normally require writing. They are within the mischief covered by the legislation if the trustees are not party to the arrangement, but not, one would have thought, if the trustees themselves are directed to transfer the interests. Nevertheless, *Grey* v *Inland Revenue Commissioners* [1960] AC 1 suggests that writing is required even in this situation, and I would suggest that the decision is not in accord with the policy described.

Grey v *Inland Revenue Commissioners*

The usual interpretation of the House of Lords case of *Grey* v *Inland Revenue Commissioners* is that a transfer of an equitable interest on its own constitutes a disposition, even if the trustees are directed to make it, and therefore must be in writing and attract consequent liability for *ad valorem* stamp duty.

Mr Hunter was beneficial owner of shares, the legal title being held by nominees. In order to transfer his beneficial interest, Mr Hunter orally directed the nominees (one of whom was Grey) to hold the shares on trust for beneficiaries under six settlements (the nominees were also the trustees under these settlements). Later the trustees/nominees executed deeds of declaration to this effect, which were of course in writing.

In effect the whole scheme was a tax-avoidance device, which may account in part for the House of Lords reasoning (though I argued above that it should not in principle). If the oral direction had transferred the shares no *ad valorem* stamp duty was payable; if the transfer had been effected by the written declaration, however, it was.

It should be noted that stamp duty is imposed, not upon a transaction itself, but upon the written instrument by which property is transferred. The amount of *ad valorem* duty was calculated as a proportion of the value of the interest being transferred. If the value of such interest was nothing, as (for example) where a bare legal estate carrying no right to beneficial enjoyment was transferred, no *ad valorem* duty was payable, but taxpayers obviously preferred to avoid transferring the valuable beneficial interest in writing if they could.

In deciding in favour of the Inland Revenue, the House of Lords held that a direction by a beneficiary to the trustees, to transfer his interest to someone else constituted a disposition and must therefore be in writing. While on a literal interpretation it may be difficult to regard this as being other than a disposition, it does not fall within the mischief of the legislation, as a request to trustees can hardly constitute a secret transaction.

Lord Radcliffe's view was that s. 53(1) did not merely consolidate the earlier Statute of Fauds: this was a disposition, whether or not it was also within the mischief of s. 9 of the earlier statute.

Problem question

A has equitable title to shares in X Co. and Y Co. and wishes to transfer his interests to B. His shares in X Co. and Y Co. were conveyed by D to C (a nominee) some time ago, on trust for A.

In order to effect the transfer of his equitable title in the shares in X Co. A orally surrenders his interest to C. He tells C that he would like C to hold the share on trust for B, and C does so.

A orally declares himself trustee for B of his equitable interest in the shares in Y Co.

Has A effectively transferred his beneficial interest in the shares to B?

This question, which was recently set as one part of a multi-part question, is intended to get you to examine some variations on *Grey*.

If surrenders of equitable interests do not require writing (on which, see above), A's transfer of X Co. would illustrate an easy method of avoiding the consequences of *Grey* v *Inland Revenue Commissioners*. if Mr Hunter had surrendered his interest this would probably not have required writing. But of course the trustees could immediately have declared new trusts, and would presumably have done so had Mr Hunter asked them, these not requiring writing. This therefore allows for an easy way to achieve a *Grey* disposition without attracting stamp duty.

This only works, of course, if surrenders do not require writing, and that is what this part of the problem is about. On this issue, see the discussion above.

On the question of the transfer of Y Co. the issue is this. Suppose a beneficiary declares that he himself will hold his interest on trust for another (rather than directing the trustees to do so), so creating, in effect, a subtrust. A commonly held view is that the issue depends on whether the equitable owner effectively gives away the totality of his interest, so that he, like the trustees who hold the legal title, becomes in turn a merely nominal owner. If so, this is in reality a case of substitution of a new beneficiary, for which on policy grounds formality ought to be required.

If, on the other hand, the equitable owner purports to assume the active role of a trustee of his equitable interest, for example, by declaring discretionary trusts, the case resembles a straightforward subtrust, and should arguably be regarded as a declaration of trust, and not a disposition of an equitable interest at all.

The *Vandervell* litigation

I have suggested that in principle, the merger of legal and equitable interests, extinguishing rather than disposing of the equitable interest, should not require writing, on the grounds that it is not a hidden transaction of the type which the law would wish to prevent. On the same principle, it should also be possible for an equitable owner orally to direct the trustees to transfer *both* their legal and his equitable interest to a single third party. In this event also, the equitable interest is extinguished, and the transaction cannot be secret from the trustees. The House of Lords came to this conclusion in *Vandervell* v *Inland Revenue Commissioners* [1967] 2 AC 291.

There are two *Vandervell* cases, both arising out of a scheme which was originally intended to transfer money to endow a chair without attracting taxation, in this case surtax.

Vandervell No. 1

Mr Vandervell wished to endow a chair of pharmacology. He was also equitable owner of a substantial number of shares in Vandervell Products Ltd, a private limited liability company which he controlled. The legal interest in Vandervell's shares was held by a bank as nominee.

In order to endow the chair, he arranged with the bank orally (presumably to avoid stamp duty) to transfer both legal and equitable interests in these shares to the Royal College of Surgeons (RCS). It was not Vandervell's intention that the College should receive the shares absolutely, with all the implications that would have had for control of Vandervell Products Ltd. The intention, rather, was that it should receive large dividends on these shares, upon which, as a charity, it was not liable to pay tax. It actually received some £266,000 by these means. Vandervell retained an option to repurchase the shares themselves for a nominal amount (£5,000), however. He did not retain it in his own name, for that would have left him liable to pay surtax on the dividends. Instead, he set up a trustee company, Vandervell Trustees Ltd, to whom the option was granted.

At this stage, therefore, the legal interest in the shares had been transferred to the RCS. Vandervell Trustees Ltd had the legal interest in the option. If the equitable interest in either remained in Vandervell himself, however, he would be liable to surtax.

The shares and the option should be considered separately.

The shares   The Revenue initially claimed surtax from Mr Vandervell on the ground that he remained the equitable owner of the shares, although the legal interest had clearly been vested in the RCS, in the absence of a separate disposition in writing, of his equitable interest. This argument was rejected by the House of Lords, which held that s. 53(1)(c) had no application to the case where a beneficial owner, solely entitled, directs his bare trustees with regard to the legal and equitable estate. This is the most important part of the *Vandervell* litigation for formality purposes, and is in line with the policy discussed. As far as the shares themselves were concerned, therefore, both legal and equitable interests had been validly transferred despite lack of writing.

A interesting aside is that *Re Rose* was approved (see chapter 3): the transfer was effective as soon as Vandervell had performed his last act.

The option   Vandervell was liable to surtax nevertheless, because the House of Lords also held (Lords Reid and Donovan dissenting) that he had not succeeded in divesting himself of the equitable interest in the option, the legal interest of which was now in the trustee company, as this was held on resulting trust for him, along with liability to pay surtax on the dividends.

This did not raise a formalities point, however, but was the result simply of Vandervell's failure to state where the equitable interest was to go. Lord Wilberforce noted that the trusts upon which the option was supposed to be held were undefined and in the air, possibly to be defined later. The trustee company itself was clearly not a beneficiary, and an equitable interest cannot remain in the air, and so the only possibility was a resulting trust in favour of the settlor.

Vandervell No. 2

In order to avoid further surtax liability, Vandervell in 1961 instructed the trustee company to exercise the option and repurchase the shares, and this gave rise eventually to further litigation (*Re Vandervell's Trusts (No. 2)*

[1974] Ch 269, CA) about whether Vandervell had divested himself of the option and the whereabouts of the equitable interest in the shares thereby purchased.

Clearly the legal interest in the shares was now vested in the trustee company, Vandervell Trustees Ltd, because it had purchased the shares. They were also trustees under a separate trust for Vandervell's children. The £5,000 purchase money came from the children's settlement, and the trustee company regarded themselves as holding the shares on trust for the children under this settlement. In other words, they regarded the equitable interest in the shares as being in the children.

Liability to surtax now depended on the whereabouts of the equitable interest in the shares during that period (although in the event the Inland Revenue was excluded as a party to the action, and the taxation point was not in fact the main issue). It was argued that, as before, it remained with Vandervell. Again, let us consider separately the option and the shares.

The option The Court of Appeal held that the option was destroyed when it was exercised by the trustee company in 1961, so Vandervell's equitable interest in it (resulting from the earlier litigation) was extinguished. This was not a disposition within s. 53.

The shares The Court of Appeal held that the children had the equitable interest. The shares had been placed by the trustee company on the trusts of the children's settlements, and the Court of Appeal held that Vandervell had now succeeded in divesting himself of the entire interest in these shares, there being no longer a resulting trust in his favour. This was because

'Vandervell now justifiably fed up with his scheme'

the later trusts were precisely defined, in favour of the children's settlements, so that it was no longer necessary for the equitable interest to remain in the settlor.

Lord Denning MR analysed the position as a termination of the resulting trust of the option in favour of Vandervell, and a fresh trust of the shares declared (presumably by the trustee company) in favour of the children. He thought that as to the first part, writing is not required to terminate a resulting trust, and that since the new trust was not of land no formalities were required for its creation.

So far as the formality aspects of the *Vandervell* decisions are concerned, at no stage did s. 53 operate to defeat a transaction in either case. Since none of the transactions could have been kept secret from the trustees this is in accord with the policy of the section.

In 1965 Vandervell, presumably by now justifiably fed up with his scheme, clearly relinquished by deed any interest, legal or equitable, he may still have had in the shares.

Oughtred v Inland Revenue Commissioners

The point which arose in a third important House of Lords case, *Oughtred v Inland Revenue Commissioners* [1960] AC 206, is logically quite separate from that which arose in the above cases. It is virtually a pure taxation case, though in general policy terms I suppose that if Oughtred had won, the possibility might have arisen of secret transfers of beneficial interests, at any rate for the short time between a contract for sale and the actual transfer.

Contracts for the sale of personalty (unlike land: see below) do not require writing, but equity recognises that the buyer has an interest as soon as the contract is made. A possible route round s. 53 (and therefore stamp duty) might therefore be to have an oral contract for the sale of (say) shares, followed later by a formal transfer. The argument is that the oral contract, not the written transfer, conveys the equitable title; the formal transfer merely conveys the bare legal title, which is worth hardly anything for the purposes of *ad valorem* stamp duty.

This was the essence of the scheme in *Oughtred v Inland Revenue Commissioners*. Mrs Oughtred owned 72,700 shares in William Jackson & Son Ltd absolutely; 200,000 shares in the same company were held on trust for Mrs Oughtred for life, thence for her son, Peter absolutely. The parties orally agreed to swap, so that Mrs Oughtred would obtain Peter's reversionary interest (she would then have 200,000 shares outright), and in exchange Peter would obtain Mrs Oughtred's 72,700 shares. Peter therefore stood to gain an immediate interest in a small number of shares, and to lose a reversionary interest in a large number of shares. The contract was later performed.

The Revenue claimed stamp duty on the transfer of the reversionary interest in the 200,000 shares, the actual transfer of which involved writing. Oughtred's argument was that the equitable interest was transferred on the oral contract for sale, and that the later writing transferred only the bare legal title.

The argument was rejected by the House of Lords, Viscount Radcliffe and Lord Cohen dissenting. The essence of the majority view was that though equity, in appropriate circumstances, can grant specific performance of a contract of sale, and though in that case a constructive trust arises immediately in favour of the purchaser, the buyer does not have a full beneficial interest until the formal transfer. The situation was regarded as analogous to a sale of land, where the deed of conveyance is the effective instrument of transfer (and so liable to stamp duty). The minority view, on the other hand, was that the purchaser obtained a full beneficial interest immediately.

Essay question

Examine the exact nature of the interest of a prospective purchaser of land, after the contract for sale has been concluded but before legal title has been conveyed.

This question clearly invites discussion of the majority and minority views in *Oughtred*, and little else. It is a short question, and was recently set as one part of a multi-part question.

The equitable doctrine of part performance

The equitable doctrine of part performance allows for limited avoidance of formality provisions. It developed originally from the principle that equity would not allow a statute to be used as a cloak for fraud. In recent years, however, it appeared to be developing away from a purely fraud-based doctrine into an evidential doctrine, with its own detailed rules. These rules were arguably both unsatisfactory and uncertain, and the Law Commission (Law Com. No. 164: 'Formalities for Contracts for Sale, etc. of Land') accordingly recommended the abolition of the doctrine, at any rate in relation to contracts for the sale or other disposition of land, or interests in land. Their proposals were brought into effect by the Law of Property (Miscellaneous Provisions) Act 1989, which also tightened up on formality provisions affecting land.

It seems generally to be accepted that insofar as part performance had become a rigid evidential doctrine, that has not survived the 1989 Act. But the question still arises: what if formality provisions are being relied upon to promote a fraud? If seems unlikely that the 1989 Act was ever intended to affect the fundamental principle that equity will not permit a statute to be used as a cloak for fraud. Or suppose the provisions of the 1989 Act itself are used to promote fraud? It must be presumed that the original fraud basis of the doctrine survives the 1989 Act.

Remember that the 1989 Act applies only to formality provisions concerning land. Insofar as the part performance doctrine applies to other dispositions, and declarations of trust, it has not been affected by the 1989 Act.

The following question appeared on a recent exam paper, not as a whole question but as one part of a two-part question:

> What authority (if any) is there for the principle that equity will not allow a statute to be used as a cloak for fraud? If there is authority, how does the principle apply, and has its application been in any way curtailed by section 2 of the Law of Property (Miscellaneous Provisions) Act 1989?

It is not proposed here to examine in detail the authority for the proposition that equity will not allow a statute to be used as a cloak for fraud, not least because much of it is discussed elsewhere in the book, and in particular in chapter 6. Additionally, secret and half-secret trusts (chapter 7) may well be based on this principle. The other main area which is based on this principle is the doctrine of part performance itself, however. This doctrine allows trusts (and contracts) to be enforced in spite of non-compliance with statutory writing requirements.

Though the doctrine can be used to avoid s. 53 of the Law of Property Act 1925, by virtue of s. 55(d), the main cases arise from attempts to enforce a contract for a leasehold or freehold estate in land, despite non-compliance with the formalities required by the (now repealed) Law of Property Act 1925, s. 40:

> (1) No action may be brought upon any contract for the sale or other disposition of land or any interest in land, unless the agreement upon which such action is brought, or some memorandum or note thereof, is in writing, and signed by the party to be charged or by some other person thereunton by him lawfully authorised.
>
> (2) This section applies to contracts made before or after the

commencement of this Act and does not affect the law relating to part performance, or sales by the court.

Like s. 53, s. 40 replaced earlier provisions deriving from the Statute of Frauds 1677, so cases before 1925 were equally authoritative on s. 40.

There are two important points to note about s. 40. First, in the absence of the required formalities it merely prevented an action being brought upon a contract for the sale or other disposition of land or any interest in land, but did not render the contract void. Secondly, s. 40(2) expressly preserved the old equitable doctrine of part performance.

In the context of estate contracts, the part performance doctrine was used to stop people relying on formality provisions to get out of contracts from which they have had a benefit. An important point was that it only avoided formality provisions, and did not, for example, validate a purported contract that was unenforceable for any other reason (e.g., that there was no consideration, or that one of the parties was a minor). The same would still be true in s. 53 cases — the doctrine would not validate a disposition if the reason for invalidity were anything other than lack of writing (e.g., a certainty or constitution problem).

Originally the doctrine was subject to very strict requirements, and indeed even in recent years it has not always been lightly invoked. As Walton J observed in *Re Gonin (deceased)* [1979] Ch 16:

> After all, the doctrine of part performance is one which enables the court to disregard the express provisions of an Act of Parliament, and it would appear that it ought to be a somewhat narrow doctrine accordingly.

The view originally taken that the acts of part performance must unequivocally point to the existence of a contract concerning land, and (virtually) had to be explicable on no other basis. Only then would it clearly be fraudulent to rely on the formality provisions. If the acts of part performance were explicable on the basis of a contract, but not necessarily one relating to land, then no great injustice would be caused by enforcing that contract, rather than the contract relating to land. Payment of money alone was never regarded as a sufficient act of part performance, since apart from the fact that fraud could always be averted by its repayment, its payment need not be related to any contract, let alone one relating to land.

A strict approach to the doctrine also ensured that the mischief behind the formality requirements would not be subverted, since the acts of part performance would provide evidence which was almost as good as that which writing itself would provide.

This, then, was the approach taken by the courts in the earlier cases, such as *Maddison* v *Alderson* (1883) 8 App Cas 467. In *Maddison* v *Alderson* the same view was taken of provision of services as of payment of money, where a housekeeper continued in service on the basis of an agreement that the house would eventually be conveyed to her. In effect, a change in possession of the land was considered necessary.

The sort of case where the application of formality provisions may well have caused great injustice was *Wakeham* v *Mackenzie* [1968] 1 WLR 1175, where a widow gave up her council flat to look after a widower for no wages, on condition that he would convey his house and contents to her in his will. This contract was held enforceable, even in the absence of writing, on the basis of the part performance doctrine. Another, similar case is *Kingswood Estates* v *Anderson* [1963] 2 QB 169, where also there had been a change in possession of the property. A widow had vacated rent-controlled premises in favour of others provided by her landlord under an oral agreement that she would be permitted to stay there for rest of her life, and the acts of part performance were held sufficient. A clear fraud would have been perpetrated had the landlord been permitted to rely on the statutory formality provisions.

There are statements in *Kingswood Estates* v *Anderson*, however, suggesting a relaxation in the doctrine. The Court of Appeal did not consider it necessary that the acts of part performance had to indicate the *terms* of the contract alleged. It was necessary only that they pointed to the existence of a contract, and be consistent with the contract. It is doubtful whether there really was any relaxation of the requirements, however, and the case is probably consistent with *Maddison* v *Alderson*. In *Re Gonin* (see below), the case was explained in terms of existing principles, and Walton J did not think it broke new ground.

The same cannot be said, however, for the view taken by the majority (Lord Morris of Borth-y-Gest dissenting) in the leading decision of the House of Lords in *Steadman* v *Steadman* [1976] AC 576, noted by Professor Wade (1974) 90 LQR 433. In this case the doctrine operated although no change had taken place in the possession of any land, and the case clearly extended the scope of the doctrine, although if *Re Gonin* is correct (see below), probably not very much.

A summary of the position before *Steadman* v *Steadman* was that, first, the act of part performance alleged must unequivocally point to the existence of an agreement, although it need not show all its terms, and secondly, that the act alleged must unequivocally indicate that the contract relates to land.

Steadman v *Steadman* concerned a post-divorce battle for a share in the matrimonial home. The wife applied for an order to sell. The husband (who was in arrears in maintenance by £194) orally agreed to buy out the wife's share for £1500. By another term of the oral agreement, the husband was not required to pay any further maintenance, apart from £100 of the arrears.

The acts relied upon for the purposes of the part performance doctrine were:

(a)   A variation of the maintenance order by the magistrates' court.

(b)   Payment of the £100 arrears.

(c)   The drawing up of a draft agreement to purchase by the husband's solicitors.

The wife refused to sign the draft agreement, and held out for £2000 (no doubt property prices had risen). She sued for an order to sell the matrimonial home under the Married Women's Property Act 1882, s. 17, but eventually lost in the House of Lords. The House held that the original oral agreement was enforceable.

The decision laid down that, for the doctrine to operate, it is necessary that:

(a)   Taking all the acts of part performance together, they pointed unequivocally to the existence of a contract. No special standard of proof was required, merely the ordinary civil standard of balance of probabilities.

(b)   The payment of money by itself was insufficient, though it could be relevant when considered along with other acts of part performance (as in the case itself).

The case did not make clear whether the acts of part performance must indicate that the contract relates specifically to land. Their Lordships split 2-2 on this question (Lord Salmon and the dissenting judge, Lord Morris of Borth-y-Gest thought so; Lords Reid and Dilhorne thought not), with the fifth (Lord Simon) expressing no firm view, on the grounds that it was unnecessary to determine the point in the case itself (because the contract clearly related to land).

This allowed Walton J to consider the matter afresh in *Re Gonin* [1979] Ch 16. He agreed with Lords Salmon and Morris, and indeed took a very traditional view of the doctrine. The facts were similar to *Maddison* v *Alderson*: there was an oral promise that in consideration of the plaintiff going to live with and look after her parents the parental home should become hers on their deaths. Walton J refused to invoke the doctrine.

The case was relatively weak on its facts. The plaintiff had no home of her own to give up, and was merely returning home after the call of war. Walton J seemed to think that there was no real evidence that there was any connection bewteen returning home and the agreement: probably the plaintiff would have returned anyway. If so, the alleged acts of part performance may well not have been referable to a contract at all, let alone a contract relating to land. Nevertheless, the case could well have acted as a brake on the development of a wide part performance doctrine, since if Walton J's reassertion of the traditional approach was correct, *Steadman* v *Steadman* was authority for very little, other than that payment of money could in limited circumstances be relevant.

Nevertheless, *Steadman* v *Steadman* clearly worried the Law Commission, not least because it had left the law in an extremely uncertain state. They also took the view (at p. 3) that whereas the part performance doctrine was a blunt instrument for doing justice despite non-compliance with statutory formalities, equity had developed more flexible ways (see next section) of dealing with the position if formalities were not observed. Accordingly, they recommended the abolition of the part performance doctrine.

The recommendations of the Commission led to the enactment of the Law of Property (Miscellaneous Provisions) Act 1989, s. 2 of which provided:

> (1)   A contract for the sale or other disposition of an interest in land can only be made in writing and only by incorporating all the terms which the parties have expressly agreed in one document or, where contracts are exchanged, in each . . .
>
> (8)   Section 40 of the Law of Property Act 1925 (which is superseded by this section) shall cease to have effect.

Apart from the tightening up of the formalities provisions in this section, it differs from its precursor in not making any provision for the part performance doctrine. However, although s. 40 was repealed and s. 40(2) not replaced, the part performance doctrine was not abolished expressly. It should also be remembered that the doctrine did not derive from s. 40(2), but from an earlier, fundamental equitable principle. Since it does not derive from statute, and since it has not been expressly abolished, is it therefore possible to argue that it still survives?

No doubt in interpreting the new statute the courts will take account of the Law Commission's recommendations, which clearly favoured the abolition of the doctrine. It is also worth noting that the section does not merely render unenforceable any contract which does not comply with its provisions, but that contracts failing to comply are void. The Commission

took the view (at p. 23) that the doctrine of part performance would cease
to have effect in contracts concerning land, presumably because there would
be nothing for it to operate on. This was also the view taken by Professor
P.H. Pettit ([1989] Conv at 441):

> It is an inevitable consequence of section 2 that the doctrine of part-
> performance no longer has a role to play in contracts concerning land.
> The simple fact is that under the new law if section 2 is not complied
> with there is no contract for either party to perform;

My own view is that, insofar (if at all) as the doctrine had evolved from
its fraud-based beginnings, the effect of the 1989 Act is to curtail those
developments. But what about cases like *Wakeham* v *Mackenzie* and
Kingswood Estates v *Anderson*? In such cases, reliance on the statutory
formality provisions could perpetrate a clear fraud. Is it likely that equity
will allow that to happen because of a new statute, which does not expressly
abolish the doctrine? As yet it is too early to predict how the courts will
react to the 1989 Act, but I would suggest that such a conclusion is most
unlikely. Nor do I think it is a bar to the operation of the doctrine that
the contract is rendered void rather than merely unenforceable, since it
is only rendered void by the operation of a formality statute whose provisions
are being used as a cloak for fraud. I cannot see how that change of legislative
technique can make any difference.

It is arguable, however, that equity has evolved other devices for dealing
with the genuinely fraudulent case, and no longer needs to rely on the
part performance doctrine. To that argument we turn in the next section.

Alternatives to part performance

Proprietary estoppel

It is also worth pondering whether, in a situation where the part performance
doctrine may have applied prior to the 1989 Act, there are any alternative
equitable doctrines which may be capable of producing a just result. Another
recent exam question (which was again one part of a two-part question)
was as follows:

> In its report (Law Com. No. 164: 'Formalities for Contracts for Sale,
> etc. of Land'), the Law Commission took the view (at page 18) that
> if the part performance doctrine were abolished, many of the cases where
> injustice might be caused by an inability to plead the doctrine could
> be resolved by the application of the equitable doctrine of estoppel.

In your view, does the estoppel doctrine apply sufficiently extensively in land law to enable this view to be supported?

The question concentrates on equitable estoppel, but for completeness it should also be noted that the Commission also considered various common-law actions. For example, recovery of money paid by a prospective purchaser would normally be recoverable on the grounds of total failure of consideration. If work had been carried out, a *quantum meruit* claim might be made.

So far as estoppel is concerned, the effect of the doctrine (in essence) is that where one party makes a representation upon which another party relies to his detriment, the party making the representation may be estopped from later denying it. It may well be, therefore, that in a case like *Wakeham* v *Mackenzie*, considered in the previous section, the widower might be unable to deny his intention to convey his house and contents to the widow in his will. The widow has obviously relied on the promise to her detriment, and, it might be thought, in principle, therefore, ought to be able to enforce it.

The problem with estoppel is one of remedies. In most of the cases it is invoked as a defence, usually to a possession action. The widow would need to be able to use the doctrine as a *cause* of action in a case like *Waskeham* v *Mackenzie*, however, in order to force the widower to convey the house and contents to her. Full discussion of the estoppel doctrine is beyond the scope of this book, but any student of the law of contract knows that, in general, an estoppel can be used as a shield but not as a sword. However, there is some authority that this limitation does not apply to proprietary estoppels, and that proprietary estoppels are protected by a wide range of remedies.

Clearly the Commission was of the view (at p. 19) that the remedies for proprietary estoppel were sufficient to prevent injustice in most situations where previously the part performance doctrine may have operated. Among the cases cited were *Dillwyn* v *Llewelyn* (1862) 4 De GF & J 517 and *Pascoe* v *Turner* [1979] 1 WLR 431, in both of which cases conveyance of the fee simple *was* awarded as a remedy. Many writers find these cases, and in particular *Pascoe* v *Turner*, convincing for a wide view of proprietary estoppel, but I would suggest that a note of caution should be sounded. A close reading of *Dillwyn* v *Llewelyn* reveals that the decision was not based on estoppel at all, but that the reasoning is in contractual terms. It appears, indeed, that there was an estate contract in this case. In *Pascoe* v *Turner*, Cumming-Bruce LJ, delivering the judgment of the court, clearly does reason from proprietary estoppel, and this is certainly the stronger authority. On the other hand, he also reasons from the older, common-law acquiescence doctrine, which, it is usually accepted, is based on finding an implied contract.

It has to be concluded that there is no *conclusive* authority for the proposition advanced by the Law Commission. In cases where a conveyance of land has been ordered by the court, either the entire reasoning is contractual, or there is alternative contractual reasoning (or at any rate, acquiescence reasoning). If the true analysis of these cases is that there was a contract, then we are back to requiring writing, unless of course, the detrimental reliance also counted as a sufficient act of part performance.

It is also pertinent to note that, insofar as the Law Commission was worried about uncertainty in its criticism of the part performance doctrine, it can hardly be said that the equitable estoppel doctrine is a particularly certain alternative.

There may also be difficulties with estoppel reasoning where third parties are involved. In the part performance and estoppel cases already discussed there was no third party (e.g., purchaser), and the only question was whether the other party to the contract, or in the estoppel cases the party who had made the representation, was bound. But estate contracts can also bind third parties (subject to the registration requirements of the Land Charges or Land Registration Acts), whereas contractual licences do not (see chapter 6), and estoppel licences may well not either (see, e.g., [1981] Conv 347). In any problem question involving a third party, therefore, estoppel reasoning may not be a satisfactory alternative to the part performance doctrine.

Estoppel comparisons may also operate in reverse. Cases that look at first sight like estoppel (or indeed contractual) licences, may in reality be estate contract cases. *Pascoe* v *Turner* is one (see [1981] Conv 347). A better example, perhaps, is *Errington* v *Errington* [1952] 1 KB 290, one of the many cases in this section also discussed in chapter 6. A father purchased a house on a mortgage, and agreed with his son and his new wife that if they occupied the house and paid all the instalments, he would then transfer the property to them. The young couple went into occupation and paid the instalments. Later, the father died, and his widow inherited the property. Then the son left his wife, who continued to live in the house, paying the mortgage instalments. The widow sought possession from the daughter-in-law, and lost.

The case raises a number of difficulties, but for present purposes we are only concerned with why the widow was bound by an arrangement that had been made not by herself, but by her predecessor in title. It is often explained as a contractual licence case, but this reasoning is weakened by the views of Fox LJ in *Ashburn Anstalt* v *Arnold* [1988] 2 All ER 147 (see chapter 6), who held that contractual licences do not create interests in land and do not bind third parties. Arguably, the widow was a third party to the arrangement, so that if the daughter-in-law had no more than a contractual licence, she should not have been bound. But the agreement was to convey the house to the young couple upon payment of all the instalments. Surely, therefore, this was an estate contract, which is clearly an interest in land, capable of binding the widow.

The contract was oral, so to succeed on this basis the daughter-in-law would have to argue part performance. Were there sufficient acts of part performance (this was of course before the 1989 Act)? The couple went into occupation, and started to pay off the mortgage instalments. Even on the traditional reasoning described at the beginning of this section, these acts surely point to the existence of a contract, referable to land. I suggest that there was sufficient part performance.

Estate contracts need to be registered (in *Errington* v *Errington* under the provisions of what is now the Land Charges Act 1972) in order to bind purchasers, but the widow was not a purchaser. She had simply inherited the house. Non-registration is no objection to the estate contract theory, therefore, and I would suggest that this is the true explanation of *Errington* v *Errington*.

Constructive trust

Another possibility, closely related to the discussion in the previous section, is that a constructive trust might protect against any injustice that might arise from the abolition of the part performance doctrine. It seems that constructive trusts *may* arise in similar circumstances to proprietary estoppels, and there is no doubt that a full range of equitable remedies is available to protect a beneficiary under a constructive trust. Constructive trusts also give rise, unlike (probably) proprietary estoppels, to full beneficial interests, and so are capable of binding third parties also.

In *Re Basham* [1986] 1 WLR 1498, for example, the facts were very similar to those in *Re Gonin*, but the plaintiff, Mrs Bird, won. Edward Nugee QC followed *Re Cleaver* [1981] 1 WLR 939, considered in the mutual wills section in chapter 6, and held that a proprietary estoppel giving rise to a constructive trust arose, the plaintiff thereby obtaining the conveyance of the estate to her. He said that proprietary estoppel was a form of constructive trust which arose when A acted to his detriment on the faith of a belief known to and encouraged by B that he had or was going to have a right over B's property, so that B was prevented by equity from insisting on his strict legal rights if to do so would be inconsistent with A's belief. If this case is correct, then any act by the plaintiff, in reliance upon an alleged agreement (or even a mere representation by the defendant), would enable the plaintiff to succeed on constructive trust reasoning and indeed the constructive trust doctrine would potentially be far wider than the doctrine of part performance has ever been. The reasoning in *Re Basham* is also similar to that adopted in *Re Sharpe* [1980] 1 WLR 219, although that case is not mentioned in Edward Nugee's judgment.

In *Re Sharpe*, an 82-year-old lady, who was not in good health, loaned a large sum of money (£12,000) to her nephew to enable him to purchase a house in which they could both live. The nephew later went bankrupt, and the question arose whether the old lady's money was secured, or whether it formed part of the nephew's assets, to be divided among his general creditors. Browne-Wilkinson J found for the old lady, on the basis that she was a beneficiary under a constructive trust, which bound the trustee in bankruptcy. His views on when a constructive trust might arise were, like those later expressed in *Re Basham*, very wide. Browne-Wilkinson J thought that a constructive trust can be imposed simply because a licensee expends money or otherwise acts to his detriment. If the reasoning in this case is correct, almost any reliance on a promise relating to the occupation of property could give rise to a constructive trust. Such reasoning may well apply to cases similar to *Re Gonin*.

Re Gonin was decided before either *Re Cleaver* or *Re Sharpe*. Would the result have been different had it been decided later, and the reasoning of those later cases applied?

Both *Re Sharpe* and *Re Cleaver* have been criticised, however, and may well be wrong, or explicable on other grounds. *Re Cleaver* is discussed in chapter 6. *Re Sharpe* may well be better explained on other grounds. For example, if it was the intention of the aunt and nephew that the old lady should have an interest in the property, then she may well have an interest on conventional resulting trust principles, as discussed in chapter 6. Alternatively, it has been argued by Jill Martin [1980] Conv 207 that an estoppel licence or proprietary estoppel was created, and that this is the true explanation of the decision. As already explained, a detailed discussion of estoppel licences and proprietary estoppels is outside the scope of this book (they are traditionally land law), but I would suggest that there are problems with this approach, in particular whether estoppel licences can in fact be proprietary, so as to bind a trustee in bankruptcy.

The constructive trusts reasoning in *Re Sharpe* was treated dismissively by Fox LJ in *Ashburn Anstalt* v *Arnold* [1988] 2 All ER 147 (at p. 166b), but he did not elaborate, since the case before him was sufficiently different not to be affected directly by *Re Sharpe*. *Ashburn Anstalt* is also considered in detail in chapter 6.

Alternatives to the part performance doctrine are analysed in detail by Lionel Bently and Paul Coughlan in (1990) 10 Legal Studies, at p. 325.

SIX

RESULTING AND CONSTRUCTIVE TRUSTS

The situations in which resulting and constructive trusts arise are many and diverse. It is not intended to cover all aspects of resulting and constructive trusts in this chapter, since it is often more convenient to deal with them as they arise elsewhere in the book. Resulting trusts have already been alluded to in chapter 4, for example, since a resulting trust can be a consequence of lack of certainty, and resulting trust arguments were also examined, in a different context, at the end of that chapter. There was a resulting trust of the shares in the first *Vandervell* case, considered in the last chapter, and there is also a resulting trust if a secret trust fails (see chapter 7). Examples of constructive trusts can be found in chapters 9 and 10, and if all aspects of resulting and constructive trusts were dealt with here, this would be a very wide-ranging chapter indeed.

The areas of law which are included in this chapter were chosen primarily because they do not fit in easily elsewhere. They might well be regarded as frontier areas, since the law appears still to be developing (although the law can be stated with greater certainty today than a few years ago). They are the basis upon which matrimonial property, and the property of unmarried cohabitees, is held, and the so-called 'new model' constructive trust.

Beneficial interests of cohabitees

Until about five years ago, the law in this area was very difficult to state with any degree of certainty. Then the position was greatly improved by the two Court of Appeal decisions of *Burns* v *Burns* [1984] Ch 317 and *Grant* v *Edwards* [1986] Ch 38. Unfortunately, however, reconciling these two cases, which appeared at first sight to be contradictory, was not very easy, especially since *Grant* v *Edwards* was not a model of clarity. Also, the authority of the House of Lords was really needed finally to resolve the law in an area where one of the main problems was the profusion of apparently irreconcilable Court of Appeal decisions.

The House of Lords has now stepped in, with a remarkably clear statement by Lord Bridge in *Lloyd's Bank plc* v *Rosset* [1990] 1 All ER 1111. Because of this decision, the conclusion that could previously have been deduced only with difficulty, that there are two completely different types of case, can now be stated with absolute certainty. That does not mean, of course, that all the complications of the area have been removed, because there can still be difficulties in distinguishing between the two varieties, and deciding into which category a particular set of facts falls.

Approaching the exam

Two principles should guide you towards exam preparation. First, since this is still a developing areas, make sure you are fully up to date—this means checking the *All England Law Reports* or *Weekly Law Reports* periodically right up to the day of the exam. This cannot be over-emphasised. *Grant* v *Edwards* [1986] Ch 638, considered in detail below, was reported in the *All England Law Reports* on 13 June 1986. This would have been just before many trusts exams for that year were sat. The same is true of *Ashburn Anstalt* v *Arnold* [1988] 2 All ER 147, another important case which is considered below, which was reported in the *All England Law Reports* on 13 May 1988. Apart from being interesting cases in their own right, consider the advantages a candidate would have had who knew the cases over one who had not. Decisions like these render all existing textbooks out of date, and there could well be further decisions of similar import before your own exams. It may even be worthwhile checking the law reports in *The Times* just before the exams: in *City of London Building Society* v *Flegg* [1988] AC 54, the House of Lords reversed the Court of Appeal over the nature of beneficial interests under a statutory trust for sale. It was not fully reported until October 1987, but *The Times* report appeared just before the 1987 exams.

Secondly, there are relatively few really important cases. You should aim to know them thoroughly. In particular, consider how far their reasoning extends. Try the same cases with the variations that the (male) legal owner has gone bankrupt, and the dispute is between his cohabitee and his trustee in bankruptcy, or that he has sold the house to a third-party bona fide purchaser for value without notice of his cohabitee's rights (if any). Would the result be the same? Should it be?

Sometimes questions will be of the problem variety, probably closely tied into the facts of one of the main cases, perhaps with one of the variations discussed in the last paragraph. Typically Mr A and Miss B will be living together in a house the legal title to which is vested in A. A may have provided some spurious excuse for not vesting the house in joint names. B will not have provided any part of the purchase money but will have contributed in some other way. There may be children. Later the relationship splits up. What is the extent of Miss B's beneficial interest, if any, in the home?

The parties are usually unmarried, to avoid complications caused by the Matrimonial Causes Act 1973, s. 23, which gives the courts discretion to vary the beneficial interests.

Had B made a direct financial contribution to the purchase price there would have been a presumption that she acquired an equitable interest by virtue of the resulting trust doctrine. Similarly if B made financial contributions in other respects, for example, by payment of part or all of the mortgage repayments. Again, the problem is usually framed to avoid this possibility.

The problem may ask you specifically about the extent, if any, of B's beneficial interest in the property. Or it may be necessary for B to show a beneficial interest to win on the given facts. It certainly helps to be able to claim a property interest if a third party is involved, for example, if A subsequently mortgages the property without B's knowledge, as in *Williams & Glyn's Bank Ltd* v *Boland* [1981] AC 487, or if A has gone bankrupt, and the issue arises between B and A's trustee in bankruptcy, as in *Re Sharpe* [1980] 1 WLR 219 (see previous chapter). Some form of property interest is essential for B to win in third-party cases, though the possibility of an estoppel licence should not be overlooked (it was, for example, one of the unsuccessful arguments in *Bristol & West Building Society* v *Henning* [1985] 1 WLR 778).

A full beneficial interest might also be necessary even where no third party is involved, for example, where B wishes to obtain an order for the sale of the property under s. 30 of the Law of Property Act, to realise her 'share' of the proceeds.

But sometimes B may have alternatives to the full beneficial interest, in which case you must consider those alternatives also. It may be, for example, that A had left and B simply wishes to remain in the property. Again, an equitable interest is to her advantage, but a contractual or estoppel licence may do just as well, at any rate if no third party is involved.

Unless the context otherwise requires, in the following discussion it will be assumed (as is usually indeed the case) that legal title is vested in the male partner, but that the female partner is claiming a beneficial interest in the property.

The two different types of case

The following essay question appeared recently on a university examination paper:

Critically examine the meaning of the following passage, taken from Lord Bridge's speech in *Lloyd's Bank plc* v *Rosset* [1990] 1 All ER 1111, at 1118–1119:

The first and fundamental question which must always be resolved is whether, independently of any inference to be drawn from the conduct of the parties in the course of sharing the house as their home and managing their joint affairs, there has at any time prior to acquisition, or exceptionally at some later date, been any agreement, arrangement or understanding reached between them that the property is to be shared beneficially. The finding of an agreement or arrangement to share in this sense can only, I think, be based on evidence of express discussions between the partners, however imperfectly remembered and however imprecise their terms may have been. Once a finding to this effect is made it will only be necessary for the partner asserting a claim to a beneficial interest against the partner entitled to the legal estate to show that he or she has acted to his or her detriment or significantly altered his or her position in reliance on the agreement in order to give rise to a constructive trust or proprietary estoppel.

In sharp contrast with this situation is the very different one where there is no evidence to support a finding of an agreement or arrangement to share, however reasonable it might have been for the parties to reach such an arrangement if they had applied their minds to the question, and where the court must rely entirely on the conduct of the parties both as the basis from which to infer a common intention to share the property beneficially and as the conduct relied on to give rise to a constructive trust. In this situation direct contributions to the purchase price by the partner who is not the legal owner, whether initially or by payment of mortgage instalments, will readily justify the inference necessary to the creation of a constructive trust. But, as I read the authorities, it is at least extremely doubtful whether anything less will do.

In this passage Lord Bridge clearly distinguished between two types of case. The first type is where there is evidence of an agreement to share the property beneficially. The agreement need not be formal, and its terms need not be particularly precise, but it appears that it must be based on evidence of express discussions between the partners. More importantly, the evidence of the agreement must be independent of the conduct of the parties in the course of sharing the house as their home, or in other words independent of any improvements or contributions, whether financial or otherwise, either may have made to the home, or to expenses such as housekeeping, or contributions such as giving up employment in order to look after the children. If there is such evidence, then it is not necessary to look at the conduct of the parties in order to establish either the existence of a beneficial interest, or its size. The agreement tells you both of those.

The second type of case is where there is no evidence, independently of the conduct of the parties (e.g., contributions to the home), of any such agreement. *Rosset* itself was such a case. Here, if any inference is to be drawn of an intention to share the beneficial interests, it can only be drawn on the basis of the contributions themselves. Thus, the contributions are used to establish the existence of a beneficial interest, and also its size, there being no other evidence for either. Lord Bridge is of the opinion that in this situation, it is likely that only direct contributions to the purchase price by the partner who is not the legal owner, whether initially or by payment of mortgage instalments, will do.

The conduct of the parties is also relevant in the first type of case, but it is of far lesser importance than in the second type. Also, the conduct need not necessarily be in the form of direct contributions to the purchase price. Since the agreement to share is shown independently of the parties' conduct, the only function of the conduct is to get around the formalities requirements of s. 53(1)(b) of the Law of Property Act 1925 (see previous chapter). It should be borne in mind that there is unlikely to have been any written agreement in this type of case, and the inference to be drawn is that (usually) the male cohabitee has declared himself trustee for himself and the (usually) female cohabitee. Section 53(1)(b) of the Law of Property Act 1925 requires such a declaration to be in writing, unless there is an implied, resulting or constructive trust, in which case by virtue of s. 53(2), the provisions of s. 53(1)(b) do not apply. There will be a constructive trust if the female cohabitee has acted to her detriment or significantly altered her position in reliance on the agreement. All that is required, therefore, is to show detrimental reliance, in order to get around the formality provisions.

This is made clear elsewhere in Lord Bridge's speech in *Rosset*:

Even if there had been the clearest oral agreement between Mr and Mrs Rosset that Mr Rosset was to hold the property in trust for them both as tenants in common, this would, of course, have been ineffective since a valid declaration of trust by way of gift of a beneficial interest in land is required by s. 53(1) of the Law of Property Act 1925 to be in writing. But if Mrs Rosset had, as pleaded, altered her position in reliance on the agreement this could have given rise to an enforceable interest in her favour by way either of a constructive trust or of a proprietary estoppel.

It is obvious, then, that it is a matter of some importance to establish into which of the two categories a particular case falls, and indeed this has generally been the issue in the cases that have arisen post-*Rosset*. We are now going to expand on the fundamental distinction drawn by Lord Bridge, but in the reverse order. It is easier to consider first cases where there has been no independent agreement, and then to look at the independent agreement cases by way of contrast.

No independent agreement

Where there is no independent agreement, in the absence of a presumption of advancement (on which, see below), the usual presumption will be that the beneficial interests are to be shared in the proportions in which the parties contribute to the purchase price of the property. It is very unlikely that this presumption will be rebutted by the conduct of the parties, so that in general, beneficial interests will indeed be shared proportionately with the *financial* contributions of the parties.

The reason for this is that where there is a voluntary transfer of the legal title to property (i.e., not a transfer for value), then unless there is a presumption of advancement (see below), the presumption is that the equitable title does not follow the legal title, but remains in the settlor, i.e., there is a resulting trust. In the present context, where Mr A and Ms B contribute half each to a house, legal title to which is conveyed into the name of Mr A alone, the presumption is not that Ms B is giving a half share of the property to A. Equitable title does not follow legal title, the presumption being that it remains where it is. In other words, each will be entitled in equity to a half share.

In *Hodgson* v *Marks* [1971] 1 Ch 892, considered again later in this chapter, an old lady (Mrs Hodgson) conveyed the legal title of her house to her lodger (Evans), purely as a device in order (or so Evans said) to protect him against her nephew, who disapproved of him. This was a voluntary transfer of the legal title, and in the Court of Appeal, Russell LJ took the view that only the bare legal title was conveyed to Evans. Equitable title remained with Mrs Hodgson, who thereby had an interest by way of a resulting trust.

Presumption of advancement

The opposite presumption (i.e., that the equitable title *does* follow the legal title) prevails where there is a presumption of advancement.

Presumptions of advancement occur where the relationship between the parties is such as to impose a moral obligation upon one to provide for the other. Examples are the obligation of a husband to support his wife, and the obligation of a father to support his children.

The effect of the presumption is that where there is a voluntary conveyance of the legal title (i.e., without consideration, in effect a gift), the equitable title passes also. In other words, the presumption is that an out-and-out gift is intended, to fulfil the moral obligation to give, whereas in other voluntary conveyances there is a presumption of resulting trust.

So, for example, if a husband provides the money for a home which is conveyed into the name of his wife, an out-and-out gift of the home is presumed. Or if it is conveyed into the joint names of husband and wife, the presumption will be that the equitable title also will be jointly held, even if the husband has provided all the purchase money.

The presumption only applies between husband and wife and between father and son or daughter (or any other person to whom he stands *in loco parentis*, e.g., an adopted child). It does not apply from wife to husband, nor at all between unmarried couples.

The position as between mother and son, or mother and daughter, is less clear. In *Bennet* v *Bennet* (1879) 10 Ch D 474, Jessel MR having observed (at p. 476) that the presumption of gift arises from the moral obligation to give, went on to say:

[T]he father [of a child] is under that obligation from the mere fact of his being the father, and therefore no evidence is necessary to shew the obligation to provide for his child. In the case of a father, you have only to prove that he is the father, and when you have done that the obligation at once arises . . .

He continued (at p. 480):

In the case of a mother . . . it is easier to prove a gift than in the case of a stranger: in the case of a mother very little evidence beyond the relationship is wanted, there being very little additional motive required to induce the mother to make a gift to her child.

In other words, a weaker form of the presumption applies, it being easier to prove an intention to make a gift than in the case of a stranger.

The presumption is based upon intention, and can therefore be rebutted. A presumption of advancement between mother and daughter was rebutted recently in *Sekhon* v *Alissa* [1989] 2 FLR 94. The daughter bought a house which was conveyed into her sole name for £37,500, but of that £37,500 she had contributed only £15,000, her mother having contributed the remaining £22,500. It appeared that the only reason the house was conveyed into the name of the daughter alone was because the mother thought that there would be a capital gains tax advantage to her. Hoffman J considered all aspects of intention and came to the conclusion that the mother did not intend the entire beneficial interest to be conveyed to the daughter.

Another example of rebuttal of the presumption of advancement may be if a wife is allowed to draw cheques on a joint banking account for the convenience of the husband, perhaps because the husband is ill, as in *Marshall* v *Crutwell* (1875) LR 20 Eq 328. Clearly in such a case there is no intention to make a gift to the wife, unlike, for example, *Re Figgis* [1969] 1 Ch 123, where an otherwise similar arrangement on a joint account was not merely for convenience. It also appears that bank guarantees, for example, where a husband guarantees his wife's overdraft, do not attract the operation of the presumption, but that ordinary rules of contract apply: *Anson* v *Anson* [1953] 1 QB 636.

Relevance of marriage

Because of the operation of the presumption of advancement, it can be relevant whether or not the parties are married. Suppose, for example, a matrimonial home is purchased in the name of the husband alone, but his wife has contributed to the purchase price (either the deposit or mortgage repayments). There being no presumption of advancement from wife to husband, the equitable interests remain in proportion to the contributions, and the husband will therefore hold the legal estate on trust for both himself and his wife in proportion to their contributions. They will thus hold the land as joint tenants or tenants in common in equity, and a statutory trust for sale will arise under the provisions of the Law of Property Act 1925, ss. 34–36. The same result obtains, of course, if the parties are living together but not married.

Suppose instead, however, that the man contributes to the purchase money, the property being conveyed into the woman's name alone. It now matters whether the parties are married. If so, the presumption of advancement applies, and (in the absence of evidence rebutting the presumption) the wife will obtain both legal and equitable title. If the parties are unmarried, the opposite result obtains, the presumption being that the man retains an equitable title under a resulting trust.

There is also legislation which applies to married but not to unmarried couples. Section 37 of the Matrimonial Proceedings and Property Act 1970, entitled 'Contributions by spouse in money or money's worth to the improvement of property', allows for the beneficial interests of husbands and wives, but not unmarried couples, to be varied by substantial contributions 'in money or money's worth to the improvement of real or personal property in which . . . both of them has or have a beneficial interest'. Sections 24 and 25 of the Matrimonial Causes Act 1973 allow the courts significantly to alter the property interests of married (but not unmarried) couples in the event of divorce, a decree of nullity of marriage or a decree of judicial separation. In that event, the importance of the prior property interests of the spouses is reduced, since they will no longer be conclusive. The Matrimonial Causes Act 1973 applies only on the breakdown of marriages, however, and if the question of the existence or otherwise of a beneficial interest arises during the course of the marriage (for example, where a third party is involved, as in *Rosset* itself), the issue will be determined on the basis of the ordinary principles of equity discussed in this section.

Non-financial contributions

It is obvious from the above discussion that, in the absence of a presumption of advancement, great significance is attached by the courts to financial contributions, which are referable to the acquisition of the property. These contributions may take the form of provision of the initial deposit, or payment of mortgage instalments.

By comparison, other contributions are arguably undervalued. Generally speaking, this operates to the disadvantage of the woman living in the home, since it is still far more likely that the man will earn more money than the woman, and it is accordingly likely that his financial contributions will be the greater. On the other hand, the woman may contribute in other ways. She may, for example, give up her job to bring up the children, pay the household expenses, or provide furniture or domestic services. Because it undervalues these other contributions, the law appears to work unjustly against the woman (which is presumably why legislation was thought necessary for married couples).

Yet it is clear that little weight is attached to non-financial contributions. Should it be? On the one hand, it might be argued that the courts should exercise a discretion based on some abstract notion of justice. It has also been argued that equity is a flexible instrument. 'Equity,' said Lord Denning MR in *Eves* v *Eves* [1975] 1 WLR 1338, at p. 1340, 'is not past the age of child bearing'. It might therefore be thought possible for the courts to move away from strictly property-based criteria in cases of this type.

On the other hand, the exercise of a wide discretion by the courts would inevitably give rise to uncertainty. Remember that it is property rights that are being created. Not only would it be more difficult to advise the parties themselves, but third parties could be adversely affected. Conveyancing could become more difficult, and the policy behind the 1925 property legislation could thereby be subverted.

It is now reasonably clear that the courts will not exercise a discretion of this nature. Indeed, a rigidly property-based approach was taken by the House of Lords over 20 years ago, in *Pettit* v *Pettit* [1970] AC 777 and *Gissing* v *Gissing* [1971] AC 886. Mrs Gissing, for example, had been married to Mr Gissing for 16 years, and had paid a substantial sum towards furniture and the laying of a lawn, but the house had been conveyed into the name of Mr Gissing alone, and Mrs Gissing had made no direct contributions towards its purchase. On their divorce, the House of Lords held that she had no interest (the case was decided before the enactment of the Matrimonial Causes Act 1973). The main importance of the case is that the House refused to exercise a discretion simply in order to do 'justice'. The interests of the parties were determined on the basis of their intentions at the time of acquisition of the property, and not by their subsequent conduct.

A number of Court of Appeal decisions appeared subsequently to alter the position, however. The basis of these decisions is a passage from Lord Diplock's speech in *Gissing* v *Gissing* [1971] AC 886, which has been quoted out of context. The essence of the passage is that:

A resulting, implied or constructive trust — and it is unnecessary for present purposes to distinguish between these three classes of trust — is created . . . whenever the trustee had so conducted himself that it would be inequitable to deny to the *cestui que trust* a beneficial interest in the land acquired.

The Court of Appeal took the view that this passage allowed them a great degree of flexibility. The nature of the interest depended on all the equities of the case, and the law might consider not mrely financial contributions at the time of acquisition of the property, but all types of contribution, whether at that time or subsequently.

However, the Court of Appeal restated the conventional view in *Burns* v *Burns* [1984] Ch 317, the facts and results of which were similar to *Gissing*, except that though the parties had lived together as husband and wife for 19 years, they were unmarried. All the 1970s cases (except one) were explained on conventional property-based reasoning. The plaintiff, Valerie Burns, had been living with the defendant for 19 years, 17 in the house which was the subject of the dispute. She and the defendant, Patrick Burns, had never married, however. The house had been purchased in the name of the defendant, and he paid the purchase price. The plaintiff made no contribution to the purchase price or the mortgage repayments, but had brought up their two children, performed domestic duties and recently contributed from her own earnings towards household expenses. She also bought various fittings, and a washing machine, and redecorated the interior of the house. The plaintiff left the defendant and claimed a beneficial interest in the house.

Since the couple had never married the provisions of the Matrimonial Causes Act 1973, ss. 24 and 25 did not apply, and the Court of Appeal held that the plaintiff's case rested on orthodox property principles. In the absence of a financial contribution which could be related to the acquisition of the property, for example, to the mortgage repayments, or a contribution enabling Patrick Burns to pay the mortgage instalments, she was not entitled to a beneficial interest in the house.

Burns v *Burns* was upheld by the House of Lords in *Winkworth* v *Edward Baron Development Co. Ltd* [1988] 1 WLR 1512. The House of Lords refused to infer that Mrs Wing had an equitable interest in the matrimonial home, situated in Hayes Lane, and the case is a restatement of conventional orthodoxy. She and her husband were the sole directors of Edward Baron Development Co. Ltd, which owned the house in which they lived. Mr and Mrs Wing had sold their former matrimonial home, which they owned jointly, but the proceeds (£8600 after the mortgages had been redeemed) had not gone directly to the acquisition of the new matrimonial home in Hayes Lane, but to pay off the overdraft of Edward Baron Development Co. Ltd.

The reason the case arose was because Edward Baron Development Co. Ltd mortgaged Hayes Lane to Winkworth. Mrs Wing knew nothing of this, and her signature, which was necessary to effect the mortgage, was forged by Mr Wing. The company subsequently became insolvent, and Winkworth brought an action for possession of the property. Mr Wing did not attempt to claim an interest based on his *own* contribution (which was the same as his wife's, i.e., half the proceeds from the sale of the previous property), presumably because his claim was tainted with fraud. No such fraud affected Mrs Wing. She nevertheless lost, because the payment of the £8600 was not referable to the acquisition of the house in Hayes Lane. Lord Templeman, whose speech was the only speech of substance, purported expressly to follow the reasoning in *Burns* v *Burns*.

An interesting point to note about the *Winkworth* case is that although the parties were married, the legislation outlined above did not apply, and indeed it is unlikely that the Matrimonial Causes Act will ever apply where a beneficial interest is claimed against a third party.

The conclusion that can be drawn from these cases, therefore, is that in the absence of an agreement between the parties to share the property, and in the absence also of financial contributions referable to the acquisition of the property, it is very difficult for the party without legal title to claim an equitable title. Other contirbutions, hweover substantial, are unlikely to suffice. The decision of *Thomas* v *Fuller-Brown* [1988] 1 FLR 237 is a good illustration, where the Court of Appeal held that a man had no interest in the house in which he lived with a woman (who had legal title), although in the view of Slade LJ (at p. 240):

> [The work he did] was obviously quite substantial . . . *inter alia*, he designed and constructed a two-storey extension, created a through lounge, carried out minor electrical and plumbing works, replastered and redecorated the property throughout, landscaped and reorganised the garden, laid a driveway, carried out repairs to the chimney and the roof and repointed the gable end of the property, constructed an internal entry hall at the property, rebuilt the kitchen and installed a new stairway.

It seems to have been assumed that this work was not referable to the acquisition of the property, and no doubt that it was no more than any man would do about the house!

Finally, there is *Rosset* itself. Mr and Mrs Rosset decided to purchase a semi-derelict farmhouse for £57,000. Mrs Rosset understood that the entire purchase money was to come out of a family trust fund, the trustees of which insisted that the house be purchased in the husband's sole name (this appears to have been the only reason for the legal title being vested in Mr Rosset alone). The house required renovation, and it was intended that this should be joint venture. The vendors allowed Mr and Mrs Rosset to enter the property a number of weeks before completion in order to begin repairs, and render the house habitable.

During this period Mrs Rosset spent a lot of time at the house, urging on the builders and attempting to co-ordinate their work (until her husband insisted that he alone should give instructions), going to the builders' merchants to obtain material required by the builders, delivering the materials to the site, assisting her husband in planning the renovation and decoration of the house (she was a skilled painter and decorator), wallpapering two bedrooms, arranging the insurance of the house, arranging a crime prevention survey, and assisting in arranging the installation of burglar alarms.

Unbeknown to Mrs Rosset, Mr Rosset was unable to fund the purchase and repairs entirely from the trust fund, and obtained an overdraft of £18,000 from Lloyd's Bank, execuring a legal charge on the property in their favour on the same day as completion. He later defaulted on the repayments, and the bank sought possession. Mrs Rosset claimed a beneficial interest in the property, binding the bank by virtue of her actual occupation, as an overriding interest under the Land Registration Act 1925, s. 70(1)(g).

Notice that like *Winkworth*, although the parties were married, the

legislation outlined above did not apply, since again it was claimed that
the beneficial interest was capable of binding a third party. The Matrimonial
Causes Act will only usually apply in two-party cases.

In the Court of Appeal in *Rosset*, most of the discussion revolved around
whether Mrs Rosset was in actual occupation when the charge was created,
in order to be able to rely upon s. 70(1)(g). While this discussion is of
some importance to land law students, it is of no relevance for present
purposes. The House of Lords was able to avoid all discussion of s. 70(1)(g),
simply holding that Mrs Rosset had no beneficial interest. There was no
evidence of any agreement between the parties to share the beneficial interest,
and the wife's contributions were regarded as *de minimis*. The principles
discussed in this section were applied.

The cases suggest, then, that for a beneficial interest to be acquired in
this type of case, the contributions must be referable to the *initial* acquisition
of the property. Presumably, however, there is no reason in principle why
the respective beneficial interests of the parties should not be capable of
being varied after acquisition. Suppose, for example Valerie Burns (in *Burns
v Burns*) had, 10 years after acquisition, paid for an extension, doubling
the value of the property. Clearly, this is not referable to the initial
acquisition, and since the parties in *Burns* were unmarried, the Matrimonial
Proceedings and Property Act would not apply. There are no cases where
anything like this has actually occurred, but surely it is inconceivable that
the courts would not infer a beneficial interest in such circumstances. Surely
beneficial interests are capable of being varied after initial acquisition. No
doubt the courts would require very strong evidence before inferring such
a variation, since otherwise the nature and size of the beneficial interests
could be constantly changing. In principle, however, it ought to be possible
to infer an agreement to vary existing beneficial interests in the event, for
example, of one party making a substantial capital improvement.

The other way in which conduct after initial acquisition can be relevant
even in this type of case, is that repayment of mortgage instalments is
regarded as being referable to initial acquisition.

Cases where there is an agreement to share

By contrast with the cases discussed in the previous section, where conduct
apart from financial contributions referable to the acquisition of the property
will hardly ever suffice, there is another type of case where even parties
who have contributed very little have been held entitled to quite a large
share.

In these cases, it is possible to infer an agreement, from evidence apart
from the conduct relied upon, between the parties to share the beneficial

interests. In such a case, it is unecessary to rely on the conduct itself in order to draw that inference. The existence of the beneficial interest, and its size, are determined by the agreement and not by the conduct.

That is not to say that the conduct is entirely irrelevant, because a declaration of trust by the legal owner falls foul of the formalities provisions of s. 53(1)(b) of the Law of Property Act 1925, unless in writing. However, resulting and constructive trusts are expressly exempted from the formality requirements by s. 53(2). In order to invoke s. 53(2), it is necessary for the party claiming that it would be inequitable for the legal owner to renege on the agreement. All that is required is detrimental reliance, however. There is no additional need for the conduct to be substantial, or referable to the acquisition of the property.

The leading case is the decision of the Court of Appeal in *Grant* v *Edwards* [1986] Ch 638. In 1969 a house was purchased for the plaintiff, Mrs Linda Grant, and the defendant, George Edwards to live in as if married (although Linda Grant was actually married to someone else). The house was purchased in the name of Edwards and his brother. Edwards told Grant that her name would not go on the title for the time being because it would cause prejudice in the matrimonial proceedings pending between Mrs Grant and her husband. In reality, he had no intention of conveying any legal title to the plaintiff.

The defendant paid the deposit on the house, and most, but not all, of the repayments on the two mortgages, He paid the deposit and all the mortgage instalments on the first mortgage, but the plaintiff paid some instalments under a second mortgage. The plaintiff also made substantial contributions towards general household expenses, provided housekeeping and brought up the children. In 1980 the couple separated, and the plaintiff claimed a beneficial interest in the property.

The Court of Appeal held that Edward's statement that Mrs Grant's name would have appeared on the title except that it could cause prejudice in the matrimonial proceedings was evidence of a common intention that Mrs Grant should have beneficial interest (a half share) in the property. Mrs Grant had relied to her detriment on the common intention, so that she was entitled to a half share on a resulting or constructive trust.

It may be observed that Linda Grant's contributions were not particularly significant, and would certainly not have justified a half share, or probably any share, on the principles discussed in the previous section. The crucial element in the case was the statement by the defendant as to why the plaintiff's name would not go on to the title. The Court of Appeal took the view that this statement could only be explained on the basis of a common intention that she was to have a half share. At first sight this seems rather a surprising conclusion, since Edwards clearly intended no such thing, but the representation was interpreted (in effect) as meaning: 'your name would go on the title but for the fact that it would prejudice your matrimonial proceedings'. Had Edwards intended to say: 'the house is to be mine alone', there would have been no need for an excuse. By this somewhat tortuous reasoning, therefore, the court was able to infer, independently of her contributions, a common intention that she was to have a half share, and the case depended on this.

Because there was evidence of a common intention (independent of the contributions themselves), Linda Grant's contributions (unlike those of Valerie Burns), were relevant only in order to get round the formality provisions of s. 53 of the Law of Property Act 1925. It was necessary only for Grant to show that she had relied on the agreement to her detriment, by acting in a manner which was explicable only on the basis that she was to have an interest in the house, for a constructive trust to arise in her favour.

This is a far less stringent requirement than that adopted in *Burns* or *Rosset*, where there was no outside evidence of any agreement, so that evidence of intention could only be inferred from the contributions themselves. Furthermore, the value of the beneficial interest was determined by the common intention (as evidenced by the defendant's statement), and not by the value of Linda Grant's contributions.

Mention was made in the previous section of *Eves* v *Eves* [1975] 1 WLR 1338. In that case, Lord Denning MR reasoned that equity was still capable of developing, and that the courts had a discretion to depart from strictly property-based criteria in order to achieve what they saw as 'justice'. It is now clear that the case cannot be explained on that basis, but while in *Grant* v *Edwards* Lord Denning MR's reasoning in *Eves* v *Eves* was expressly rejected, the decision itself was upheld, and it seems that it is in fact a case of this type.

Janet Eves, who was under 21 and separated from her husband, went to live with a man whose marriage had also broken down. They had a child together, and shortly afterwards found a house with the intention that they would live there together. The man told her that if she had been 21 he would have arranged for the house to be conveyed into their joint names, but in reality this was simply an excuse for having the house conveyed into his name alone. The house was in a dilapidated state, and Janet did a great deal of heavy building work improving it, including wielding a 14lb sledgehammer to break up the concrete in the front garden, so that it could be levelled and turfed. When the relationship broke down, Janet Eves was held to be entitled to a quarter-share. As in *Grant* v *Edwards*, the case depended upon the representation made by the man: there would have been no need for him to make an excuse had he intended to say: 'the house is to be mine alone'. As Brightman J explained (at p. 1345):

> The defendant clearly led the plaintiff to believe that she was to have some undefined interest in the property, and that her name was only omitted from the conveyance because of her age.

The cases of *Grant* v *Edwards* and *Eves* v *Eves* were explained by Lord Bridge in *Rosset*, who also made clear what inference was to be drawn from the representations, and what was the importance of the subsequent conduct of the female partner:

> Outstanding examples on the other hand of cases giving rise to situations in the first category [i.e., where there is an agreement to share] are *Eves* v *Eves* [1975] 1 WLR 1338 and *Grant* v *Edwards* [1986] Ch 638. In both these cases, where the parties who had cohabited were unmarried, the female partner had been clearly led by the male partner to believe, when they set up home together, that the property would belong to them jointly. In *Eves* v *Eves* the male partner had told the female partner that the only reason why the property was to be acquired in his name alone was because she was under 21 and that, but for her age, he would have had the house put into their joint names. He admitted in evidence that this was simply an 'excuse'. Similarly, in *Grant* v *Edwards* the female partner was told by the male partner that the only reason for not acquiring the property in joint names was because she was involved in divorce proceedings and that, if the property were acquired jointly, this might operate to her prejudice in those proceedings. As Nourse LJ put it (at 649):

>> 'Just as in *Eves* v *Eves*, these facts appear to me to raise a clear inference that there was an understanding between the plaintiff and the defendant, or a common intention, that the plaintiff was to have some sort of proprietary interest in the house otherwise no excuse for not putting her name onto the title would have been needed.'

The subsequent conduct of the female partner in each of these cases, which the court rightly held sufficient to give rise to a constructive trust or proprietary estoppel supporting her claim to an interest in the property, fell far short of such conduct as would by itself have supported the claim in the absence of an express representation by the male partner that she was to have such an interest. It is significant to note that the share to which the female partners in *Eves* v *Eves* and *Grant* v *Edwards* were held entitled were one-quarter and one-half respectively. In no sense could these shares have been regarded as proportionate to what the judge in the instant case described as a 'qualifying contribution' in terms of the indirect contributions to the acquisition or enhancement of the value of the houses made by the female partners.

In *Grant* v *Edwards*, Nourse LJ (at p. 646) drew the following distinction, which essentially summarises the above discussion, between the relevance of the woman's conduct in *Grant* v *Edwards* itself, and its relevance in a case like *Burns* v *Burns*:

> In most of these cases the fundamental, and invariably the most difficult, question is to decide whether there was the necessary common intention, being something which can only be inferred from the conduct of the parties, almost always from the expenditure incurred by them respectively. In this regard the court has to look for expenditure which is referable to the acquisition of the house (see . . . *Burns* v *Burns* [1984] Ch 317). If it is found to have been incurred, such expenditure will perform the twofold function of establishing the common intention and showing that the claimant has acted upon it.
>
> There is another and rarer class of case, of which the present may be one, where, although there has been no writing, the parties have orally declared themselves in such a way as to make their common intention plain. Here the court does not have to look for conduct from which the intention can be inferred, but only for conduct which amounts to an acting upon it by the claimant. And although that conduct can undoubtedly be the incurring of expenditure which is referable to the acquisition of the house, it need not necessarily be so.

Elaborating on the question of what conduct would suffice, he referred to *Eves* v *Eves*, and said:

> So what sort of conduct is required? In my judgment it must be conduct on which the woman could not necessarily have been expected to embark unless she was to have an interest in the house. If she was not to have such an interest, she could reasonably be expected to go and live with her lover, but not, for example, to wield a 14 lb sledge-hammer in the front garden. In adopting the latter kind of conduct she is seen to act to her detriment on the faith of the common intention.

The requirement for this type of case is detrimental reliance, therefore. In *Burns* v *Burns*, by contrast, the court had to look for expenditure which was referable to the acquisition of the house. It is obvious that it is far easier to satisfy the requirement in *Grant* v *Edwards* than it is to satisfy the requirement in *Burns* v *Burns*.

Post-Rosset litigation

Given that it is far more difficult for an interest to be acquired in the *Burns* or *Rosset* situation than where an independent agreement, or common intention, can be inferred, it is not surprising that post-*Rosset* disputes have essentially been about into which category a particular case falls.

It is obvious from the discussion in the previous section that evidence for the independent agreement, or common intention, need not be in writing (otherwise no detrimental reliance would be required at all), and indeed it is not even necessary for the parties expressly to have agreed to share the property. In neither *Grant* v *Edwards* nor *Eves* v *Eves* was there any evidence of the parties sitting down to make such an agreement, and indeed, in both cases a common intention was inferred from an excuse being made for *not* putting the woman's name on the title. Since the cases often arise many years after the acquisition of the property (in *Burns* v *Burns*, the parties had been living together for 19 years), recollection of old conversations is likely to be extremely scanty. Yet it is upon such recollections that the outcome of the case will probably depend.

One such case is *Ungurian* v *Lesnoff* [1990] Ch 206. Mrs Lesnoff, who was a Polish academic, gave up a flat in Poland of which she could have remained in occupation for life, her Polish nationality and her career, in order to live with Mr Ungurian. Ungurian bought a house in London, registered in his sole name, in which he and Mrs Lesnoff lived as man and wife for four years. During that time Mrs Lesnoff installed or supervised the installation of central heating, and the re-wiring and re-plumbing of the house, in addition to other works of improvement and redecoration. Mrs Lesnoff remained in occupation, and when Ungurian brought an action for possession and the case finally came to court many years later, Vinelott J held that Mrs Lesnoff had an interest, but the case depended upon obscure recollections of conversations which were over 20 years old:

In Beirut, over Christmas 1968 and subsequently in London by the plaintiff to the first defendant on a number of different occasions, *inter alia*, the plaintiff used the following words of which the following are a translation from Polish to that effect, 'We will have to look for and buy a house for us in London so that you will feel secure and happy, having lost your house in Poland', and 'You'll have to decide and find the house which you like. I want you to feel that you have something to rely on if anything happens to me'.

From this obscure recollection, and other circumstances surrounding the purchase of the house, and the subsequent conduct of the parties, was inferred a common intention, not that Mrs Lesnoff should have a share of the fee simple, but that she should have the right to reside in the house for life.

The consequences of this were startling: because Ungurian's interest was subject to Mrs Lesnoff's prior life interest, there were thereby necessarily successive interests in the property, and the house therefore became settled land within the Settled Land Act 1925. Accordingly, Mrs Lesnoff as tenant for life was entitled to call for the execution of a vesting deed and the appointment of trustees, and, once the house was vested in her, to sell it and to re-invest the proceeds in the purchase of another house or to enjoy the income therefrom.

In reaching this view (which was not necessary for the actual decision) Vinelott J followed the majority view, and not the view of Lord Denning MR, in *Binions v Evans* [1972] Ch 359, a case which is considered in detail in the following section. If he is correct, then Mrs Lesnoff was entitled to sell the house, a consequence certainly infinitely more far-reaching than anything envisaged in the obscurely-recollected conversation that took place in Beirut in December 1968.

Whether or not Vinelott J's view on the application of the Settled Land Act *is* correct is considered in more detail later in the chapter. It can be concluded, however, that although Lord Bridge's speech in *Rosset* has done much to clarify an area of law that was previously rather obscure, the detailed application of *Rosset* principles might still be fraught with difficulties.

New developments in constructive trusts

Another frontier area is the recent extension of the law relating to constructive trusts, particularly where informal arrangements are concerned regarding land.

As with beneficial interests of cohabitees, any statement of the law in this area will be highly controversial, and there is definitely not any right answer; and as with beneficial interests of cohabitees there are not very many really vital cases, and the trick is to know those few very well, and to consider exactly how far they go.

A general fraud doctrine?

Later on in this chapter we will consider a problem question on this subject, but it is worth examining some of the general assumptions first. One such assumption, often made, is that property obtained by fraud is to be held on constructive trust for the victim of the fraud. Many of the recent cases extending the imposition of constructive trusts assume the existence of a general principle of this nature. Yet this assumption is at best highly questionable, so it is worth in the first place examining exactly how far equitable fraud jurisdiction goes.

The issue encompasses a number of areas dealt with elsewhere in the book, which is why the exam question mentioned in the first chapter:

'Equity will not permit a statute to be used as a cloak for fraud.' Discuss.

shows up the penalties of concentrating too narrowly during exam revision. It is unwise to attempt this question unless you are reasonably confident about a substantial proportion of the syllabus.

Clearly there would be little point in repeating large chunks of the book for the purposes of this discussion, so I would suggest you cross-refer for the details of the part performance doctrine (chapter 5) and secret and half-secret trusts (chapter 7). Only general observations on these areas will be made here.

In fact the principle stated in the above question is a good starting-point for discussion. It is an important equitable principle which was developed by the courts of equity to prevent people from taking unfair advantage of statutory formality provisions, which are of course intended to prevent, rather than encourage fraud. It is quite an old principle, dating back certainly as far as the Wills Act 1837, and possibly back to the Statute of Frauds 1677.

Yet important though it is, the principle that equity will not permit a statute to be used as a cloak for fraud is not authority for a more general fraud principle for the imposition of constructive trusts. In the first place, it generally concerns the enforcement of express rather than constructive trusts. In the second place, it is limited to the abuse of statutory provisions, and not even all statutes appear to be covered.

An early but oft-quoted example is the decision of the Court of Appeal in *Rochefoucauld v Boustead* [1897] 1 Ch 196. The plaintiff was the Comtesse de la Rochefoucauld. She owned some estates producing coffee in Ceylon (present-day Sri Lanka), but these properties were subject to a considerable mortgage, which the Comtesse was having difficulty in repaying. In order to stop the mortgagee from foreclosing, an arrangement was made whereby the defendant purchased the estates subject to the mortgage. The precise circumstances of this transfer were disputed, but the Court of Appeal accepted on the basis of both oral evidence and letters that the defendant took the land as trustee for the plaintiff.

'a terrible blight of leaf disease'

He treated it as if it were his own, however, and raised more money on it by way of mortgage without the plaintiff's consent. Unfortunately, a 'terrible blight of leaf disease' occurred which destroyed the coffee enterprise, and the defendant was bankrupted (though eventually discharged). The plaintiff asserted her equitable title, and claimed an account of profits, but the defendant claimed that he was beneficial owner of the property.

Various arguments were advanced by the defendant, all of which were rejected, but the interesting one for our purposes was that the trust claimed by the plaintiff was not evidenced in writing signed by the defendant, as required by the Statute of Frauds 1677, s. 7, which was the precursor of the Law of Property Act 1925, s. 53. This argument was rejected on the principle quoted in the exam question above.

The case is not authority for a wide general principle applicable to constructive trusts. Presumably the trusts, being based as they were on oral evidence and letters, were express rather than constructive in nature. Also, the reasoning of Lindley LJ, who delivered the judgment of the court, does not expressly extend beyond the particular statute: the court 'will not allow the Statute of Frauds to be made an instrument of fraud'.

Nevertheless, it would probably apply where there is an attempt to use any statute intended to prevent fraud as a means of perpetrating a fraud. Thus the reasoning probably applies to any statutory formality requirement, not just s. 53 of the Law of Property Act 1925 (the present-day equivalent of the Statute of Frauds). It does not follow that it applies to all statutes of any type, however, still less that it applies even where no statute at all is involved.

It should also be noted that the reasoning of Lindley LJ would enable even express trusts to be established despite lack of writing within the s. 53 criteria.

Nor is the doctrine of part performance—another application of the maxim discussed in chapter 5—authority for any more general principle. Most of the cases are about the Law of Property Act 1925, s. 40, though the doctrine applies also to s. 53. All the cases considered in chapter 5 refer to express trusts, so the doctrine cannot be used as authority for any proposition about constructive trusts.

Fraud and secret trusts

What of other applications of the doctrine that equity will not allow a statute to be used as a cloak for fraud? Another strand of cases concerns secret and half-secret trusts, where the fraud principle avoids the formality provisions of what used to be the Wills Act 1837 (see chapter 7). These are arguably constructive, and so could be used to provide support for a general theory, but could just as easily be examples of express trusts. If so, of course, they also provide no authority for any general principle of imposition of constructive trusts.

We will see in chapter 7 that one theory for the basis of enforcement of both fully and half-secret trusts is the fraud of the trustee. The argument that they are express is that both varieties implement the express intentions of the testator, even though those intentions may not be expressed correctly, in writing, signed and attested etc.

The argument for classifying them as constructive is that the formality requirements of the Law of Property Act 1925, s. 53(1) (see chapter 5) apply to express, but not (by virtue of s. 53(2)) constructive trusts. Section 53(1)(b) requires express trusts of land to be declared in writing, yet a fully secret trust of land was enforced in *Ottaway* v *Norman* [1972] Ch 698 despite being oral. Further, that case ostensibly rested on constructive trust principles. This is therefore apparently authority that at any rate fully secret trusts are constructive.

It is possible that the case applies directly only to fully secret trusts, and indeed, *Re Baillie* (1886) 2 TLR 660 suggests that writing is required for half-secret trusts of land. The distinction (with which the author does not agree) will be elaborated in the following chapter.

But whether or not writing is required for a secret trust of either variety, it does not follow that they should be classified as constructive. As we have already seen, express trusts can also be exempted from statutory writing requirements if to do otherwise would be to promote fraud. This necessarily follows from *Rochefoucauld* v *Boustead*.

Hodgson v Marks

Another example is *Hodgson* v *Marks* [1971] Ch 892. An old lady (Mrs Hodgson) was cajoled into making a voluntary conveyance (i.e., not for value) of her house to her lodger (Evans). Evans then sold the property to a third party (Marks). Two issues arose: first, did Mrs Hodgson have an equitable interest in the property, and secondly, did that interest bind Marks? Both issues were decided in favour of Mrs Hodgson in the Court of Appeal. The second issue is of more importance to land law than trusts, because of the application of s. 70(1)(g) of the Land Registration Act 1925. This aspect of the decision was upheld by the House of Lords in *Williams & Glyn's Bank Ltd* v *Boland* [1981] AC 487. Here we are interested in the first issue.

In the Court of Appeal Russell LJ, who gave the only substantive judgment, and with whom Buckley and Cairns LJJ agreed, thought that Mrs Hodgson's interest was by way of resulting trust. If it was, then the decision would be of no help for this discussion: resulting trusts are expressly exempted from the operation of s. 53, and we are only interested in the question whether express trusts can also be.

Mrs Hodgson did not argue a resulting trust, however, but an express trust, and this was the basis of Ungoed-Thomas J's decision in the High Court. It should be noted that though Ungoed-Thomas J was reversed in the Court of Appeal, the reversal was only as to the interpretation of the Land Registration Act 1925, not on the question of the existence of a trust. Ungoed-Thomas J relied on *Rochefoucauld* v *Boustead* [1897] 1 Ch 196, so at this stage *Hodgson* v *Marks* was no more an authority on constructive trusts than is the earlier case.

Russell LJ seemed unsure whether the *Rochefoucauld* v *Boustead* principle could apply to Marks, the third-party purchaser. This is why he preferred to base his decision on resulting trust reasoning, but he would have been happy to apply Ungoed-Thomas J's reasoning to Mr Evans, the original lodger:

Quite plainly Mr Evans could not have placed any reliance on s. 53, for that would have been to use the section as an instrument of fraud.

It seems, then, that even express trusts are outside the scope of s. 53 if the section is being used to prevent proof of fraud. Thus, whether secret and half-secret trusts are express or constructive, they are not affected by any enactment requiring formality. Therefore, they cannot be used directly as authority for any constructive trust reasoning.

It may well be then that any fraud principle is limited to trusts which are express, but which would otherwise fail only because of a statutory formality provision. There may also be further limitations to the doctrine. For example, it probably applies only where there is an attempt to use a statute intended to prevent fraud as a means of perpetrating fraud.

Conclusions on the fraud doctrine

Far from being of general application, therefore, the fraud principle may not even apply to every statutory provision. Indeed, it would be difficult to argue that it applies to the Land Charges Act 1972 (replacing the 1925 Act, which was intended to simplify conveyancing, not prevent fraud), following the House of Lords decision in *Midland Bank Trust Co. Ltd* v *Green* [1981] AC 513. There a sham sale between husband and wife, intended specifically to defeat a third party's valuable option to purchase a farm, succeeded in its purpose, solely because the option had not been properly registered under the Act. Lord Wilberforce said (at p. 531) that in general it is not 'fraud' to rely on legal rights conferred by Act of Parliament. Thus equity's intervention is by no means as universal as some of the recent cases suggest.

There is another principle relating to fraud, which is that he who seeks equity must come to the court with clean hands. This principle prevents people from enforcing fraudulent trusts. It, too, has nothing to do with the imposition of constructive trusts.

Mutual wills are the exception, in that they are clearly regarded as constructive. The special problems relating to them are considered in the following paragraph. It will be seen that though they clearly give rise to constructive trusts, the reasoning is directed to a specific problem, and is not of general application.

The problem of mutual wills

Mutual wills cases may seem to provide the necessary authority for constructive trusts being based upon a general fraud principle.

They are unlike secret and half-secret trusts in three main respects. First, they give rise to what are clearly constructive trusts. Secondly, whereas the enforcement of secret trusts prevents the use of a statute, intended specifically to prevent fraud (Wills Act 1837, as subsequently amended), actually to perpetrate a fraud, mutual wills are not otherwise unenforceable merely because of a statutory formality provision. Thirdly, secret trusts are imposed only on the property actually received by the secret trustee, whereas with mutual wills (as will appear below), all the property of the trustee, present and future, is subject to the trust.

Yet despite the apparent generality of reasoning in this area, it can in fact be seen that constructive trusts are imposed for a very specific reason, and that these cases are in fact not authority for a general rule.

Mutual wills are agreements, usually but not necessarily between husband and wife. Wills are made (or the parties agree to make them) by each party in (usually) the same terms, and there is a mutual agreement that neither party will revoke, but the essence of the transaction is an agreement that each party will settle his or her property in a particular (usually the same) way.

Suppose for the following discussion that Mr X and Miss Y marry, and enter into a transaction whereby each agrees to settle part of his/her estate on the other party on his/her death. Mutual wills are made then, and each undertakes that it will be his/her last. Sometime later, Y dies. X, later in life marries Z, and there are children of the second marriage. The effect of the agreement is that Z and any children of the second marriage are deprived of some benefit under X's will, whereas Y's next of kin can claim against X's estate, the extent depending on the terms of the original arrangement.

The law on mutual wills was recently reviewed by Nourse J in *Re Cleaver* [1981] 1 WLR 939, noted by Hodkinson [1982] Conv 228 (and also discussed in all the main textbooks). The reasoning in this case is by no means new, and is in fact a restatement of principles which are centuries old. The leading case, for example, is regarded as *Dufour v Pereira* (1769) Dick 419.

While X and Y are both still alive each can revoke his/her will. That revocation will be valid, but may be in breach of contract. This depends on the construction of the agreement, and is an application of the general law of contract.

On Y's death X becomes absolutely entitled to any money received under Y's will (unless the will gives him a life interest only), but on the other hand he is bound by a trust regarding his other property and future earnings. He cannot later revoke his will (which he made before Y's death). Further, he becomes constructive trustee on the terms of the will, which, of course, he undertook would be his last.

The reason for the constructive trust is that X received property under Y's will because of the agreement. His conscience demands, therefore, that he be subject to the agreement, so that a constructive trust is imposed on all his other present and future property. Otherwise he would have received the property by fraud. The fraud arises from the causal relationship between X's receipt of the property under Y's will and the making of the mutual wills agreement, and is therefore a much wider concept than fraud in the criminal law sense, which requires an element of intention, and has connotations of dishonesty.

If one were to generalise from the law on mutual wills, then, one could assert that a constructive trust is imposed on anyone who receives property through fraud. Further, to show fraud in this sense it is enough to show that receipt of the property was subject to an agreement. So the question is: can one generalise from these cases?

I would suggest not, and that mutual wills are special cases. The basic problem is that X, the survivor, is often Y's executor. It is possible that the reasoning in the early cases was influenced by the fact that before the Executors Act 1830, executors were entitled to retain the residuary estate for themselves, so X would have been residuary legatee under Y's will. It is also quite likely that he would only have been executor, and therefore residuary legatee, because of the promises made at the time of the mutual wills. So a possible reason for imposing a constructive trust would have been to prevent him benefiting personally from the residuary estate, especially if he had promised to use it for Y's next of kin.

A more likely explanation, however, is that if X is Y's executor, it has been assumed that there is no other way of binding X to his original agreement (because X himself is the only person who can enforce it), though this assumption is probably mistaken.

In principle X should be unable to renege on his promise even after Y's death, because he continues to be contractually bound. The contract is enforceable by Y's estate (as in *Beswick* v *Beswick* [1968] AC 58, considered in chapter 3). When X dies, the action is by Y's estate against X's estate. In practice, however, there are difficulties with the contractual action, and this may be the real reason for continuing to impose a constructive trust today.

In the first place, those whom Y intended to benefit cannot themselves enforce the contract, as they are not a party to it (only Y is). In effect, they are in the *Re Plumptre's Marriage Settlement* situation (see chapter 3), and actually it is difficult to see why, in principle, they should be put into any better position than any other volunteer.

Enforcement of the contract is in fact at the discretion of Y's personal representative, but this causes problems if he is X. There is a solution, however, because if X does anything inconsistent with the terms of the agreement, he will be liable, in his capacity as personal representative, directly to the intended beneficiaries. Thus it would seem that the contract can be enforced, albeit by a tortuous route.

There is another difficulty, however, because specific performance has to be available as a remedy. No theoretical difficulties arise if the contract can be construed as one to settle property on X's death. If, however, it is construed as a contract not to revoke an existing will, specific performance is unlikely to be available.

One difficulty is that wills are revoked automatically on marriage. X may well wish to remarry after Y's death, but an agreement not to revoke the will could be construed as one in restraint of this second marriage. If so, not only would it not be specifically enforceable, but it would be void as an illegal contract on public policy grounds.

In the end it all depends on construction of the agreement. In principle mutual wills can be made which are contractually enforceable, but the difficulties may be a justification for the imposition of a constructive trust. If so, the justification is not of general application.

A general principle of fraud?

Since even the reasoning in mutual wills cases seems to be directed at a specific mischief (the problems of an alternative contractual enforcement), it follows that the development of any general principle seems unwarranted by earlier authority. It can also cause injustice. It must be remembered that the imposition of a constructive trust is an extreme step. As between the parties, it creates the incidents of a trustee-beneficiary relationship. More importantly, it creates a property interest, which binds third parties also.

The case most often relied upon for a general principle, and on which later cases have been based, is the Court of Appeal decision of *Bannister* v *Bannister* [1948] 2 All ER 133. It is an important case, and should be mastered in its entirety. You will probably find first, that the judgment of Scott LJ is more limited in its scope than later cases would lead you to suppose, secondly that there are other (better?) reasons for the decision, and thirdly that the imposition of a trust leads to consequences which are more extreme than are either necessary or desirable.

The defendant was negotiating to sell two cottages to the plaintiff, her brother-in-law, and it was understood that after the sale she would be able to continue to live in one of the cottages rent-free for as long as she wished. Because of this oral arrangement the plaintiff obtained the cottages for only £250, as compared with their true market value of around

£400. No written agreement to this effect was included in the conveyance, however. After the sale, the plaintiff claimed possession of the cottage. Obviously the plaintiff had obtained the property cheaply by fraud. The Court of Appeal therefore decided that he held it as constructive trustee of the defendant for her life.

How extensive is this authority? Certainly there are passages in the judgment which appear to suggest a general principle. Nevertheless, the case is actually about an attempt to use the writing provisions of the Law of Property Act 1925 as a cloak for fraud. It is really only an application of the principles considered earlier in this chapter, and is not unlike *Rochefoucauld* v *Boustead* [1897] 1 Ch 196 or *Hodgson* v *Marks* [1971] Ch 892.

The trust imposed was said to be constructive. Perhaps, though, this was only because such trusts are expressly exempted from s. 53 of the Law of Property Act 1925 (requiring writing, which there was not in the case). We saw earlier in the chapter, though, that express trusts can also probably avoid the provision.

At the beginning of this chapter (p. 90), I suggested that you should always consider the possibility that the same result could be reached without resort to trusts reasoning at all. For example, where no third party is involved, the same result can often be reached on contract reasoning, without the necessity for any kind of trust. What about *Bannister* v *Bannister* itself? There were only two parties, i.e., no complications involving purchasers, and there was clearly a contract. Why could not the Court of Appeal have reached the desired result by treating the agreement as giving rise to a contractual licence to remain in one of the cottages? Contractual licences do not need to be in writing, and the defendant would have had exactly what she had bargained for. By contrast, the constructive trust reasoning actually adopted by the court gave her far more, as will become apparent below.

Perhaps the case was not argued on this basis because it was not clear at that time that it was possible, in circumstances such as these, to have a contractual licence, not in writing, giving a right of exclusive possession in land. Not until the early 1950s, with decisions such as those of the Court of Appeal in *Foster* v *Robinson* [1951] 1 KB 149, and *Errington* v *Errington* [1952] 1 KB 290, did the courts begin to elaborate circumstances where a contract giving a right of exclusive possession of property might be construed as creating a licence, rather than (for example) an equitable lease. A contract to create a lease (or, in other words, an equitable lease) may well not have served in *Bannister* v *Bannister*, since writing was required by the Law of Property Act 1925, s. 40 (subject to the part performance doctrine discussed in chapter 5), and of course the arrangement was oral.

If similar facts to those in *Bannister* v *Bannister* were to arise again today, however, I would suggest that contractual licence reasoning would be the most appropriate to adopt. It is true that in recent years the courts have somewhat curtailed the scope of contractual licences where exclusive possession is granted (as, for example, in *Ashburn Anstalt* v *Arnold* [1988] 2 All ER 147, a case considered in greater detail below), but not in cases like *Bannister* itself. No rent was payable by the defendant, nor was there any obligation on the defendant to continue in occupation of the cottage, and there was no ascertainable term. It would have been quite inappropriate, therefore, to construe the arrangement as giving rise to an equitable lease, and indeed the case is virtually on all fours with *Foster* v *Robinson* [1951] 1 KB 149, where the Court of Appeal held that a contractual licence had been created.

This case also shows how the imposition of a constructive trust can be an extreme remedy. Its effect was that the defendant became a tenant for life under the provisions of the Settled Land Act 1925, and therefore had powers to sell it. Clearly this is a much more extreme result than the parties intended.

Problem question

A has legal title (in fee simple) to Blackacre, and agrees with B, who is a 90-year-old lady, that if she (B) decorates and looks after the place, she can live there as long as she wishes. B, who is remarkably alert for her age, asks A whether the agreement between them will still apply if A sells the property, and A agrees that it will. B decorates and looks after the place, and has lived there ever since.

Later A agrees to sell, and conveys Blackacre to C. Although before the sale C is unaware of the exact terms of B's arrangement with A, he is aware of the presence of B in the house. Further, A tells C that one of the reasons for selling to C in particular is that he is confident that he (C) will allow B to remain in the property. C does nothing to disabuse A of this notion.

Advise B whether she has a beneficial interest in the property, and if so the extent of that interest.

Would your answer be different if the case was appealed to the House of Lords?

Leaving aside the last paragraph for the moment, this question invites you to consider the case of *Binions* v *Evans* [1972] Ch 359, and subsequent developments based on that decision. You are asked only about beneficial interests in the land, whereas a similar type of question in a land law exam may also invite you to consider contractual and estoppel licences, or further ramifications of the Settled Land Act 1925.

Binions v *Evans* is another case which should be mastered in its entirety. Though the decision of the Court of Appeal was unanimous it is complicated by the fact that there were alternative, and even conflicting reasons given by each of the three judges in the case. It is therefore a good example of the pitfalls of reading only one judgment, especially if, like many students, you decide to concentrate on the judgment of Lord Denning MR. This is one of the many cases where his reasoning is at variance not only with that of the other judges in the case, but is also out on a limb in a more general sense.

You should also remember that *Binions* v *Evans* was truly a frontier case, and you really cannot expect certain answers. Views can legitimately differ, not only as to whether the case was correctly decided, but also as to what it decided, and you will not be penalised for disagreeing with the view of the examiner. It is important that whatever view you take has an internal logic (i.e., contains no contradictions) and is well-argued. Also, you ought probably to form a view.

Nearly everyone remembers the facts of *Binions* v *Evans*, and they are set out briefly below. But do not take immense trouble to remember the facts at the expense of the legal issues involved. You are examined on the latter, not the former.

The trustees of the Tredegar Estate, which is near Newport in South Wales, entered into an agreement with Mrs Evans (the defendant). Her husband had worked on the estate for many years, and had a tied cottage, and shortly after his death the trustees agreed that Mrs Evans could continue to live in the cottage for the rest of her life. In return Mrs Evans was required to keep the property in a proper manner.

The trustees later sold the cottage to the plaintiffs, Mr and Mrs Binions, expressly subject to Mrs Evans's 'tenancy agreement'. The plaintiffs, having thereby obtained the cottage more cheaply, six months later claimed possession from Mrs Evans. The Court of Appeal unanimously decided that they should fail.

Though the three members of the court were unanimous about the result, the reasoning of the Master of the Rolls is quite different from that of the other judges.

Lord Denning MR started with the assertion that Mrs Evans had a contractual licence, which bound the purchasers with notice. This is really a land law point, and also outside the scope of the question, which is limited to the discussion of beneficial interests. If his reasoning were correct, then it would have been unnecessary for the Court of Appeal to consider whether Mrs Evans also had a beneficial interest, and there would have been no need for any discussion of constructive trusts at all. However, it would be difficult today to argue that contractual licences bind third-party purchasers of land, following the Court of Appeal decision in *Ashburn Anstalt* v *Arnold* [1988] 2 All ER 147, a case considered further below. So if *Binions* v *Evans* is correct, it is almost certainly not on the basis of Lord Denning's contractual licence reasoning.

Even at the time, the preponderance of authority was probably against the proposition that contractual licences could bind purchasers, and Stephenson LJ doubted whether this line of reasoning was correct in *Binions* v *Evans* itself. It was because of such doubts that the case was also decided on constructive trusts reasoning. Even Lord Denning was not prepared to rely exclusively on contractual licence reasoning, and accordingly he too adopted another approach.

This was that, because Mr and Mrs Binions had purchased expressly subject to the agreement, equity would impose upon their conscience, and require them to hold the property on constructive trust for Mrs Evans. This approach, ostensibly based on *Bannister* v *Bannister* [1948] 2 All ER 133, differs from the earlier case, however, and from the views of the other two judges, in that the trust arose not under the original agreement, but only on the sale of the property to the plaintiffs. Also, the other points made above about *Bannister* v *Bannister* (lack of writing) could not apply in *Binions* v *Evans*.

The precise scope of this approach is unclear, and obviously the examiner intends that you should discuss it, since the exact facts of *Binions* v *Evans* are not reproduced. One view is that it depends on the purchaser taking *expressly* subject to an agreement enforceable between the other two parties, and if so then B is not protected. However, the Master of the Rolls himself thought that to take *impliedly* subject to an enforceable agreement would be enough, in which case C is bound so long as the original agreement is enforceable. You may think that there are consideration difficulties about the agreement between A and B, however (and indeed, for that matter, about the original agreement in *Binions* v *Evans*).

Parts of Lord Denning's judgment are more radical, however. He thought that a constructive trust could be imposed whenever the trustee had conducted himself in an inequitable manner. This would give enormous discretion to the courts, and presumably would protect B.

The reasoning of Megaw and Stephenson LJJ was entirely different, though in some respects it can lead to even more startling conclusions. In their view, the original agreement between the trustees and the defendant created a life tenancy. Thus, even at this stage the trustees held the property on trust for Mrs Evans for her life, thereafter for the Tredegar Estate in fee simple. Because this was a succession of equitable interests, Mrs Evans had an interest in land coming within the provisions of the Settled Land Act 1925. The purchasers were therefore bound by an existing trust, on the ordinary principles of the equitable notice doctrine.

Applying this reasoning to the problem (assuming that you can construe the original agreement in the same way), B, as tenant for life, could have the legal estate vested in her and would have extensive powers to sell the land, overreaching C's interest. Such a result is clearly far more extreme than the parties intended. It should be noted that Lord Denning MR thought that the Settled Land Act 1925 did not apply, because he said it applies only to expressly created settlements (though the Act does not say this).

As noted in the previous section, however, in *Ungurian* v *Lesnoff*, Vinelott J reviewed all the judgments in *Binions* v *Evans* and on this issue, preferred that of the majority to that of Lord Denning MR.

There have been two cases subsequent to *Binions* v *Evans*. Lord Denning's view was adopted in part by the High Court in *Lyus* v *Prowsa Developments Ltd* [1982] 1 WLR 1044, and again by the Court of Appeal in *Ashburn Anstalt* v *Arnold* [1988] 2 All ER 147.

In *Lyus* v *Prowsa Developments Ltd*, the plaintiffs, Mr and Mrs Lyus, had an estate contract, as prospective purchasers of property from a firm of builders. The builders became insolvent before completion, and the mortgagee, National Westminster Bank, exercised its power of sale under the mortgage. From this point, the plaintiffs were entirely at the mercy of the bank, and no longer had any enforceable rights.

The defendants were purchasers from the bank, who purchased subject to the plaintiffs' contract, in so far as it was originally enforceable. Dillon J held, on the basis of *Binions* v *Evans*, that they therefore held the benefit of the original estate contract on trust for the plaintiffs, and that Mr and Mrs Lyus were entitled to specific performance of it.

Dillon J limited *Binions* v *Evans* to cases where the purchaser took subject to a right. It is not enough that he merely knew of it. This case is therefore of direct relevance to the problem. On Dillon J's view, C is presumably not bound.

In one respect *Lyus* v *Prowsa Developments Ltd* represents an extension of *Binions* v *Evans*: the plaintiffs had no rights at all before the purchase from the bank, as they were before then entirely at the mercy of the bank. Here the right was apparently created by the sale. This could be relevant to the problem if you took the view that B has not provided sufficient consideration for an enforceable contract with A (but you would have to reject Dillon J's other limitation).

The recent decision of the Court of Appeal in *Ashburn Anstalt* v *Arnold* [1988] 2 All ER 147, comprehensively noted by M.P. Thompson [1988] Conv 201, is probably more important to students of land law than to trusts, but nevertheless it contains important *dicta* which bear on the present problem. At first sight the facts appear to be quite complex, but stripped of non-essential detail, and so far as is relevant to this problem, they were as follows.

Arnold & Co. agreed in February 1973 with Matlodge (Ashburn Anstalt's predecessors in title), on the sale of a sublease on the property (shop premises) to Matlodge, that Arnold & Co. could remain in occupation 'as licensees'. Matlodge had no immediate need for the premises, but wished eventually to demolish it for development. The agreement allowed Arnold & Co. to remain, rent-free but paying all outgoings, until 29 September 1973, and thereafter until Matlodge gave three months' notice, certifying that it was ready forthwith to demolish the property for development.

By October 1985, as a result of various transactions, both the head lease and sublease on the property had merged in the freehold, which was purchased by Ashburn Anstalt. Arnold & Co. were still in occupation, and claimed to be entitled to remain on the terms of the original agreement. The land was registered, and they claimed that the agreement gave them an overriding interest, under s. 70(1)(g) of the Land Registration Act 1925, which was binding on Matlodge's successors in title. In other words, they claimed that Ashburn Anstalt were bound by the 1973 agreement, despite not being party to it. Ashburn Anstalt, on the other hand, sought possession.

Only interests 'subsisting in reference' to land come within s. 70(1)(g), so the main issue was whether the agreement created such an interest. There was another agreement, also considered in the case, which is not relevant to the problem.

The judgment of the court was delivered by Fox LJ. He held that the agreement created a lease, rather than a contractual licence. This disposed of the case, because a lease is an interest in land, and hence within s. 70(1)(g). This aspect of the case is of greater importance to land law students than students of trusts, and it is likely to be controversial, because the lease was, to say the least, very unusual. The difficulty was not so much that rent was not payable, because in principle it is possible to lease property rent-free, but that the agreement did not appear to be for a certain duration after 29 September 1973. It could only be terminated (on three months' notice) in certain circumstances (intention to demolish the property for redevelopment), which may never have occurred. Thus, it seemed that one of the most fundamental requirements for a lease, certainty of maximum duration, was not present. Nor was Arnold & Co. under any obligation to remain in occupation of the property. Nevertheless, relying heavily on the three-month notice provision, Fox LJ held that a periodic tenancy had been created.

Fox LJ went on, however, to consider the position on the basis that he was wrong on the main issue. This is technically *obiter dicta*, of course. The main interest for land lawyers is the categorical statement that contractual licences are not interests in land, and do not bind third-party purchasers. Statements of Lord Denning MR to the contrary in *Errington* v *Errington* [1952] 1 KB 290 were disapproved, and Fox LJ thought that if the decision in *Errington* was correct, it could only be justified on grounds other than those adopted by Lord Denning. Other possibilities that have been canvassed are that there was an estate contract (to convey the property on completion of the mortgage repayments), or that there was an estoppel which bound the third-party purchaser—see further the discussion of this case at the end of chapter 5. For present purposes, assuming Fox LJ's views are correct, it follows that *Binions* v *Evans* also could not be justified on Lord Denning's contractual licence reasoning, and can only be supported on the basis either that there was a constructive trust, or some other ground altogether (see below).

On the constructive trust question the court took the view that it would only impose a constructive trust where it was satisfied that the conscience of the purchaser was affected. This required more than mere notice, even express notice of the contractual licence. Even a purchaser who took 'subject to' a contractual licence would not necessarily be bound. There must be a clear undertaking on the part of the purchaser, and the obligation must be imposed expressly in the conveyance. While Fox LJ supported the decision in *Binions* v *Evans*, he would virtually have limited it to its facts. On his view, a constructive trust will only be imposed where the conveyance to the purchaser is made *expressly* subject to the contractual licence, and he also thought that the fact that the purchaser had paid a reduced price in *Binions* v *Evans* significant. None of these factors was present in *Ashburn Anstalt*, so no constructive trust arose. Nor on this view (I would suggest) would a constructive trust arise in the present problem.

By now, therefore, it should be clear that to do well on this question you must have read at any rate all the judgments in *Binions* v *Evans*, and also both *Lyus* v *Prowsa Developments Ltd* and *Ashburn Anstalt* v *Arnold*. You should also make sure you are fresh for the exam itself, because you will have to consider how to apply the cases in the exam room, and cannot prepare entirely in advance.

The last paragraph invites more wide-ranging discussion. The House of Lords can reconsider the issue afresh, and is not bound by the existing authorities. It may do so on grounds of general policy. Clearly, it is very hard on someone in Mrs Evans's position to be deprived of a remedy, especially in view of the Binions' behaviour. The question is whether the constructive trust is the best means of redress.

Bear in mind that a constructive trust creates a property interest, which is capable of binding anyone who comes on to the land. It may also reduce the value of the land. The policy of the 1925 legislation was to make land more saleable, and this policy demands that purchasers can easily discover precisely what interests affect the land they are purchasing. Informally created interests, that are difficult to discover, are clearly undesirable. In *Ashburn Anstalt*, Fox LJ noted (at p. 167) that 'In matters relating to the title to land, certainty is of prime importance. We do not think it desirable that constructive trusts of land should be imposed in reliance on inferences from slender materials.'

Of course, a purchaser will necessarily be aware of a licence to which the conveyance is made expressly subject, so the *Ashburn Anstalt* solution would not cause any injustice in this regard, at least so far as the first purchaser is concerned. However, presumably once a constructive trust has been imposed on the first purchaser, subsequent purchasers will also be bound, subject only to the ordinary equitable notice rule. Uncertainty can still arise, therefore, on second and subsequent conveyances.

Another difficulty with the imposition of constructive trusts is that it can lead to extreme results. For example, as we saw above, it is arguable that the Settled Land Act 1925 applied in both *Binions v Evans* (both Megaw and Stephenson LJJ though so) and *Bannister v Bannister*. If so, then someone in B's position gets a considerably greater interest than anyone conceived.

One answer would be to regard the constructive trust as something less than a full proprietary interest. Lord Denning's citation of American authority (Cardozo J) suggests that he regarded such a trust as a remedy only, without the wider property consequences usually attendant upon creation of trusts. There is little authority that this is the position taken by English law, though there is some authority for its adoption in the United States. It might get round some of the difficulties in the area, but it still leaves the law vague (especially a problem where property interests are concerned).

Perhaps there are better answers anyway, for example the interference with contract reasoning alluded to by Megaw LJ in *Binions v Evans* itself. There was a contract between the trustees of the Tredegar Estate and Mrs Evans, giving her an irrevocable licence. That remained binding on the trustees even after the sale to the plaintiffs, because otherwise the trustees could have evaded their obligations by the unilateral act of selling the property. The plaintiffs knew of this contract and deliberately caused it to be broken. They were therefore guilty of the tort of interference with contract.

Megaw LJ wondered whether the principles of the tort action would apply in a land law situation, but it is difficult to see why they should not, and in some respects this is a better solution than to impose a constructive trust. Not all third parties would be bound; the tort seems to require express knowledge of the existence of a contract, and constructive knowledge of its terms (*Emerald Construction Co. Ltd* v *Lowthian* [1966] 1 WLR 691). Because of the express knowledge requirement, the difficulties of conveyancing are not significantly increased. Also, subsequent purchasers would not be bound (unless they too had express notice of the contract) because no proprietary interest would have been created.

Lyus v *Prowsa Developments Ltd* is altogether more difficult to explain, and still more difficult to justify. There could have been no interference with contract because there was no enforceable contract before the sale. The best view may well be that this case is simply wrong. Unlike the earlier case it is not clear that any policy demanded that the plaintiffs should win. The dispute was essentially about money, as the property had significantly increased in value. The effect of the decision was therefore a substantial windfall for the plaintiffs, and probably a substantial loss for the defendants.

SEVEN

SECRET AND HALF-SECRET TRUSTS

The fact that there has been very little litigation on secret and half-secret trusts in recent years in no way diminishes the enthusiasm of examiners for this topic. Nor, I think, should it be assumed that secret trusts no longer have any practical relevance, although no doubt the reasons for using them have changed. It is less likely today that a testator will wish to keep hidden the existence of an extra-marital sexual partner, or an illegitimate child, and the Mortmain considerations (on which, see below) behind many of the early cases are clearly no longer applicable. Nevertheless, particularly with the increase in step-parenthood, informal secret trusts may well have a place even today. One spouse may be prepared to leave all his or her property to the other (current) spouse on the understanding that he or she will ensure that children of a previous marriage are adequately provided for, and may prefer to proceed in this way rather than risk upsetting the relationship, by making a new will. This could give rise to a secret trust, just as surely as the mistress and Mortmain cases of the nineteenth century.

Questions tend to fall into two types. The first is an essay which requires you to explain and account for the differences which exist between the rules governing fully and half-secret trusts: the second is a problem which demands that you remember exactly what those differences are and can apply them to a (usually uninspiring) set of facts. The two types of question involve different considerations, and it is as well to approach them separately.

Underlying principles and the different rules for secret and half-secret trusts

Almost any essay on this topic will seek to cover the basis of secret and half-secret trusts, and the different rules the courts have worked out for them although it is possible to slant the question towards various angles. Though the following discussion centres around an essay question, you will almost certainly not be able to put together a good, as opposed to merely passable, answer unless you have been prepared to go beyond the textbooks and lecture notes during study and revision.

In the first place the question is likely to be framed so as to encourage a comparison of differing opinions, and in any case you should be conscious of the range of views attributable to various academic writers. You should also have gained an impression of how these views fit together, where they clash, and on what terms it might be possible to reconcile some or any of them. If you lack this basic knowledge of the field, you might be advised to look for a different question to answer.

Essay question

Can any rational principles be offered to justify the different rules developed by the courts with regard to fully secret and half-secret trusts?

Because it is an essay and not a problem this sort of question often attracts very mediocre candidates. A common mistake is simply not to think about the question at all, or even to read it properly. Even a relatively poor candidate knows that all the textbooks say the distinction is illogical, so all that is necessary is to agree and to trot out all the standard cases on secret trusts mentioned in the textbooks, in the hope that somewhere in that lot will lie the reason why the distinction can be labelled illogical.

Such a candidate will get a poor second if there is nothing in the answer that is flagrantly wrong, or at best a third if there are substantial omissions or errors in the recital. The problem is simply that the question does not ask for a textbook treatise of the area, but is directed specifically towards discussion of principles. Obviously if you have thought about these during revision so much the better, because an examination is not an ideal situation in which to consider complex matters for the first time. But even if you have not given the matter much thought you should have close regard to the wording of the question (or do another question). The textbook treatise is frankly not an answer to the question at all, yet candidates who answer in that way are extremely common, and probably never even realise why they do not obtain a better result.

As with any other essay question you must determine its central point and its limits, so as to be able to judge how much information you can safely include without drifting into irrelevance. Also, though you ought to cover all arguments, you would be well advised to form a view yourself as to which view is correct. Before you start to write, decide where you are going, what authority you intend to use to get you there, and what arguments for the opposing view you will have to deal with on the way.

The question asks whether there is any rational principle which can account for the distinction, so the following discussion concentrates on reasons of principle upon which equity undertakes to enforce these trusts. Clearly, if there is no difference in principle between the grounds for enforcing fully and half-secret trusts, the assertion that the distinction is illogical is greatly strengthened. There are two principal theories on which enforcement of secret trusts can be justified, and both need to be examined.

In the following discussion, 'he' includes 'she' and 'himself' includes 'herself'.

What are the different rules between secret and half-secret trusts?

If you are asked to ascertain whether there are any rational principles which justify the different rules developed by the courts with regard to fully secret and half-secret trusts, quite a good starting point is an explanation of how the rules for the two in fact differ (assuming, of course, they do differ).

The main difference between the courts' treatment of fully secret and half-secret trusts concerns the time of communication of the terms of the trust of the secret trustee. For fully secret trusts it appears to be necessary for the existence of the secret trust to be communicated to the trustee before the death of the testator, and there is some authority that the terms also have to be communicated before the testator's *death* (below). Whether or not these communications precede or succeed the date of the *will* is irrelevant, however, to the enforcement of a fully secret trust.

For fully secret trusts, the authorities are *Wallgrave* v *Tebbs* (1855) 2 K & J 313, and *Re Boyes* (1884) 26 Ch D 531. In *Wallgrave* v *Tebbs* (1855) 2 K & J 313, the testator had left property to close friends without informing them in his lifetime that he wished the land to be used for a religious charitable purpose. The court held that the friends were entitled to the property beneficially—a decision which, surprisingly enough, was most likely to give effect to the wishes to the testator, since if a secret trust had been found to exist it would have been void under the (now repealed) Statutes of Mortmain. As it was, the friends were free to carry out the testator's wishes. If, as the testator's relatives had argued, a secret trust had been created, they would have had to hold property on resulting trust *for those relatives*, the purpose of the trust being unlawful. Hence the surprising situation that the very last people who might be expected to argue for a secret trust (the relatives) did so in that case, and in other cases to which the Statutes of Mortmain applied.

The case is authority for the proposition that for a fully secret trust to be enforced, the intended trustee must be told of the existence of the trust before the testator's death. In *Re Boyes* (1884) 26 Ch D 531, however, the intended trustee was told of the existence of the trust before the testator's death, but was not told its terms, which were in favour of the testator's mistress. Kay J held that the intended trustee held the property on a resulting trust for the testator's estate.

If *Re Boyes* is correct, then not only the existence, but also the terms of a fully secret trust must be communicated to the trustee before the date of the testator. Kay J said (at p. 536):

> If the trust was not declared when the will was made [i.e., fully secret trust], it is essential in order to make it binding, that it should be communicated to the devisee or legatee in the testator's lifetime and that he should accept that particular trust.

For fully secret trusts, there is no authority that the date of the will is of any relevance. In the case of a half-secret trust, however, it appears that the terms of the trust have to be finalised before the date of the will. The leading authorities are *Re Keen* [1937] Ch 236 and *Re Bateman* [1970] 3 All ER 817. In *Re Keen*, a clause in the testator's will gave £10,000 on trust to two persons, who were directed to dispose of it 'as may be notified by me to them or either of them during my lifetime'. In fact, some months prior to the will, the testator had given one of the two trustees a sealed envelope containing a sheet of paper on which he had written the name and address of the proposed secret beneficiary (a lady to whom the testator was not married).

The Court of Appeal held that no valid half-secret trust had been created, and the £10,000 fell into residue. One reason was that, simply as a matter of construction, the clause in the testator's will referred to a *future* direction, whereas the direction had by then *already* been communicated to one of the two trustees. Therefore, the express terms of the will were inconsistent with the terms of the trust being contained in the sealed envelope. Had that been the only ground for the decision, the case would have created no difficulties, and the position for half-secret trusts would have been identical to that for fully secret trusts.

Lord Wright MR also said, however, that the testator having declared the existence of the trust in the will, should not be able to reserve to himself the power of making future dispositions without a duly attested codicil simply by notifying them during his lifetime. If that is correct, it follows that the terms of a half-secret trust must be finalised by the date of the will. In *Re Bateman's WT*, the trustees were directed by a clause in the will to dispose of the income from the testator's estate 'to such persons and in such proportions as shall be stated by me in a sealed letter in my own handwriting and addressed to my Trustees'. As in *Keen*, this refers to a *future* direction, but unlike *Keen*, the trustees in *Bateman* received their instructions by means of a sealed letter after the will, but before the death of the testator. Therefore, the express terms of the will were not inconsistent with the timing of the communication.

Nevertheless, the Court of Appeal held that the direction to trustees was invalid. The only possible explanation for the case, and indeed the one actually adopted by Pennycuick V-C, was that as a general principle, a half-secret trust is enforceable only where its terms are known at the date of the will.

There may be other differences between fully and half-secret trusts, but in this chapter we will concentrate on the main one, the timing of the communication of the terms of the trust in relation to the date of the will.

The differences having now been explained, we can return to the question to see whether they can be justified.

Basis of enforcement of secret and half-secret trusts

The authorities suggest that the basis of enforcement of fully and half-secret trusts is the same, that equity imposes upon the conscience of the secret trustee for the prevention of fraud. This is clear from the speech of Viscount Sumner in *Blackwell* v *Blackwell* [1929] AC 318 (at pp. 335–6):

> For the prevention of fraud equity fastens on the conscience of the legatee a trust, a trust, that is, which otherwise would be inoperative; in other words it makes him do what the will in itself has nothing to do with; it lets him take what the will gives him and then makes him apply it, as the Court of conscience directs, and it does so in order to give effect to wishes of the testator, which would not otherwise be effectual.

Blackwell v *Blackwell* is, of course, the leading authority on half-secret trusts, but it is clear that Viscount Sumner treats the two varieties as the same, and that these comments are intended to apply to both.

From the quote three propositions can be gleaned. First, the reason equity fastens on the conscience of the legatee is for the prevention of fraud. Secondly, the effect of the trust is to make the legatee 'do what the will in itself has nothing to do with'; in other words, the trust operates independently of the will. Thirdly, in order to prevent fraud, equity directs the legatee to give effect to wishes of the testator. This point is of some importance. The fraud whose commission is being prevented is not the taking of the property beneficially by the legatee, but, having taken it, not giving effect to the wishes of the testator.

Relevance of and nature of fraud

The need for fraud can be seen clearly in the House of Lords decision in *McCormick* v *Grogan* (1869) LR 4 HL 82, where Lord Hatherley LC and Lord Westbury emphasised that the doctrine should be limited to cases where the intended trustee had committed a personal fraud upon the testator, by inducing the bequest on the clear representation that he would hold the property on behalf of the intended beneficiary. Lord Westbury in particular emphasised the need for a '*malus animus*' to be 'proved by the clearest and most indisputable evidence'.

But this immediately raises the question: if the object is merely to prevent the intended trustee from taking the property for himself, on what ground should equity disregard the requirement of the Wills Act 1837 by giving effect to the testator's oral instruction that the property should go to someone not named in the will? If the defeat of the intended trustee's fraudulent profit was all that was desired, it would be sufficient simply to compel him to hold the property on a resulting trust for the testator's estate. In fact, however, this is not all that is desired.

A historical reason why a resulting trust would not have provided a satisfactory solution is that, prior to the Executors Act of 1830, an executor was entitled to take as residuary legatee all property not specifically disposed of in the will. If, as might well happen, the intended trustee was also the executor, a resulting trust would merely have the effect of granting him indirectly what the court refused to allow him to take directly.

'someone whose existence the testator would prefer to keep hidden from his family'

An early example is *Thynn* v *Thynn* (1684) 1 Vern 296. Here, the testator had made his wife his sole executrix, but his son, on a fraudulent pretext, persuaded her to step down in his favour. The court compelled him to hold the property on trust for the wife. If it had not enforced the trust, but allowed the property to result to the estate, the fraudulent son (as executor) would have taken beneficially, so this solution would clearly have been inappropriate.

By the time *McCormick* v *Grogan* was decided, the Executors' Act had altered the rule. Nowadays, the effect of a resulting trust in favour of the testator's estate will be to pass the property to the person named as residuary legatee, or, if there is none, to those close relatives of the testator who are entitled to take in the event of his total or partial intestacy. There can still be problems, as in *Re Rees* [1950] Ch 204, where the intended trustee (the solicitor who had drafted the will) was also the named residuary legatee, but such problems are less likely to arise today.

Nevertheless, the House of Lords in *McCormick* v *Grogan* would have been prepared to enforce the secret trust on its terms, though on the facts of the case no trust was held to have been created. Again, this may be explicable in the light of social considerations. A common reason for setting up a secret trust is the desire to benefit someone whose existence the testator would prefer to keep hidden from his family, such as a mistress or, as in *McCormick* v *Grogan* itself, an illegitimate child. A resulting trust would divert the property to the very last people whom the testator wished to benefit (his legitimate family). But for the court to give weight to this sort of consideration involves accepting that the testator's wishes are of sufficient importance to justify ignoring the clear terms of a statute in order to enforce the trust.

Hodge [1980] Conv 341 has a different explanation. He argues that the nature of the fraud lies not simply in keeping the property personally, but in the fact that it was the promise to carry out the testator's wishes *in their exact terms* which induced him to leave his property to the intended trustee. It is the intended trustee's failure to do this which makes the fraud, not the element of greed. He would be just as fraudulent with regard to the testator's confidence if he gave the property to a charity, as he would be if he kept it for himself. And the testator would be no less defrauded if the intended trustee were to (say) hand over the gift intended for the testator's mistress to his innocent and long-suffering wife. A deception practised out of high moral principle is still deceit. Therefore, nothing less than the enforcement of the testator's wishes will suffice to avert a fraud in this situation.

This explanation of the true meaning of fraud has the backing of authority. It is clear from the quote from *Blackwell* v *Blackwell* already considered, that fraud in this context does not necessarily require the trustee to keep the property beneficially, but merely for him, having taken the property, not to carry out the testator's wishes. A similar statement can be found in Lord Sterndale's judgment in *Re Gardner* [1920] 2 Ch 523 (at p. 529): 'The breach of trust or the fraud would arise when [the secret trustee] attempted to deal with the money contrary to the terms on which he took it.' It is not necessary for him to attempt to keep it beneficially, and indeed, in *Re Gardner* itself, he had no intention of so doing.

Lord Westbury's requirement in *McCormick* v *Grogan* was for a '*malus animus*' to be proved by clearest and most indisputable evidence. This seems to suggest that an deliberate intention to deceive him must be shown on the legatee's part (for example, where he had deliberately induced the testator to leave the property to him in the will, on the clear representation that he would hold it in trust for the secret beneficiary). It also appears that the standard of proof is as in common-law fraud; in other words, a very high standard indeed is required.

Lord Westbury's remarks were not essential to the decision in *McCormick* v *Grogan*, and indeed, seem not to have been adopted in later cases. For example, in the later House of Lords authority, *Blackwell* v *Blackwell* [1929] AC 518, Lord Buckmaster thought that all that was required to show a fraud was:

(a) the intention of the testator to subject the intended trustee to an obligation in favour of the intended beneficiary;

(b) communication of that intention of the intended trustee; and

(c) the acceptance of that obligation by the intended trustee, either expressly or by acquiescence.

In *Ottaway* v *Norman* [1972] Ch 698, Brightman J, relying on the criteria above, enforced a trust of land without any suggestion that the intended trustee had procured her prior life interest by deceit. At the time of the arrangement between herself and the testator, Ottaway, she clearly intended to carry out her promise to leave the land to Ottaway's son in her own will. Her failure in the event to do this might be rated as a breach of trust, and it is clearly a fraud in the sense that it defeats the intention of the testator, but no question of '*malus animus*' arose. Nor did Brightman J see any reason to depart from the ordinary civil standard of proof, i.e., balance of probabilities.

Is '*malus animus*', and the requisite higher standard of proof, therefore irrelevant? In *Re Snowden* [1979] Ch 528, Megarry V-C appears to suggest that it may have to be shown in some circumstances, but unfortunately these are not elaborated upon. This aspect of the case may in any event be limited to issues of proof: if the only way that a would-be beneficiary can assert the existence of a trust in his favour is to allege facts which necessarily impute fraud to the alleged trustee, then inevitably '*malus animus*' will need to be shown, and the standard of proof will be high. If the three elements listed earlier can be shown without proof of '*malus animus*', however, presumably he may still succeed on the balance of probabilities.

Secret and half-secret trusts take effect independently of the will

It is also clear from *Blackwell* v *Blackwell* [1929] AC 518 that secret and half-secret trusts operate independently of the will. It is possible that they operate as express trusts created *inter vivos* by the agreement reached between the testator and the intended trustee, the function or relevance of the will being to vest the property in the intended trustee at the agreed time for the assumsption of his office. From the passage in Viscount Sumner's speech, however, to which allusion has already been made, it seems more likely that after the will has transferred legal title to the legatee, the court fastens on the conscience of the legatee by imposing on him a trust. This is probably best analysed as a constructive trust, imposed in order to prevent fraud.

A similar analysis was adopted by Lord Westbury in *McCormick* v *Grogan* (at p. 97).

> The Court of Equity has, from a early period, decided that even an Act of Parliament shall not be used as an instrument of fraud; and if in the machinery of perpetrating a fraud an Act of Parliament intervenes, the Court of Equity, it is true, does not set aside the Act of Parliament but it fastens on the individual who gets a title under that Act, and imposes upon him a personal obligation, because he applies the Act as an instrument for accomplishing a fraud.

Whichever analysis is correct, whether secret and half-secret trusts are express *inter vivos* trusts or constructive trusts imposed once the legatee has received the property, the will does no more than constitute the trust, transferring the legal property to the secret trustee. It seems likely that the trust could also be constituted by intestacy, in the absence of any will, if the settlor refrains from making a will in the knowledge that the property will pass to the intended trustee by virtue of the Administration of Estates Act 1925, rather than using a more usual form of transfer for an *inter vivos* trust.

It is undoubtedly correct to say that the mechanism by which secret and half-secret trusts are enforced has nothing to do with the will. But to describe the mechanism is not the same thing as providing a reason for their enforcement. The reason that equity imposes on the conscience of the legatee is fraud, and the mere fact that the mechanism operates independently of the will in no way affects that requirement.

The operation of secret and half-secret trusts independently of this will does have other consequences, however. In *Re Young* [1951] Ch 344 a half-secret trust was enforced despite the fact that the beneficiary had witnessed the will, which under s. 15 of the Wills Act 1837 would normally have the effect of invalidating the gift to the witnessing beneficiary. Since he took outside the will, however, this rule did not apply. Dankwerts J commented:

> The whole theory of the formation of a secret trust is that the Wills Act has nothing to do with the matter. . ., since the persons do not take by virtue of the gift in the will, but by virtue of the secret trusts imposed upon the beneficiary, who does in fact take under the will.

In *Re Gardner (No. 2)* [1923] 2 Ch 230, a secret trust in favour of a beneficiary who had predeceased the testator was upheld. It is not possible to leave property to a dead person by will, and it is difficult to justify this decision even on the basis that the will has nothing to do with the matter. The usual analysis is that, at the very least, the will constitutes the trust by transferring legal title to the secret trustee. Romer J saw no reason why a declaration of trust by the secret trustee should not have occurred at the moment of communication of the trust to him (at p. 233):

> The rights of the parties appear to me to be exactly the same as though the husband [secret trustee], after the memorandum had been communicated to him by the testatrix. . ., had executed a declaration of trust binding himself to hold any property that should come to him upon his wife's [settlor's] partial intestacy upon trust as specified in the memorandum.

If Romer J's view is correct, then the consequences are not limited to an ability to make a secret or half-secret trust in favour of a beneficiary who predeceases the testator. If the trust comes into force from the moment of communication, then it must also follow that it is irrevocable from that moment, and the secret trustee would be unable later to change his mind. This would be an unfortunate consequence if the communication was made many years before the testator's death and circumstances had changed radically in the meantime. Suppose, for example, the secret beneficiary ran off with the secret trustee's wife. Could not the secret trustee inform the testator that he was no longer prepared to accept the property on the original terms? Or, if he were no longer able to get in touch with the testator, could he not refuse to take the property under the will? One would have thought that, in principle, he should be able to change his mind, but if Romer J is right, and the trust is created from the moment of communication, then it may well be that he cannot.

There is another difficulty with Romer J's analysis. The secret trustee must be declaring himself trustee of after-acquired property, since only the testator's death is legal title vested to him. The conventional view is that trusts of future property are void (see further Chapter 3). The orthodox view is that *Gardner (No. 2)* is wrong.

Can the distinctions between secret and half-secret trusts be justified?

There is no particular difficulty in justifying the decision in *Wallgrave* v *Tebbs*, since if the intended trustee knew nothing about the trust until after the testator's death, there could have been no fraud in the procuring of the bequest, and thus no reason for the court to compel the intended trustee to do anything in particular with what is now his own property. Another justification is that any other decision would have permitted the testator to derogate from his grant. A bequest ought not to be 'snatched back' after it has been made, any more than a birthday present could be later reclaimed.

Re Boyes is more difficult to justify, since there appears to have been a fraud on the testator, but it is clear from Kay J's judgment that his understanding of the basis of enforcement was substantially that outlined above:

> The essence of [the early cases on secret trusts] is that the devisee or legatee accepts a particular trust which thereupon becomes binding upon him, and which it would be a fraud in him not to carry into effect.

Further, the intended trustee was willing to carry out those terms. It seems that the case must be explained as one in which the scope of any possible fraud was limited to denying the existence of the trust. The intended trustee could hardly be said to have procured the bequest by a promise to adhere to its terms, since he did not know them. All he knew was that the testator wished him to take the property in the capacity of trustee and not beneficially, so by compelling him to hold as trustee the court had done all it needed to in order to make him comply with the terms on which the bequest had been granted. If the intended trustee had known where the terms of the trust could be found (e.g., in a letter to be opened after the testator's death) then it could be said that he accepted those terms and was bound by them. In this situation, he would hold the property on the terms of the secret trust (*Re Keen* [1937] Ch 236, 242).

There is nothing in the fraud basis of enforcement, however, which would require that an intended trustee must know the terms of the trust by the time the will is executed. There is no real difference between making a bequest on the strength of the intended trustee's promise, and leaving that bequest unrevoked on the strength of his later assurance. So there is no reason to refuse to enforce the trust where the intended trustee becomes aware of its terms only after the execution of the will. All that is necessary is that he should be aware of them, or where they are to be found, before the bequest takes effect, i.e., upon the testator's death.

It is also obvious that justifications for *Keen* and *Bateman* become even more difficult given that secret and half-secret trusts operate outside the will.

It is therefore difficult to justify *Keen* and *Bateman* simply on the basis of the principles of enforcement of secret and half-secret trusts. Are there any other justifications for these cases, therefore, or can they be justified by a policy which outweighs any of the above discussion?

Other justifications for Keen and Bateman

It is sometimes argued that the fraud theory ought to draw a distinction between fully and half-secret trusts, on the ground that there is no possibility of an intended trustee of a half-secret trust claiming the property for himself, since the fact of the trust is plain from the will. All that is needed to avert fraud, therefore, is to compel him to hold on resulting trust for the testator's estate.

This may be an argument against enforcing half-secret trusts at all, but it is no argument for the rule regarding time of communication. To impose a resulting trust would be the same thing as refusing to enforce the trust, because a resulting trust is what would happen in any case where a testamentary bequest failed for whatever reason. But it is clear that the courts do enforce half-secret trusts, provided that the terms are communicated prior to or contemporaneously with the making of the will. It is also clear that they do this partly out of a desire to prevent fraud: see the speeches of the House in *Blackwell v Blackwell* [1929] AC 318.

In any case it is simply not adequate to say that a resulting trust would suffice to avert fraud; as suggested earlier, it would still amount to a fraud on the testator. Can we say that it is only a fraud on him if the intended trustee has assented to the scheme before the will was made, and so procured the bequest? Hardly—there is no difference between making the bequest and leaving it unrevoked on the strength of the trustee's later acquiescence.

To argue that the rule regarding time of communication can serve to prevent fraud seems simply illogical.

A possible justification for the *Re Keen* distinction is that because the existence of a half-secret (but not fully secret) trust is openly declared in a formal testamentary bequest, any later addition or change to the statement that the property is to be held on trust must also be made in a properly attested will or codicil. Therefore, if the testator chooses to declare the terms of his trust later than the date of executing his will, he is committed to using the correct formalities. This argument only applies, of course, to half-secret trusts.

It has a superficial attraction, as it takes account of the fact that the problem of adequate proof is one which bedevils the whole area of secret trusts. If a testator has blandly asserted that property is to be held on trust, it is obviously vital to ensure that any other statements he may have made regarding the precise terms of that trust are indeed referable to that particular trust, and no other. B. Perrins [1985] Conv 248 explains the timidity of the courts in accepting evidence which post-dates the will.

In this, they appear to have been influenced by the probate doctrine of incorporation by reference. This, in brief, permits the incorporation into a will of any document which was in existence at the time the will was executed, and was referred to as such in the will itself. It is a useful doctrine in that it saves the bother of copying out lengthy trust documents in the will itself, merely for the purpose of adding a fresh sum to those trusts by way of bequest. The testator can instead simply refer to those documents and rely on a short declaration that the bequest is to be held on the terms set out in those documents. He cannot, however, incorporate a document which is not yet in existence at the time of making the will: to allow this would be to tempt fraudulent claims that this or that document was the one to which the testator meant to refer.

It is therefore easy to see why the courts, conscious of the wisdom of these limits to the doctrine of incorporation by reference, may have thought it prudent to import those limits into the enforcement of half-secret trusts. But as a principled justification for the communication rules, the explanation has defects.

It should be noted, for example, that it is not necessary to the enforcement of a half-secret trust that any document at all should exist to declare the terms of the trust. So long as he communicates the terms before signing his will, the testator is free to rely on a purely oral communication, which must be even more susceptible to later misrepresentation than a document. Further, since the courts are prepared to accept the existence of fully secret trusts on quite slender evidence, e.g., *Ottaway v Norman* [1972] Ch 698, it would be odd if they refuse to accept oral evidence to show the terms of a half-secret trust: the chance of a fraudulent claim is certainly no greater in the latter case.

In any case, to argue that the testator, having once committed himself to formality, remains bound by the need for further formality if he wishes to expound the terms of his trust later than the date of making his will, is merely to penalise him for partial compliance with the Wills Act 1837, while allowing the testator who ignores that Act entirely (by creating a fully secret trust) to have his wishes enforced. This seems to fall short of being a rational justification, therefore.

Another, related argument which was stated in *Blackwell* v *Blackwell*, and repeated in *Re Keen*, is that to permit a testator simply to state the existence of a trust and communicate its terms at his leisure would be to permit a will to be freely altered by unattested dispositions, thus defeating the policy of the Wills Act 1837.

The argument reflects a respect for the policy of the Wills Act, and it has been argued that the same policy ought to apply also to fully secret trusts (see T.G. Watkin [1981] Conv 335). This, it is argued, would allow the testator who has made up his mind where he wants his property to go, but wishes its destination to be secret, to fulfil his desires by making his communication prior to the will, while defeating the testator who is merely indecisive and wants the luxury of changing his will without the trouble and expense of making fresh testamentary provisions.

Whatever can be said for this view, as Watkin acknowledges, the practice of permitting indecisive behaviour via a fully secret trust is so firmly entrenched that a statute would be required to effect the change. In any case the argument, even if sound in principle, provides no reason for treating fully and half-secret trusts differently; indeed it is a strong argument for treating them in the same way.

Though the question does not ask for it, since I have concluded that there is no rational justification for the distinction, it is worth considering whether there is any possibility of reform.

The chances of any reform in this area are limited to statutory intervention to bring the two species of secret trust in line, and/or the possibility that the House of Lords may one day review *Re Keen* and decide that, after all, there is no sound basis for the distinction drawn in that case. It is arguable that the time of communication was not the true basis of the decision in *Re Keen*, since the alleged communication did not anyway match the description given in the will, but the rule derived from *Re Keen* has since been applied in *Re Bateman's WT* [1970] 1 WLR 1463. However, the question is still open to review by the House of Lords.

These, then, are some of the issues which a good answer to our hypothetical question ought to cover. It is not intended to be a model answer, however,

and other views are possible. Model answers are in any case a bad thing.
You should not attempt to parrot-learn a stock answer, but would be better
advised to examine the above reasoning, and pick holes in it where you
can.

Problem questions

A typical problem question on secret trusts will attempt to test you on
several points. Almost inevitably, it will introduce the distinction between
half and fully secret trusts discussed above. Other possible complications
for which you should look out may include:

(a)   The form of wording used to indicate a half-secret trust. Has the
testator referred to the trust as something already known to the intended
trustee, or has he made the *Re Keen* style error of using language which
could be taken to indicate a future communication? If the examiner has
chosen to use words which do not precisely match those in any decided
case, you may have to use your own judgment here and be prepared to
argue for your chosen interpretation.

(b)   Possible contradictions between the words of the will and the
directions given by the testator to the intended trustee. For example, the
testator may have left property 'to X on trust', but informed X that only
part of that property is to be held for the beneficiary and that X can
keep the rest. You then have to consider whether X will be allowed to
do so, and if not, what happens to the property—will it go to the beneficiary,
or pass on resulting trust?

(c)   More than one intended trustee. This raises issues concerning the
rules for joint tenants and tenants in common (see B. Perrins (1972) 85
LQR 225) and perhaps whether they can be applied by analogy in the
case of half-secret as well as fully secret trusts.

(d)   The later addition of a codicil which has the effect of republishing
the will. Can this affect a situation where the testator communicates with
his intended trustee only after making the will which contains a half-secret
trust?

(e)   *Ottaway* v *Norman* complications. If the obligation imposed upon
the intended trustee is to leave the property in his own will, what is the
status of the trust in the lifetime of the intended trustee? Can property
other than that received under the testator's will be bound by the trust?

(f)   The issue of whether a secret trust of land can be enforced without
writing as required by s. 53(1)(b) of the Law of Property Act 1925, or
possibly, whether a secret trust of an equitable interest can be created,
and if so whether this requires writing by virtue of s. 53(1)(c).

(g)   The 'sealed envelope' situation. How far must the intended trustee be aware of its contents, and will it suffice if the envelope is not to be opened until the testator's death?

You would be very unlucky indeed to be faced with a problem which contained all of these elements together, but you should be ready to tackle all or any, if necessary. By way of example, let us consider such a problem. In order to cover all these aspects, the following problem is inevitably rather clumsy, but it may suffice for illustrative purposes.

Problem question

In 1980, Tom made a will which contained the following dispositions:

(a)   My house, Blackacre, to Alice, absolutely.
(b)   My farms, Whiteacre and Brownacre, to Benjamin and Cecil jointly.
(c)   My country cottage, Greenacre, to Damion on trust to carry out my wishes.
(d)   All my personal property to Edgar on the trusts privately communicated to him by me.
(e)   All my residuary estate to Fenella.

Prior to making the will, Tom had told Damion that he wanted him to hold Greenacre on trust for George, Tom's illegitimate son. In 1982, Tom told Alice that he had left her Blackacre so that she would be assured of a home for life, but that he expected her to leave Blackacre, and any other property she might possess at her death, to George in her own will. He then told Benjamin, but not Cecil, that he wanted them to hold Whiteacre on trust for George, but that they could keep Brownacre for themselves. Finally, he wrote a letter to Edgar, telling him that he wished him to hold certain items of the personal property on trusts which he would find contained in a sealed envelope, which should not be opened until after Tom's death. The envelope contained the direction that Edgar should hold 10,000 shares on trust for George, but that he could keep the rest of the personalty for himself.
In 1985, Tom won £10,000 on the football pools, and executed a codicil, which left the £10,000 'to Edgar, on the trusts known to him'. Damion died in 1986, a fortnight before Tom also died.
Advise all the parties.

This is simpler than it looks to work through, so long as you do not confuse the parties with one another. A rough plan, showing who gets what, and on what terms, is strongly recommended. It should also note the issues raised, after which it is simply a matter of working your way through the apparent jungle of legal issues in your list.

Depending on how much time is available, some students like to open a problem with a short résumé of the area of law. In the context of a monster problem like this, this practice is unlikely to be helpful, since you would need to cover practically every aspect of secret trusts in your 'short' résumé. Let us jump straight in, then, and start with Alice.

Alice exists simply to fulfil the role of Miss Hodges, the housekeeper in *Ottaway* v *Norman* [1972] Ch 698. Miss Hodges was employed by Mr Ottaway who left her his bungalow in his will, on terms that she would leave it by her own will to Mr Ottaway's son. According to the evidence given by the son and his wife, she also undertook to leave them the furniture and other contents, including her money.

It was established in *Re Gardner (No. 1)* [1920] 2 Ch 523 that an agreement to make provision for beneficiaries after one's death could be enforced. In that case, a wife had left her estate to her husband who had agreed to divide the property among beneficiaries on his death, but he died before making his will. The Court of Appeal found that he held the property for himself for life, and for the beneficiaries after his death.

Brightman J, in *Ottaway* v *Norman*, accepted that there had been an arrangement between old Mr Ottaway and Miss Hodges that she should leave the bungalow to the son, and was prepared to enforce that agreement by imposing what he called a constructive trust upon the bungalow in the hands of Miss Hodges's executor (she having later changed her mind and left her property to a cousin). He also accepted that the trust comprised such furnishings and fixtures as Miss Hodges had received under Mr Ottaway's will, but not that it included all Miss Hodges's other property and cash from whatever source.

In respect of the last, it seems that he was not convinced that so far-reaching an obligation had in fact been envisaged in the agreement, but if, as in our problem, the intended trustee has clearly accepted such an obligation, it may well be, on analogy with mutual wills (on which, see chapter 6), that this obligation also could be enforced against her estate.

This raises the issue of the status of the trust during Alice's lifetime. In *Ottaway* v *Norman*, Brightman J employed the concept of a 'floating trust', derived from the Australian case of *Birmingham* v *Renfrew* (1937) 57 CLR 666, which would remain in suspense during the life of the trustee and crystallise on her death, attaching to whatever property was comprised within her estate. This, as the learned judge noted, would seem to preclude Alice from making even a small pecuniary legacy in favour of her relatives

or friends. Compare the views of Nourse J in *Re Cleaver* [1981] 1 WLR
939 in the context of mutual wills, discussed in chapter 6.

George can enforce the secret trust, therefore, at least with regard to
Blackacre, and perhaps also with regard to Alice's other property, as it
seems she accepted this obligation. The fact that the trust is not contained
in writing ought, I would suggest, to be no bar to its enforcement, despite
the Law of Property Act 1925, s. 53(1)(b). In *Ottaway* v *Norman* itself the
section was avoided as the executor was held to be a constructive trustee
of the bungalow. Whether or not this analysis was correct, in principle
a fully secret trust of land should be enforceable despite the absence of
writing, either on the assumption that such trusts are to be regarded as
constructive since they are imposed on the ground of conscience, or more
probably becaue equity will not allow a statute intended to prevent fraud
to be used as a cloak for fraud.

The devise of the farms to Benjamin and Cecil raises the issue of whether
communication to one of several trustees can bind them all. Where a gift
is made (as here) to trustees as joint tenants, the orthodox view is that
if communication is made before the execution of the will, all will be bound,
whereas if communication is made after the execution of the will but before
the death of the testator, only those who have accepted the trust are bound
by it, on the basis that the gift to an intended trustee who does not consent
is not tainted with any fraud in procuring the execution of the will (see
Farwell J in *Re Stead* [1900] 1 Ch 237 at p. 241).

Though it does not arise in the problem, note for the sake of completeness
that where the gift is to the intended trustees as tenants in common, only
those who are aware of the trust are bound, whether they obtain this
knowledge before or after the will is executed.

This orthodox distinction lacks credibility, and B. Perrins (1972) 88 LQR
225 has argued that the true rule rests on the principle of *Huguenin* v *Baseley*
(1807) 14 Ves Jr 273, that no man may profit from the fraud of another.
On this argument, Cecil would be bound if Tom was induced to leave
the farms to him on the strength of Benjamin's promise, and the question
of when communication occurred would be a matter of evidence only. The
argument has much to commend it, but is inconsistent with *Re Stead*.

On the facts of our problem, Cecil would not on the basis of *Re Stead*
be bound by the trust, since it was not communicated to him until after
the making of the will (or indeed at all).

Benjamin can of course claim that his share of Brownacre at least is
free from the trust in favour of George, because clearly Tom intended
only to impress Whiteacre with the trust. The extrinsic evidence difficulties,
discussed below in relation to half-secret trusts, almost certainly do not
apply to fully secret trusts, so Benjamin should be permitted to adduce

evidence to show that Tom indeed intended him to take his interest in Brownacre beneficially.

Greenacre may be subject to a half-secret trust in George's favour. Tom has communicated his wishes, which Damion must be taken to have accepted, prior to the execution of the will, but there is still an issue as to whether a half-secret trust of land requires to be evidenced in writing under s. 53(1)(b) of the Law of Property Act 1925. In *Re Baillie* (1886) 2 TLR 660 it was said that a half-secret trust of land will not be enforced unless evidenced in writing, but the case is of doubtful authority, pre-dating as it does *Blackwell* v *Blackwell* [1929] AC 318 (when *Re Baillie* was decided, the enforceability at all of half-secret trusts was not beyond doubt). I would suggest that writing ought not to be required, on the same basis as for fully secret trusts (see above).

Damion has died before Tom, which makes it necessary to consider whether a secret trust can be enforced in the absence of the intended trustee. For a fully secret trust, there is some authority that it must fail, since the gift upon which it is engrafted will lapse with the death of the intended trustee (see Cozens-Hardy LJ in *Re Maddock* [1902] 2 Ch 220 at p. 251). Half-secret trusts may, however, be saved, for the trust is plain on the face of the will, and the maxim that 'Equity will not allow a trust to fail for want of a trustee' ought to impose a trust upon Greenacre in the hands of Tom's executor. He will therefore be taken to hold Greenacre for George, and not for Fenella as residuary legatee.

Edgar's situation raises several problems. Half-secret trusts must, of course, be communicated prior to, or contemporaneously with, the execution of the will, but it is only in 1982 that Tom informs Edgar that he is to hold all Tom's personal property on trust. This raises the question of the effect of the codicil. A codicil has the effect of republishing a will, i.e., it is as though the will itself had been made at the date of the later codicil. Can we therefore say that, since Edgar was aware that he was to be a trustee by the date of execution of the codicil, he is therefore bound?

In *Blackwell* v *Blackwell* itself, the gift which was subject to the half-secret trust was contained in a codicil, but in that case the gift was created for the first time by the codicil, and the trustees had been duly informed in advance. Here, the half-secret trust is originally created earlier, in the will, and the intended trustee has not been informed in advance. There is no direct authority whether the later reference to that trust in the codicil, at a time when Edgar has been informed of the trust, will suffice first to create the trust contained in the will, and secondly to add to this trust the extra £10,000.

On the method of communication, via a sealed envelope, *Re Keen* [1937] Ch 236 is authority that it is permissible, provided, as here, the trustee knows that it contains the terms of a trust and has agreed to carry out those terms, whatever they may turn out to be.

On the main issue, in favour of allowing the trust, it can be argued that the policy of the *Re Keen* rule is merely to ensure that the trust is communicated prior to some properly executed testamentary disposition which indicates its terms, and that, this being the case here, the mention of the trust in the codicil should be good enough.

Against this, however, is a possible argument based on *Re Cooper* [1939] Ch 811. In that case, a testator had left £5,000 to trustees on half-secret trust in his will, having duly informed them in advance and obtained their agreement, and later added a further £10,000 to this trust in a codicil. The Court of Appeal held that only the first amount mentioned in the will could be subject to the half-secret trust, and that the amount added by the codicil fell into residue. This might be taken to mean that a testator is obliged to inform his trustees of each and every alteration or addition, and secure their agreement prior to that alteration or addition. If this were so, it could be argued that no subsequent agreement could retroactively validate the trust in the will, despite the republication doctrine.

An alternative, and in my view better, interpretation of *Re Cooper*, is that trustees are bound by what they agree to, and that this is a question of fact to be determined on the evidence. In *Re Cooper*, the trustees had agreed to hold £5,000, and that was the limit of their obligation, since they never knew of the further obligation imposed in the codicil. As Greene MR said (at p. 818):

it was not with regard to any sum other than the £5,000 that the consciences of the trustees (to use a technical phrase) were burdened.

He seemed to envisage, however, that if the agreement had been that the trustees would hold £5,000 or whatever sum the testator finally chose to bequeath, it would have been enforceable on those terms. This also accords with the view taken by the courts that a sealed envelope may be sufficient communication, despite the fact that the terms are, *ex hypothesi*, unknown to the trustee, who assents to carry them out whatever they might turn out to be. It is suggested therefore that this case offers no obstacle to a decision that Tom's codicil is effective to create the half-secret trust in favour of George.

Even if the half-secret trust is validated by the codicil, the words in the will, 'to Edgar on the trusts privately communicated to him by me', are arguably ambiguous as to whether a past or future communication is indicated (the other ground of the decision in *Re Keen*). Presumably they would have to be construed as past if the codicil is regarded as republishing the will.

One further complication is that, on the facts of our problem, it appears that the money bequeathed by the codicil is, in fact, intended for Edgar beneficially, since the letter, when opened, directed him to hold only the shares in trust for George and to keep the rest of the personal property for himself. In principle, there seems no reason why this should be unacceptable.

Assuming that the half-secret trust might thus be held valid, there remains the issue of whether Edgar may indeed retain for himself the personalty other than the shares intended for George. The courts have shown themselves reluctant to admit any evidence to contradict the terms of a will. In *Re Rees* [1950] Ch 204, the testator had left his whole estate on half-secret trust and privately informed his trustees that they were to make certain payments and retain the surplus for themselves. Since one of the trustees was the solicitor who had drafted the will, the court was, perhaps, especially disposed towards caution in this case, holding that on the proper construction of the will, the half-secret trust was imposed upon the entire estate. The trustees would not therefore be allowed to introduce extrinsic evidence to contradict this by showing that they were intended to take beneficially subject only to making the payments. The issue seems to turn on the construction of the will. If it can be said that the will creates a conditional gift, then the trustees may take, subject to fulfilling the condition. If, however, it imposes a trust, the trustees will not be allowed to bring evidence to contradict the will.

Re Rees was in any case doubted in *Re Tyler* [1967] 1 WLR 1269. Our problem provides strong evidence, in the shape of the letter, of Tom's true intentions concerning the terms of his trust, and there is no reason in principle why the court should not enforce these terms, permitting Edgar to take the rest of the personalty beneficially. It can hardly be said that this would involve adducing evidence to contradict the will: rather, the evidence is directly *upon* its terms.

Had the facts of our problem been closer to those in *Re Rees*, however, probably no evidence in contradiction to the will could have been brought. In that case, Edgar would hold the shares for George, and the rest of the personalty for Fenella as residuary legatee.

It can be seen, then, that none of the points in the problem is especially difficult, so long as you work through it in a logical manner.

EIGHT

CHARITABLE TRUSTS

Questions on charities also often arise in problem form but it would be rare for a problem question to be limited to charities issues alone. Almost invariably knowledge of private purpose trusts and/or unincorporated associations, considered already in chapter 4, would also be required. For example:

Disaster struck the University of Gloucester when an explosion in the biochemistry department resulted in the release of a virus which caused the deaths of a number of lecturers, students and technicians, and left many more permanently incapacitated. The president of the Students' Union wishes to launch a public appeal for donations, the fund of which is to be applied for the following purposes:

(a) To compensate the bereaved families of those who died.

(b) To provide nursing care and special facilities for those victims who are incapacitated.

(c) To hold an annual memorial service for the dead, and erect a memorial tablet in the city centre.

(d) To campaign for the introduction of new legal restrictions upon research into organisms harmful to mankind.

(e) To provide scholarships in the university, with preference to be given to the relatives of victims of the disaster.

Advise him whether the fund is likely to obtain charitable status, and if not what alterations would need to be made to all or any of these purposes.

If it is not charitable, and the president is unwilling to alter the purposes in any way, what consequences, if any, would attach to the fund's lack of charitable status?

This particular problem asks you, among other things, whether the disposition is likely to be charitable, and if not, whether it might be valid as a private purpose trust. The alternative issue obviously requires knowledge of the material examined at the end of chapter 4. The question may not

address issues of validity alone, however, the following questions also asking
about distribution of surplus funds in an account:

> Mr Smith changes his name to the Rev. Why Taz Daz, and attracts
> a substantial religious following. A fund is organised to hire Wembley
> Stadium for a rally on 1 December, to celebrate the Rev. Why Taz
> Daz's infinite wisdom and immortality. Contributions are obtained from
> street collecting boxes, raffles and sweepstakes, and postal donations
> by both cash and cheque. On 25 November, by which time more than
> enough money has been raised for the hire of the stadium, the Rev.
> Why Taz Daz is run over by a bus and killed.
>
> The Charity Commissioners would like to apply the fund *cy près*.
> The Crown claims it as *bona vacantia*. The trustees of the fund would
> like to repay the money raised to the original donors.
> Discuss.

and

> In 1992 a street in Cardiff is destroyed by a gas explosion. An association
> is set up where members are invited to contribute £100 per month to
> provide temporary accommodation in Portacabins while their homes
> are being rebuilt. A and B are both among the 200 contributors to the
> fund. By 1993, however, B wishes to move to London, where he has
> obtained employment, so he ceases to contribute, and moves out of
> the Portacabin. By 1994 all the houses have been rebuilt, and the fund
> is wound up. At this time A is still a contributor. There is a substantial
> surplus.
>
> The Charity Commissioners would like to apply the moneys collected
> *cy près*, claiming that the association is a poverty charity. A argues
> that the surplus should be distributed equally among the contributors
> at the time the fund was would up. B argues that the surplus should
> be distributed among all contributors, past and present, in proportion
> to the total amount of their contributions.
> Discuss.

The only issue in each of these cases is distribution of surplus funds.
If the purposes are charitable (for the advancement of religion in the first,
and for the relief of poverty in the second question), then when pursuit
(or in the second problem, continued pursuit) of their purposes became
impossible, a *cy près* scheme ought to be effected. None of the money
ought to return to the original contributors. On the other hand, if these
are non-charitable purpose trusts, or the funds are held by non-charitable

unincorporated associations, then there can be no *cy près* scheme, but distribution will be effected among the contributors, or perhaps (in the first problem) some of it will go to the Crown as *bona vacantia*. The basis of distribution will be on the principles examined at the end of chapter 4.

The point of these two examples is to show you that it is not always possible to treat charities in isolation, and if you intend to concentrate on charities for the exam, make sure you also know about non-charitable purpose trusts and unincorporated associations. Indeed, the cases themselves often raise issues from both areas. *Re Shaw* [1957] 1 WLR 729, (the 40-letter alphabet case) was argued (unsuccessfully) as an educational charity, or alternatively (equally unsuccessfully) as a non-charitable purpose trust. *Re Hobourn Aero Components Ltd's Air Raid Disaster Fund* [1964] Ch 194, a case considered later in this chapter under self-help organisations, was entirely concerned with the distribution of surplus funds. If, as the Charity Commissioners unsuccessfully argued, the fund's purposes were charitable, a *cy près* scheme would have been appropriate. If, as was held in the Court of Appeal, the fund was not charitable, it should have been distributed among the contributors. In both those cases, issues from this chapter and issues from chapter 4 were mixed, and the last of the above problems appears to be based closely upon the *Hobourn Aero* case.

Space considerations do not permit a full review of the heads of charities, and in any case some of the issues in the above problem, and that alluded to in chapter 1, have already been considered in chapter 4. Instead, an essay question is considered, on the issue of public benefit, which is really central to the law of charities.

The requirement of public benefit

Essay question

Examine the requirement of 'public benefit' in charity, and consider its effectiveness in limiting the scope of charity to genuinely altruistic purposes.

Charitable trusts are of a public nature, in that they are publicly enforced and controlled, and enjoy certain tax concessions. It is not therefore surprising that, in order to be charitable a purpose must, in addition to falling within the *Pemsel* heads, involve a public benefit.

The *Pemsel* heads, from Lord Macnaghten's speech in *Commissioners for Special Purposes of the Income Tax* v *Pemsel* [1891] AC 531, are relief of poverty, advancement of religion, advancement of education, and other purposes beneficial to the community. The Recreational Charities Act 1958 has added an extra category, with a requirement of social welfare, which is probably similar to the public benefit requirement for the other heads.

There are therefore two requirements for a purpose to be charitable. It must confer a benefit (defined by the *Pemsel* heads) upon those who are directly the objects of the charity, and it must also confer an additional benefit upon the public at large.

For example, if a charitable purpose such as education is to be advanced, it must not only confer a benefit on those in direct receipt of the education, but must also be advanced in some way that benefits the public, or at least a substantial section thereof, rather than providing benefits for some artificially limited class of people.

However, this requirement is not applied with the same rigour to each of the four heads of charity, and in the case of the relief of poverty, its role is minimal. For this reason, the public benefit requirement will be dealt with separately under each head.

It is convenient to begin with trusts for the advancement of education, because the leading House of Lords authority concerned an attempt to set up an educational charity.

Advancement of education

Whereas in the case of relief of poverty, even benefiting a small number of people may be regarded as conferring a public benefit, with educational charities the problem of public benefit is thrown into a clearer relief. It is perhaps not surprising, then, that the leading House of Lords authority should concern this head of charity.

Obviously education constitutes a benefit to those in immediate receipt of it, but it is not self-evident that educating a few people constitutes a benefit to the general public. Indeed, given that many of the cases under this head are in reality disputes over tax relief, it would be strange if the educatin of a privileged few were to be regarded as charitable. That is why under this head in particular it is necessary that there is some additional benefit to the general public, or some appreciable sector thereof.

That is not to say that a particular form of education has to be capable of being enjoyed by everyone, so long as access to it is reasonably open. Thus public schools may be charitable as long as they are not operated as profit-making ventures, although their fees may place them beyond the means of the majority. Even scholarships or endowed chairs, which can be enjoyed only by one person at a time, present no difficulty. The problems arise where it is sought to limit the range of potential beneficiaries within a class which cannot be said to constitute a section of the public.

There are in effect two separate requirements. First, the class must be able genuinely to be described as a section of the community, rather than simply a body of private individuals. Persons following a common profession or calling, people of common nationality, religion or sex, or the inhabitants of a town or county can be described as a section of the community. Special provisions for people suffering disability are also permissible, since they are a section of the public in a meaningful sense. But in *Davies* v *Perpetual Trustee Co. Ltd* [1959] AC 459, the Privy Council held non-charitable a trust which was confined to Presbyterian youths who were descended from settlors in New South Wales who had originated from the North of Ireland. Although quite large in number, this category of potential beneficiaries was held not to be a section of the public.

Secondly, under this head, and probably under all the heads except relief of poverty, it will also be fatal if the class of potential beneficiaries (however large) is defined in terms of relation to particular individuals or a company. This approach originated in *Re Compton* [1945] Ch 123, where charitable status was denied to a trust to educate the children of three named families. It is understandable that the courts are reluctant to allow an essentially private arrangement to enjoy charitable privileges, especially tax advantages, but it seems that the principle extends to cases where the class of potential beneficiaries is defined in terms of a relationship with an employer, even where the employer is a substantial concern.

The most authoritative statements are those of Lord Simonds in *Oppenheim* v *Tobacco Securities Trust Co. Ltd* [1951] AC 297, where *Re Compton* was approved in the House of Lords. He said that first, the number of possible beneficiaries must not be negligible, and secondly, that the class must not be defined so as to depend on any relationship to a particular individual or employer.

In the trust with which the House of Lords was concerned, the number of potential beneficiaries (at least in theory) was certainly not negligible. The income of the trust fund was directed to be applied 'in providing for . . . the education of children of employees or former employees of the British-American Tobacco Co. Ltd . . . or any of its subsidiary or allied companies in such manner . . . as the acting trustees shall in their absolute discretion . . . think fit'. The number of present employees alone exceeded 110,000, so it was only the personal nexus rule which was fatal (because they were all connected with the same company).

The test is arguably inappropriate in large companies. Though perhaps the special tax concessions of charitable status should not be given to *any* arrangement for a private class, the personal link between employees is not as obvious as that between members of a family, among whom considerations of mutual interest might be considered to negate the altruistic status of the trust.

Of course, if you take a hard line on private arrangements the *Oppenheim* decision logically follows. But perhaps the real, if unstated, justification for the result was the extent of the trustees' discretion in *Oppenheim*. The benefit to 110,000 or more people may in fact have been entirely theoretical—for example, if the trustees had used the funds to pay 15% of fees to those employees who sent their sons to boarding school, only the relatively small number who could afford the other 85% would actually have benefited. Indeed, it is perhaps a pity (unless you are a hard-liner) that the test in *Oppenheim* does not address the real problem, which is the extent of the trustees' discretion to reduce the size of the class, rather than the theoretical personal nexus.

Interesting questions can arise where most but not all the fund is directed towards people connected with a particular employer. In *Re Koettgen's WT* [1954] Ch 252, an educational trust succeeded despite a direction that the trustees should give preference to the families of employees, up to a maximum of 75% of income, but a preference for the grantor's family rendered a gift non-charitable in *Caffoor v Commissioner of Income Tax, Colombo* [1961] AC 584. The trust also failed in *Inland Revenue Commissioners v Educational Grants Association Ltd* [1967] Ch 123, affirmed [1967] Ch 993, where between 76% and 85% of the income (varying from year to year) was paid for the education of persons connected with the Metal Box Co. Ltd. Pennycuick J found 'considerable difficulty in the *Koettgen* decision', and thought that a preference for a private class might always be fatal (though he did not need actually to decide that). The problem with laying down a clear rule of this nature would be that extreme cases could be envisaged (e.g., a preference up to 5% of income) where its application would further no obvious policy (unless again, of course, an objection is taken in principle to charitable status for an arrangement with *any* purely private content).

This problem is similar to that in *Oppenheim v Tobacco Securities Trust Co. Ltd* itself, i.e., that the rule is arguably too rigid. The real problem in *Oppenheim*, as has been seen, was the extent of the trustees' discretion to limit the number of people who could in practice have benefited, rather than the nexus with the company (unless again, objection is taken to *any* private arrangement). It would have been difficult to formulate a clear rule on trustees' discretion, however, where the problem is essentially one of where to draw the line, just as it is difficult to draw the line in the *Re Koettgen's WT* situation. In both cases, therefore, a rigid rule may well be the only answer.

Relief of poverty

It is unquestioned law that to relieve poverty is to confer a benefit upon the public at large, if only by mitigating the burden of support for the poor which would otherwise fall upon the community. There is no need for the *Oppenheim* v *Tobacco Securities Trust Co. Ltd* test to apply, and it does not apply in fact.

The *Oppenheim* case exempted the 19th-century 'poor relations' cases as anomalous, and left open the position regarding them. Since then the House of Lords has considered them directly in *Dingle* v *Turner* [1972] AC 601, and expressly upheld them. In that case a trust for 'poor employees of E. Dingle & Co.' was held charitable, though it would have failed under the personal nexus test.

It is clear, therefore, that the personal nexus test does not apply to this head of charity.

It is, however, necessary that the trust should be intended to benefit a class of persons, and not simply to make a gift to an individual, or group of individuals, who happen to be poor. In *Re Scarisbrick* [1951] Ch 622 Jenkins LJ (at p. 655) stated the rule thus:

I think the true question in each case has really been whether the gift was for the relief of poverty amongst a class of persons, or . . . a particular description of poor, or was merely a gift to individuals, albeit with relief of poverty amongst those individuals as the motive of the gift, or with a selective preference for the poor or poorest amongst those individuals.

This statement received the approval of Lord Cross of Chelsea in *Dingle* v *Turner*. In *Re Scarisbrick* itself the class of potential recipients was so wide as to be incapable of exhaustive ascertainment ('such relations of my said son and daughters as shall be in needy circumstances'), so the trust was charitable.

Advancement of religion

There are dicta in *Oppenheim* v *Tobacco Securities Trust Co. Ltd* [1951] AC 297 that the public benefit tests advanced in that case apply to all heads of charity except the relief of poverty. If these dicta are correct, the personal nexus rule applies to religious charities, therefore. This seems surprising because:

(a)   The rationale of the personal nexus rule, which is to deny tax and rates advantages to private educational schemes for élite family groups, does not apply as easily in the field of religion.

(b)   If a religious family group mixes actively in the community, arguably the benefit is to the community as a whole, rather than just to the family members. Therefore the *Oppenheim* test is satisfied unless the group shuts itself off from the rest of the community, as occurred in *Gilmour* v *Coats* [1949] AC 426 (see below).

In practice, therefore, there seems to be a substantial overlap between the personal nexus rule and the requirement that religion be *advanced*. Apart from requiring some positive action, it seems that there must by virtue of this requirement be an element of public contact. Private salvation, however commendable, is not charitable. Thus in *Yeap Cheah Neo* v *Ong Chen Neo* (1875) LR 6 PC 381 a provision for the performance of ancestor worship was held non-charitable (by the Privy Council), and a possible reason was that it could benefit only the family group.

The leading case is *Gilmour* v *Coats* [1949] AC 426, where the House of Lords had to consider a gift of £500 towards a Carmelite priory. The priory housed about 20 cloistered nuns who devoted themselves to intercessory prayer, and had no contact at all with the outside world. This was held non-charitable on the grounds that there was no contact with the outside world. Arguments based on Catholic doctrine, to the effect that everyone benefited from the intercessory prayers, were rejected as being not susceptible to legal proof. Nor could any benefit be found merely in the example of the piety of the women, as it was too vague and intangible. The House of Lords also rejected the argument that, entry being open to all women, the priory should be treated on analogy with an educational institution offering scholarship entry, holding that an educational establishment which required its members to withdraw from the world and leave no record of their studies would not be charitable either.

On the other hand, in *Re Caus* [1934] Ch 162, Catholic masses for the dead were held charitable. This case was doubted in *Gilmour* v *Coats*, but in principle the case seems correct, and *Caus* was applied by Brown-Wilkinson V-C in *Re Hetherington* [1989] 2 All ER 129. The point is that Catholic masses are open to the public at large even where a private function, such as a funiary rite, is incorporated into the celebration, so in principle *Caus* is distinguishable from *Gilmour* v *Coats*.

In *Re Hetherington*, Browne-Wilkinson V-C was called upon to consider a gift for the saying of masses, which did not exclude the possibility that the masses would be said in private. In practice, however, all or most of the masses would be open to public. Reviewing the cases, he said (at pp. 134-5):

1.   A trust for the . . . the advancement of religion is *prima facie* charitable, and assumed to be for the public benefit . . . This assumption of public benefit can be rebutted by showing that in fact the particular trust in question cannot operate so as to confer a legally recognised benefit on the public, as in *Gilmour* v *Coats*.

2.   The celebration of a religious rite in public does confer such a benefit because of the edifying and improving effect of such celebration on the members of the public who attend . . .

3.   The celebration of a religious rite in private does not contain the necesary element of public benefit since any benefit by prayer or example is incapable of proof in the legal sense, and any element of education is limited to a private, not public, class of those present at the celebration: see *Gilmour* v *Coats* itself . . .

4.   Where there is a gift for a religious purpose which could be carried out in a way which is beneficial to the public (i.e., by public masses) but could also be carried out in a way which would not have sufficient public benefit (i.e., by private masses) the gift is to be construed as a gift to be carried out only by the methods that are charitable, all non-charitable purposes being excluded . . .

Applying these principles to the case before him, he concluded that:

a gift for the saying of masses is *prima facie* charitable, being for a religious purpose. In practice, those masses will be celebrated in public, which provides a sufficient element of public benefit . . . The gift is to be construed as a gift for the saying of public masses only . . ., private masses not being permissible since it would not be a charitable application of the fund for a religious purpose.

In other words, he construed the gift in such a way as to exclude purposes which were non-charitable.

It follows that the mere attendance by the public at a prayer service is sufficient to distinguish *Gilmour* v *Coats*. Suppose, on the other hand, the religious organisation conducts all its affairs in private, but unlike *Gilmour* v *Coats* its members have not cut themselves off entirely from the outside world, but mix with it. This also seems sufficient to distinguish *Gilmour* v *Coats*. In *Neville Estates* v *Madden*, Cross J held charitable a trust for the members of Catford Synagogue. He thought that the rejection of example as a benefit in *Gilmour* v *Coats* would not apply to a restricted religious group if its members lived in the world and mixed with their fellow citizens, because they could thereby extend their example of religious living to the public at large.

It would seem to follow, therefore, that the requirement of public contact is not especially onerous. On Cross J's view, religion can be advanced by example, so long as one mixes in the world in a *physical* sense. *Neville Estates* is authority that no more is required.

Other purposes beneficial to the community

Under this head, where the benefit is limited to a restricted class, such a class must be a section of the public. Certainly the personal nexus test applies, and it may even be that the courts adopt a more stringent approach to public benefit under this head than under the other three heads.

For example, in *Williams's Trustees* v *Inland Revenue Commissioners* [1947] AC 447, doubt was expressed by Lord Simonds as to whether Welsh people in London could be a section of the public. In *Inland Revenue Commissioners* v *Baddeley* [1955] AC 572 it was said that the persons to be benefited must either be the whole community or the inhabitants of a particular area. If some further restriction is imposed, thus creating in effect a class within a class, the test of public benefit will not be satisfied. In *IRC* v *Baddeley*, the limitation was to Methodists living in West Ham and Leyton, and the trust was held not to be charitable.

Neither of these cases of course falls foul of the personal nexus test, and it may be that *Williams's Trustees* v *IRC* at any rate is more stringent than the test in *Davies* v *Perpetual Trustee Co. Ltd* [1959] AC 439, which applies to educational charities (see above). Viscount Simonds in *IRC* v *Baddeley* thought it possible 'that a different degree of public benefit is requisite according to the class in which the charity is said to fall', and that public benefit considerations 'have even greater weight [than in the case of educational trusts] in the case of trusts which by their nominal classification depend for their validity upon general public utility' (though Lord Reid thought otherwise in his dissenting speech).

It is possible that what constitutes a section of the public depends on the purposes of the particular trust, and the courts are more likely to strike down arbitrary restrictions which are irrelevant to those purposes, but which simply serve to exclude other sections of the public. As Lord Simonds observed in *IRC* v *Baddeley* (at p. 592): 'Who has ever heard of a bridge to be crossed only by impecunious Methodists?' He went on to say that what is true of a bridge for Methodists is equally true of any other public purpose falling within the fourth head, and of the adherents of any other creed. The point is surely that if a purpose is so clearly beneficial as to be charitable under the fourth head, the arbitrary exclusion of *any* section of the public renders the disposition in effect a private gift.

There is some authority that the test of public benefit can vary within the fourth head itself. In *Re Dunlop (dec'd)* (1984) Northern Irish Judgments Bulletin (noted by Norma Dawson [1987] Conv 114), Carswell J upheld as charitable a bequest 'To hold the remainder of my residuary estate for the Presbyterian Trust . . . to found or help to found a home for Old Presbyterian persons,' and a *cy près* scheme was ordered. There was earlier Northern Irish authority that the Presbyterians of Londonderry were not a sufficient section of the public under the fourth head, and it was accepted that there was no difference between Irish and English definitions of charity. Carswell J took the view, however, that public benefit depended upon the nature of 'the advantage which the donor intends to provide for the benefit of all of the public'. A 'bridge to be used only by Methodists should clearly fail to qualify, whereas a gift for the education of the children of members of that church might be a valid charity'. But he was also prepared to distinguish between purposes within the fourth head itself.

It should be noted that neither *IRC* v *Baddeley* nor *Williams's Trustees* v *IRC* actually turned on the issue of public benefit. In the former case the purposes were not exclusively religious, but included social purposes and the provision of playing fields, and in the latter case purposes were exclusively social and recreational. They would therefore have failed because of the inclusion of a social content, whatever view had been taken on the public benefit issue.

Recreational Charities Act 1958

This Act was in response to a number of decisions about 30 years ago, including those mentioned in the previous paragraph, where doubt was cast on the charitable status under the fourth head of a number of social trusts which had always been assumed to be charitable. It makes it charitable in certain circumstances to provide, or assist in the provision of, facilities for recreation or other leisure-time occupation. A proviso adds that nothing in the section shall be taken to derogate from the requirement of public benefit, and there is an additional requirement that the facilities are provided in the interests of social welfare (upon which requirement the Act enlarges).

In *Inland Revenue Commissioners* v *McMullen* [1979] 1 WLR 130 the Court of Appeal split on the issue of whether the recipients must, by virtue of the requirement of social welfare, by implication be 'deprived', the majority holding that the class to be benefited must be disadvantaged in such a way as to have a special need for the facilities. Bridge LJ, however, dissented, and preferred a wider view that social welfare may be promoted by benefits which extend to the better off as well as the socially deprived. The House of Lords ([1981] AC 1) left the issue open, holding the trust valid as an educational charity. Indeed, all their lordships expressly refused to decide which of the approaches adopted in the Court of Appeal was correct, and no conclusion can therefore be reached.

Presumably, social welfare indicates some element of provision for others, so that a group acting purely to benefit themselves would fail to qualify. In any event, such an enterprise would lack the necessary element of public benefit preserved by the Act.

The altruism issue

The question asks you also to consider the effectiveness of the requirement of public benefit in limiting the scope of charity to genuinely altruistic purposes. A lot of people might expect altruism and charity to go roughly hand in hand, but by no means everybody would agree that the legal definition of charity and the moral definition of altruism are the same. Sometimes, but certainly not always, the public benefit requirement has a bearing on the issue.

This is not a question capable of as precise an answer as most others on a typical equity and trusts paper, because different people can legitimately have very different ideas as to what constitutes altruism. To hark back to chapter 4, a discretionary trust in favour of altruistic members of the Somerset Cricket Club would fail on the grounds of conceptual uncertainty.

A considerable variety of good answers is therefore possible within a wide range. Some students do not like questions like this because there is no obviously 'correct' way of proceeding, but you must not ignore this part of the question (unless, of course, your fear of the vague is so great that you prefer to answer another question altogether). In fact, it is still possible to judge between different answers, not on the basis of the conclusions reached, but on the internal logical consistency of the argument (i.e., lack of contradictions), and the range of materials prayed in aid to support your viewpoint.

The discussion that follows looks at purposes which are arguably non-altruistic, and which have been considered by the courts. In some (but by no means all) cases the public benefit requirement has been a factor in deciding whether the purposes are charitable.

I must emphasise that this is certainly not intended to be a model answer to this question (there could be no such thing), but merely to throw up ideas which you may wish to consider.

Political purposes

Most people would probably argue that political purposes are not generally speaking altruistic, and the law is in the main in accordance with this view.

A trust cannot be charitable under any head if its purposes are, directly or indirectly, political. This has nothing to do with the requirement of public benefit, but is simply part of the general definition of a charitable purpose. But a wide range of purposes is regarded as political, and it is also arguable that some purposes which are genuinely altruistic fall foul of this criterion of validity.

Where the objectives involve attempting to bring about a change in the law, they will be considered political and therefore non-charitable, unless change in the law is merely ancillary to the main purpose of the trust. This was one of the reasons for the failure of the National Anti-Vivisection Society to achieve charitable status in *National Anti-Vivisection Society* v *IRC* [1948] AC 31. Lord Simonds gave as the ostensible rationale that it is for Parliament, not the courts, to decide whether any change would be for the public benefit. He also rejected the contention that alteration in the law was merely ancillary to the purposes of the trust, since in order to abolish vivisection it would have been necessary to repeal the Cruelty to Animals Act 1876 (since replaced by the Animals (Scientific Procedures) Act 1986) and pass an Act prohibiting vivisection altogether.

In *Re Bushnell* [1975] 1 WLR 1596, money was left to advance awareness of the benefits of socialised medicine and to show that its realisation was fully possible only in a socialist State. The testator had died in 1941, before the introduction of the National Health Service. One of the grounds upon which the trust was held void was its political bias in favour of socialism. Another ground for the failure of the trust in *Re Bushnell* was that in 1941 legislation would have been needed (and was of course later enacted) to introduce socialised medicine.

It was also an additional reason for the failure of Shaw's 40-letter alphabet, and accounts for the inability of, e.g., the Campaign against Racial Discrimination and the National Council for Civil Liberties to be registered. Charities may, however, campaign *against* changes in the law, which may enable some political purposes of a generally conservative nature to obtain registration.

In *McGovern* v *Attorney-General* [1982] Ch 321, Amnesty International tried to procure charitable status for some of its activities by creating a trust of those parts which were thought likely to be accepted as charitable. The objectives of the trust were the relief of needy persons who were prisoners of conscience and their relatives; seeking the release of such prisoners; seeking abolition of torture and inhuman punishment, and research into human rights and dissemination of the findings. It was held that the first and fourth objectives might be charitable but that the trust as a whole failed because of the political aspects involved in seeking release of prisoners of conscience and the abolition of torture. This necessitated reversing the policies of foreign governments, and hence the trust could not be charitable. To grant this status might prejudice the relations of the British government with foreign countries, and this consideration of policy could not be overlooked by the court.

A political taint will also be fatal to trust seeking to promote aims which most civilised nations hold to be high aspirations. In *Re Strakosch* [1949] Ch 529, the promotion of racial harmony between English and Afrikaans communities in South Africa was held non-charitable, and registration of community councils is refused where their principal aims are the promotion of interracial accord. The same will apply where the aims are harmony and peace, if such movements overtly or covertly call upon governments to promote specific policies, such as disarmament. One reason sometimes given for denying charitable status to attempts to promote moral objectives is that they necessarily involve a propagandist element biased in favour of only one side of the argument.

Campaigning, in the sense of seeking to influence public opinion on political matters, is not charitable, and in *Webb* v *O'Doherty, The Times*, 11 February 1991, Hoffman J granted an injunction restraining the officers of a students' union, which was an educational charity, from making any payments to the National Students Committee to Stop War in the Gulf, or to the Cambridge Committee to Stop War in the Gulf. On the other hand, it is legitimate for an educational charity to discuss political issues, and a political object which is merely incidental will not be fatal. In *Re Koeppler's WT* [1986] Ch 423, a testamentary gift to Wilton Park, whose main function was to organise educational conferences, was upheld as a gift for charitable purposes, although the Wilton Park's objects included the promotion of informed international public opinion and the promotion of greater co-operation between East and West. The Court of Appeal held that a political purpose which is merely incidental to the objects of a trust will not necessarily be fatal where the purposes are otherwise educational. *McGovern* v *Attorney-General* was different, because there alteration in the law was essential to Amnesty International's aims.

The Charity Commissioners have frequently expressed their willingness to advise those seeking charitable status, or doubtful as to whether proposed activities might conflict with the charitable status of existing trusts.

Value judgments in education

The public benefit requirement has a greater role to play here because whereas most people would probably regard the provision of almost any form of education as capable of being altruistic, problems arise with the education of privileged minorities. The law accords with (what I suppose is) the layman's view by making few value judgments, but the public benefit requirement was developed precisely to counteract the privileged minorities problem.

Thus, a very wide range of educational and cultural activities extending far beyond the administration of formal instruction can in theory be charitable. Schools and universities are clearly charitable, and so are nursery schools, adult education centres, societies dedicated to promoting training and standards within a trade or profession, museums, zoos and public libraries.

Nor is education limited to teaching. Learned societies which bring together experts in a field to share and exchange knowledge may be charitable. Even cultural activities such as drama, music, literature and fine arts can come within this head, on the grounds that they have a role in the cultivation of knowledge and taste.

Professional and vocational bodies which advance education, such as the Royal College of Surgeons, are also charitable, even though one of the ancillary purposes is the protection and assistance of its members. Other examples include the Royal College of Nursing, the Institution of Civil Engineers, and the Incorporated Council of Law Reporting for England and Wales. Bodies whose chief purpose is to further the interests of their members and to promote the status of the profession will not, however, be charitable, for example the General Nursing Council (see *General Nursing Council for England & Wales* v *St Marylebone Borough Council* [1959] AC 540).

Games and other leisure-time pursuits can also be charitable if educational (though physical activity which is of a purely recreational nature will not be charitable unless it falls within the provisions of the Recreational Charities Act 1958). Thus in *Re Marriette* [1915] 2 Ch 284, a gift to provide squash courts at a public school was held charitable, Eve J remarking that the playing of games at boarding schools was as important as learning from books, and that the proper education of young people can include a physical element. A similar view was taken by the House of Lords in *Inland Revenue Commissioners* v *McMullen* [1981] AC 1, a case involving the playing of football at schools and universities.

The courts can be involved in value judgments as to whether an activity is worthwhile at all in an educational sense, but the extent of these is limited. In *Re Pinion* [1965] Ch 85, the testator left his 'studio' for the purposes of a museum to display his collection of what were claimed to be 'fine arts'. However, expert witnesses thought that the paintings were 'atrociously bad', and one 'expresse[d] his surprise that so voracious a collector should not by hazard have picked up even one meritorious object'. Harman LJ described the collection as 'a mass of junk' and, reversing Wilberforce J, the Court of Appeal held the trust void, because non-charitable. In *Re Delius* [1957] Ch 299 a trust for the appreciation of the works of the composer was held charitable, but Roxburgh J made it clear that the undoubted merit of Delius's music was crucial, and the same view would not be taken of a 'manifestly inadequate' composer.

Yet while value judgments are inevitable in this area (or a school for pickpockets would be charitable), it seems that the courts do not take too stringent a view. *Re Pinion* is a fairly extreme case. In *Re Hopkins* [1965] Ch 669, on the other hand, Wilberforce J upheld as charitable a bequest to the Francis Bacon Society for the purposes of finding the Bacon-Shakespeare manuscripts. Though he observed that if found the discovery would be 'of the highest value to history and to literature', the search could equally have been futile, as not only were the manuscripts not known to exist, but Wilberforce J thought their discovery unlikely.

Thus, apart from the public benefit test there is little to restrict educational charities to altruistic purposes. It is true that a purpose which is ostensibly educational but is in reality for the advancement of political purposes will also not be charitable. Whereas education can cover political theory and philosophy, the courts draw the line where partisan propaganda is seen to be masquerading in the guise of instruction. In *Re Hopkinson* [1949] 1 All ER 346, a trust for adult education in socialist principles fell foul of this line. The Charity Commissioners commented on the problem in their Annual Report for 1967, para. 8, but seem to take a fairly generous view, regarding for example, the promotion of racial harmony as charitable.

Value judgments in religion

As with education the law is tolerant as to which religions may be charitable. The requirement of public benefit, and the related requirement (considered above) that religion be *advanced*, therefore take on a greater importance in determining the limits of charity under this head. Whether those limits are in any way coterminous with the limits of altruism depends on your view of what is altruistic.

Cross J remarked in *Neville Estates v Madden* [1962] Ch 832: 'As between different religions the law stands neutral, but it assumes that any religion is at least likely to be better than none.' In *Thornton v Howe* (1862) 31 Beav 14, charitable status was extended to a devise of land to promote the writings of Joanna Southcote, the founder of a small but fervent sect in the West of England, who had proclaimed that she was with child by the Holy Ghost and would give birth to a second Messiah. The practical effect of the decision was to bring the trust within the invalidating provisions of the mortmain legislation (which between 1736 and 1891 made testamentary gifts to charity void, and may well have been the *motive* for the courts adopting such an apparently liberal attitude) but, whatever the motive, *Thornton* v *Howe* establishes that any theistic belief, however obscure or remote, will fall within the meaning of religion for the purposes of charity law.

A more recent example is *Re Watson* [1973] 1 WLR 1472, where Plowman J held charitable a trust to publish the religious writings of a retired builder who was virtually the sole remaining adherent of a small, fundamentalist group of believers. Expert testimony regarded the theological merits of the works as very small, but confirmed the genuineness of the writer's beliefs.

Nor is it necessary that the religious beliefs in question should be Christian. Certainly the Jewish, Sikh, Hindu and Muslim faiths have been accepted. The position of Buddhism was left open in *Re South Place Ethical Society* [1980] 1 WLR 1565. In that case Dillon J remarked that religion is concerned with man's relations with God, so it seems therefore that one qualification is the need for a belief in some kind of God (or gods). High ethical principles or moral philosophy, being concerned with man's relations with man, cannot amount to a religion (though they may of course be educational, and so charitable under that head). Plowman J also thought in *Re Watson*, that doctrines which were averse to the foundations of all religion, and subversive of all morality, would not be charitable under this head.

Self-help organisations

Self-help organisations are not charitable, because they lack the necessary element of altruism. If they are not poverty charities they clearly also fail on the *Oppenheim* v *Tobacco Securities Trust Co. Ltd* personal nexus test, so the public benefit test is here tied in with the element of altruism. Hall V-C in *Re Clark* (1875) 1 Ch D 497 envisaged that they may succeed as poverty charities, where of course public benefit tests are less stringent, but this also must now be regarded as doubtful, as a second principle has developed independently of the public benefit test that the benefits of charity must be provided by bounty and not bargain. Where, as is the case with many friendly societies, the beneficiaries have, in effect, bought their entitlement in a contractual arrangement, it is again considered that the element of altruism essential to charity is lacking.

Thus in *Re Hobourn Aero Components Ltd's Air Raid Distress Fund* [1946] Ch 194, a fund established by employees to relieve members suffering in consequence of air raids on Coventry was held non-charitable on the grounds first, that the employees among whom benefit was confined could not be a section of the public, and secondly, that the fund represented a self-help arrangement in which the members' entitlement to benefit turned upon the fact of their having subscribed to the fund. In other words, even if this had been an otherwise valid poverty trust, the trust would still have been refused charitable status on the second ground, as indeed would almost any self-help organisation.

One can see why profit-making self-help organisations should not be charitable. One can also see why charitable status should be restricted, as Hall V-C thought, to those self-help organisations which relieve poverty. But the bounty not bargain argument seems harsh, even anomalous. It is, after all, accepted that some payment for benefits received from bodies which are undoubtedly charitable may legitimately be demanded; no one expects to be admitted to a public school, or the Victoria and Albert Museum, free of charge. It is still open for the courts to accept the first ground in *Re Hobourn Aero Components Ltd's Air Raid Distress Fund* while rejecting the second.

Disaster appeals

These will be valid if for the relief of poverty, otherwise, like self-help organisations, will fail on the grounds of public benefit. Here again then, it is the public benefit test which is in effect defining what is charitable, but some would question whether charity and altruism are the same thing in these cases.

The organisers of such funds are left with two alternatives. They can apply a means test criterion to the receipt of benefit, in order to fall within the poverty head, but they may regard this as invidious. The other possibility, often favoured by fund organisers (e.g., Penlee lifeboat disaster fund in 1982), is to avoid the means test and draft the appeal in such a way as to avoid charitable status altogether. In that event, of course, the tax concessions will also be foregone. Perhaps more importantly, the *cy près* doctrine will not apply, and there may be difficulties over distribution of any surplus left over after the purposes have been achieved. It may even be, that the Crown will take some or all of the surplus as *bona vacantia*, not perhaps the most fitting consequence of the altriusm of the donors.

One of the problems with disaster appeals is that they are usually set up very quickly after the disaster has occurred, often before the full legal consequences have been considered. They may well be described as charitable, and donors may believe that their contributions are going to a charitable fund, only for the organisers later to change their minds and draft the purposes so as to avoid charitable status. An interesting question might then arise as to what happens to the money already contributed, in the (probably unlikely) event of a dispute. Consider, for example, the following question (which has not yet appeared on an exam paper, but presumably could):

In 1992 an American space satellite falls to Earth, out of control. Large sections of the satellite survive re-entry into the Earth's atmosphere, one of which lands on a crowded cinema in Bradford. 500 people are killed, and many more injured.

The Bradford Cinema Disaster Appeal Fund is immediately launched, and is described on TV new programmes, and in newspapers reporting on the disaster, as charitable. Contributions are invited by the organisers, who say nothing to negate the impression that the fund is to be charitable, and a great deal of money is collected. Alan, believing the fund to be charitable, writes a cheque for £500 to the organisers.

Four days later, the organisers appreciate the consequences of the fund having charitable status, and decide to draft the purposes in such a way as to avoid it.

Alan is furious, and demands the return of his £500. The Charity Commissioners, arguing that Alan clearly intended his money to be donated for a charitable purpose, wish to apply his £500 *cy près*. The fund organisers wish to apply the £500 to the purposes of the fund.

Discuss.

This is not sufficiently weighty to be a full exam question, but it could certainly be one part of a two-part question. If Alan really was concerned, at the time of his donation, that it would be used for a charitable purpose, then it would be difficult for the fund organisers to argue that they should retain it. The issue would then be whether Alan could reclaim it, or whether it should be applied *cy près*. The issues are those applicable to an initial failure, since it appears that no charitable fund has ever been set up, and the answer would depend on whether from Alan's gift can be inferred a general (or paramount) charitable intention, in which case a *cy près* scheme would apply, or whether instead his intention was to further some specific purpose alone, in which case the £500 would go on resulting trust to Alan.

The problem illustrates the difficulties in which appeal fund donors and organisers may find themselves if they assume such funds inevitably to be charitable.

NINE

TRUSTEESHIP

The didactic cataloguing of trustees' powers and duties is the stuff of conventional textbooks, and is unsuitable for a book of this nature. Conflicts of interest have given rise to recent litigation, however, and so the area is presumably a likely exam topic. Variation of trusts also normally crops up, and in any case can give rise to some interesting conceptual difficulties.

Throughout this chapter 'he' includes 'she' and 'himself' includes 'herself'.

Conflicts of interest and the remuneration of trustees

The duty of trustees towards beneficiaries is fiduciary, and as with any fiduciary relationship the fiduciary must have no personal interest in the way the duty is performed. In other words, where a trustee has a discretion, he must not have a personal interest in exercising the discretion in a particular way. He must be motivated to benefit the trust, not himself. That is not to say that trustees are not entitled to receive any benefit for their services, but the amount of their reward must not depend on the manner in which their discretion is exercised.

In this country only the Public Trustee and a number of other trustees acting in an official capacity have any statutory entitlement to charge fees.

There are a number of ways in which trustees may be entitled to payment, but these should be regarded as exhaustive. If a trustee does not come within one of the following heads, he is not entitled to any money for the performance of his duties:

(a) The right to remuneration may be fixed by contract between settlor and trustee at the outset; banks' charging clauses are an example of this. Similarly, a director of a company who owes a fiduciary duty to the company may enter into a contract with the company for remuneration. The contract must be one that the company is empowered to make. In *Guinness plc* v *Saunders* [1990] 1 All ER 652, two Guinness directors, Thomas Ward and Ernest Saunders, claimed that they were contractually entitled to fees of £5.2 million for advice and services rendered to Guinness in connection with a take-over bid for Distillers Co. plc. The purported contract was made by a committee of three of Guinness's directors (two of whom were

Ward and Saunders), but under Guinness's articles of association the committee had no power to authorise reimbursement, and the House of Lords held that the directors were not entitlted to keep the £5.2 million that they had received.

(b) Section 30(2) of the Trustee Act 1925 entitles a trustee to reimbursement for expenses, from trust funds.

(c) The courts have a jurisdiction to authorise payment. In one of the cases involving a breach of fiduciary duty considered below, *Boardman v Phipps* [1967] 2 AC 46, though a solicitor as fiduciary to a family trust was not entitled to keep profits received as a result of his position, he was held to be entitled to liberal remuneration on a *quantum meruit* basis, which is to say, on a reasonable basis for work done for the benefit of the trust, including work that had been performed gratuitously. The Court of Appeal took a similar view in *O'Sullivan* v *Management Agency & Music Ltd* [1985] QB 428, another case involving a breach of fiduciary duty. The remuneration included even a reasonable profit element, but was not related to the actual profits obtained in breach of fiduciary duty, which had to be accounted.

In *Re Duke of Norfolk's ST* [1982] Ch 61, the Court of Appeal was prepared to exercise this jurisdiction to increase the remuneration of a trustee over the amount agreed in the original settlement. The quantity of work had increased because new property had been added to the settlement, and the tax position had been substantially altered by the introduction of Capital Transfer Tax (now Inheritance Tax) in 1975. The trustee was held entitled to extra remuneration for the increase in work.

A claim for *quantum meruit* is essentially an implied contract claim, however, and cannot be awarded to a director where the company has no power to authorise payment. The directors in *Guinness plc* v *Saunders* (above) claimed an alternative *quantum meruit* entitlement, and failed, for precisely the same reasons that their claim in contract failed: Guinness were no more empowered to enter into an implied contract to pay for the services of the two directors, than they were to enter into an express contract for the same.

In none of the above cases, however, is the amount of remuneration dependent on the manner in which the discretion (if any) of the trustee is exercised. Thus there can be no conflict between the interests of the trust and the personal interests of the trustee. Otherwise, trustees must not benefit in any way from their position as trustees. The courts refuse to allow *any possibility* that a conflict of interest may occur. Whether any conflict occurs in fact is not relevant. In other words, it is immaterial that the trust does not suffer, or even that it gains, from the activities of the trustee. The trustee has to show that there is no possible causal connection between his position and any profit made by him (outside the categories outlined above).

There are three main situations where a conflict of interest may arise between the trust and the personal interest of the trustee, which the law therefore prevents from arising. First, a trustee may not purchase trust property (or sell property to a trust). Secondly, he must not set himself up in competition with the trust even after resigning from the fiduciary position, in case he gains for himself the benefit of any goodwill acquired by the trust, and possibly also useful information. For example, in *Re Thomson* [1930] 1 Ch 203 an executor was restrained from carrying out a yacht-broking business in competition with the estate. Thirdly, he must not make any profit by virtue of his position.

Two areas in particular are likely topics for exam questions. First, the self-dealing rule, on which there has been recent important litigation. Secondly, the use by fiduciaries of information acquired in their fiduciary capacity.

A trustee may not purchase trust property

This is also referred to as the self-dealing rule, of which Vinelott J said in *Re Thompson's Settlement* [1986] Ch 99:

> It is clear that the self-dealing rule is an application of the wider principle that a man must not put himself in a position where duty and interest conflict or where his duty to one conflicts with his duty to another.

Its rationale is that if a trustee deals in trust property he abuses his position as trustee to his personal advantage. If, for example, he purchases trust property, he can buy at less than the best price obtainable. Similarly if he sells to the trust, he may be able to demand too high a price.

The rule is very strict, because there must be no possibility of the trustee taking advantage of his position, whether he does so in fact or not. The lengths to which the law goes is shown by *Wright* v *Morgan* [1926] AC 788, where a trustee who had resigned his trusteeship purchased trust property at a price that had been fixed by independent valuers. One may have thought that not even a possibility of conflict arose here. The arrangements had been made while he was still trustee, however, and the Privy Council held that this sale had to be set aside.

It is possible for purchases by trustees to be valid, but only in very exceptional circumstances. It is essential not only that the trustee paid a fair price, as he had in *Wright* v *Morgan*, but also that he took no advantage of his position, and made full disclosure of his interest. The purchase was valid, for example, in *Holder v Holder* [1968] Ch 353, where an executor, Victor, purchased two farms that were part of the estate at a fair price at an auction. He took no part in instructing the valuer who fixed the reserves, and it was clear at the auction (at least to the beneficiaries) that he participated as buyer not seller. Victor had not been active in his role as executor, and had acquired no information as a result of it. He had indeed purported to renounce his executorship, and probate had been granted to two other executors. Additionally, the plaintiff beneficiary had accepted his share of the purchase money in full knowledge of the facts, and so was disentitled from taking the action on the grounds of acquiescence.

Cross J referred to 'the very special circumstances of the case', and *Holder v Holder* should not be regarded as laying down more than the narrowest of exceptions. The rigour of the general rule was restated by Vinelott J in *Re Thompson's Settlement* [1986] Ch 99:

The principle is applied stringently in cases where a trustee concurs in a transaction which cannot be carried into effect without his concurrence and who also has an interest in or holds a fiduciary duty to another in relation to the same transaction.

Holder v Holder was distinguished, and virtually limited to its own facts. The same principles apply to sales of property to trusts by trustees.

Use of information received in a fiduciary capacity

This is an application of the wider principle that a trustee (or any fiduciary) must not make any profit by virtue of his position, the leading authority being the old case of *Keech v Sandford* (1726) Sel Cas Ch 61. The trustee took over the benefit of a lease which had been devised to the trust, when that lease expired. Presumably he would not have been in a position to do so, had he not been trustee. The lessor had refused to renew the lease for the trust, on the grounds that the beneficiary was an infant, against whom it would be difficult to recover rent. The trustee thereupon took the lease for his personal benefit, and profited from it.

There cannot have been any actual conflict of interest, because the trust itself could not have benefited, given the views of the lessor. Nor would King LC say that there was any fraud in the case, but the trustee had to assign the benefit of the lease to the infant, and account for profits received. The trustee was the one person in the world who could not take the lease for his own benefit, because by so doing he would be profiting from his position.

The general principle extends to any profits made by virtue of a fiduciary position, and if the profits are to be retained, the fiduciary must show that there is no causal connection between the position and the profit. Otherwise, any property or money acquired which can be regarded as being trust property will be held on constructive trust for the beneficiaries. Where a fiduciary has obtained incidental profits from his office, the remedy is an 'account' of profits. It is of no moment that the trust has suffered no loss; the remedy is not limited to being compensatory in nature (unlike, for example, contractual damages). It is necessary that the fiduciary accounts for all profits received in order to ensure that his duty and interest can never conflict.

Another example of the general principle is *Re Macadam* [1946] Ch 73, where trustees who used their position to appoint themselves to directorships of a company were held liable to account to the trust for all the fees they received as directors. The causal connection between position and profit must be established, however. It was not in *Re Dover Coalfield Extension Ltd* [1908] 1 Ch 65, a case similar to *Re Macadam*, but where a trustee had already become a director before becoming trustee. Similarly, in *Re Gee* [1948] Ch 284 a trustee would have been elected director anyway, by virtue of the votes of the other shareholders, however he himself had voted (he did not in fact use his trust vote, but would still have been elected even if he had voted against himself). Harman J held that the remuneration received as director was not accountable to the trust. In neither of these cases could it be said that the trustees had made any profit by virtue of their position.

Cases where profits are made from information acquired in a fiduciary position are really only a specific application of the general principles enunciated in the previous section. A case which gave rise to considerable controversy was *Boardman v Phipps* [1967] 2 AC 46. It shows how far the principle extends, even where not only does the trust not suffer, but actually benefits from the fiduciary's activities.

Boardman was solicitor to a trust, whose property included a large (but not majority) holding in a public company. He became worried about the competence of the management of the company, and tried to persuade the managing trustee of the trust to acquire a majority holding in the company. His attempts at persuasion were unsuccessful, so Boardman decided to make the acquisition himself. He did so and then, by selling off some of the assets of the newly acquired company, Boardman made a large profit for himself. Additionally, however, because the trust still had a large share in the same company, his activities resulted in a large profit for the trust as well. The fact that the trust benefited is one of the reasons for the controversy surrounding the case, but surely it is in fact irrelevant.

In most respects this was simply a personal transaction by Boardman, resulting in a personal profit to him. Unfortunately, however, it appeared that in negotiating for the majority shareholding he had, in good faith, obtained information in his capacity as solicitor to the trust, which he would not otherwise have obtained. The House of Lords therefore held (by a 3–2 majority) that he held the shares acquired as constructive trustee for the trust, and that he must account for the profit made. It was immaterial that he acted in good faith. He was, however, entitled to generous remuneration on a *quantum meruit* basis, on the principles discussed earlier in the section.

One view of the case, adopted by Lords Hodson and Guest, was that the information obtained was trust property, but this is not in fact a necessary step in the reasoning, at least so far as an account of profits remedy is concerned. The case is simply an extreme application of the principle that one must not profit from a fiduciary position. Once a causal relationship is established between information and profit the account of profits remedy follows as a matter of course.

Many commentators see Boardman as hard done by, but it should be noted that the result of the case was by no means entirely disastrous for him. He was liberally rewarded on a *quantum meruit* basis for benefiting the trust. What he could not do was to keep the speculative profits. The law allows private speculators to do so, but takes the view that those who are acting as fiduciaries accept by taking on fiduciary positions that their remuneration is limited to the categories described above, however much they benefit the other party. Though this view may appear harsh, it at least has the merit of ensuring that their discretion will be exercised in an independent manner.

Variation of Trusts Act 1958

The main conceptual areas likely to be covered in an exam are on whose behalf the court may approve a variation, and the question of what constitutes a benefit, especially where there is an element of risk. First, however, we shall consider what was the aim of the 1958 Act, and why it was thought to be desirable.

Policy behind the 1958 Act

The main reason for wishing to vary trusts today is usually to reduce liability to taxation. Equity does not generally, however, in the absence of an express power to vary the trust, allow the trustees to recast its terms. Until recent statutory reforms, therefore, and in particular the 1958 Act, powers to vary have been extremely limited, especially where tax planning is the motive.

There are nevertheless some possibilities apart from the 1958 Act. In the absence of an express power, it may be possible to invoke the rule in *Saunders* v *Vautier* (1841) 10 LJ Ch 354. Collectively, the beneficiaries, so long as they are all adult, *sui juris* and between them entitled to the entirety of the trust property, can bring the trust to an end and resettle the property on any terms they wish. They can also collectively consent to any act by the trustees which has the effect of varying the terms of the trust.

It is very important, however, to appreciate that the *Saunders* v *Vautier* doctrine depends on the beneficiaries all being collectively entitled, and able to consent. If some of the beneficiaries are infants, or if the settlement creates any interests in favour of persons who are not yet born or ascertained, variation of the trust upon this basis will not be possible. This is a serious limitation when dealing with family settlements of the usual type, which almost invariably give interests to such persons (termed non *sui juris* persons).

Even where not all the beneficiaries are adult and *sui juris* the courts will occasionally permit a variation of trust under their inherent jurisdiction. These circumstances are very limited, but it has long been recognised that the court may, in the case of necessity, permit the trustees to take measures not authorised by the trust instrument.

In *Chapman* v *Chapman* [1954] AC 429, the House of Lords indicated that this inherent jurisdiction is narrow, encompassing for the most part only emergency and salvage. It is confined to cases where some act of salvage is urgently required, such as the mortgage of an infant's property in order to raise money for vital repairs. It does not cover other contingencies not foreseen and provided for by the settlor, of which the most pertinent example would be changes in the basis of tax liability.

The court can also approve a compromise of some dispute regarding the beneficial entitlements on behalf of infant or future beneficiaries. Arguably, this is not a case of genuine variation of the trust, since the House of Lords in *Chapman* v *Chapman* held that the jurisdiction was confined to instances where a genuine element of dispute exists, i.e., where the terms of trust are genuinely unclear.

There are also statutory powers to vary trusts, apart from the 1958 Act, but these are limited to specified situations. The 1958 Act was important because it was the first provision of general application allowing variation of trusts for tax-avoidance purposes, even where not all the beneficiaries were adult and *sui juris*. The Act follows on the recommendations of the Law Reform Committee, Sixth Report (Court's Power to Sanction Variations of Trusts) (Cmnd 310). Whatever political views one holds about tax-avoidance schemes, it can at least be argued that infants and the unborn, for example, should not be deprived *for that reason* of the advantages which their adult counterparts could obtain on *Saunders* v *Vautier* principles; nor should their incapacity prevent the opportunity of gain to the trust as a whole.

The main application of the Variation of Trusts Act 1958 has been to vary the beneficial interests for tax-saving purposes, and this has been assumed to be its natural sphere of operation.

The operation of the Act (in general terms)

You ought to be aware of the general operation of the Variation of Trusts Act 1958, because essay questions will often address themselves to it.

Under s. 1(1) of the Act, the court has discretion to approve, on behalf of the following categories of person, any arrangement varying or revoking all or any of the trusts, or enlarging the trustees' powers of management and administration over the property subject to the trusts:

(a)   any person having, directly or indirectly, an interest, whether vested or contingent, under the trusts who by reason of infancy or other incapacity is incapable of assenting [i.e., infants or people mentally incapacitated], or

(b)   any person (whether ascertained or not) who may become entitled, directly or indirectly, to an interest under the trusts as being at a future date or on the happening of a future event a person of any specified description or a member of any specified class of persons, so however that this paragraph shall not include any person who would be of that description, or a member of that class, as the case may be, if the said date had fallen or the said event had happened at the date of the application to the court [in effect, the paragraph includes people who have a mere expectation of benefiting under the trusts, but those with interests, whether vested or contingent, should consent on their own behalf], or

(c)   any person unborn, or

(d)   any person in respect of any discretionary interest of his under protective trusts where the interest of the principal beneficiary has not failed or determined.

Proposals to vary the beneficial interests under a trust may thus be approved, provided (except in the case of para. (d) persons) that the court is satisfied that such variation will be for the benefit of those persons on behalf of whom approval is given.

In deciding whether to approve a proposed settlement, the court will consider the arrangement as a whole, since it is the arrangement which has to be approved, and not just those aspects of it which happen to affect a person on whose behalf the court is being asked to consent.

The application should be made by a beneficiary, preferably by the person currently receiving the income, but the settlor may also apply, and as a last resort the trustees may apply if no one else will apply and the variation is in the interests of the beneficiaries. Otherwise, it is undesirable for trustees to apply, as their position as applicant may conflict with their impartially duty to guard the interests of the beneficiaries. The settlor, if living, and all the beneficiaries, including minors, should be made parties, special attention being paid to ensure proper representation for minors and the unborn.

According to Megarry J in *Re Ball's Settlement* [1968] 1 WLR 899, the courts will not approve a proposal for a total resettlement which alters completely the substratum of the trust. This is a question of substance not form, and if Megarry J is correct the courts' jurisdiction does not therefore extend to the approval of such proposals at all.

Persons on whose behalf the court may give its approval

The way in which the Variation of Trusts Act 1958 works is to allow the court to give consent on behalf of non *sui juris* beneficiaries, but the principles underlying the rule in *Saunders* v *Vautier* were preserved by the Act, inasmuch as the court will not provide a consent which ought properly to be sought from an ascertainable adult, *sui juris* beneficiary. Hence the limits placed on s. 1(1)(b).

The difficulty with para. (b), which limits the discretion of the courts, arises with interests which are very remote, such as interests in default of appointment, or in the event of a failure of the trust. There is no problem over, for example, potential future spouses, since they clearly have a mere expectation of succeeding. They clearly come within para. (b), and the court can consent on their behalf. But if somebody is named in the instrument as having a contingent interest, however unlikely that contingency is to arise, the court cannot consent on their behalf. They must consent themselves to any variation.

This can seriously limit the scope of the 1958 Act, and *a fortiori* the discretion of the courts. For example, in *Re Suffert's Settlement* [1976] Ch 1, the court could not consent on behalf of a cousin who benefited only if Miss Suffert died without issue, and even then subject to a general testamentary power of appointment. Other examples are *Re Moncrieff's ST* [1962] 1 WLR 134, and *Knocker* v *Youle* [1986] 1 WLR 934. In the latter case the court could not consent on behalf of sisters who would benefit only in the event of failure or determination of the trust, and Warner J felt constrained to adopt a fairly literal interpretation of the Act.

What is benefit?

It is not possible to state categorically what the court will regard as benefit, except that it will adopt the test of what a reasonable *sui juris* adult beneficiary would have done in the circumstances.

Financial benefit is clearly included, and most tax-saving schemes will satisfy the requirement, since such saving preserves the total quantum of property available for distribution among the beneficiaries.

In assessing financial benefit, the court may have to balance short-term against long-term factors, and to take account of the character on whose behalf approval is sought. In *Re Towler's ST* [1964] Ch 158, Wilberforce J was prepared to postpone the vesting of capital to which a beneficiary was soon to become entitled, upon evidence that she was likely to deal with it imprudently. In *Re Steed's WT* [1960] Ch 407, the proposed scheme was for the elimination of the protective element in a trust relating to land. The principal beneficiary, who was a life tenant (but not *sui juris* because of the protective element), wanted a variation such that the trustees held the property on trust for herself absolutely. Clearly this was in theory to her financial advantage, but evidence suggested that advantage would in fact be taken of the life tenant's good nature by the very persons against whose importuning the settlor had meant to protect her, and the Court of Appeal refused its consent.

It may be wondered why the court needed to be satisfied of a benefit in this case, since as noted above, there is no express statutory requirement of benefit for para. (d) persons. It is here that it should be remembered, however, that once it is clear that the court has jurisdiction, it has an unfettered discretion to exercise its powers under the Act '*if it thinks fit*'. In *Re Steed* the Court of Appeal (commenting that the Variation of Trusts Act 1958 conferred upon the courts a 'very wide, and indeed, revolutionary discretion') refused its consent even in a para. (d) case, where it thought no benefit was shown. In effect, whereas the court obviously cannot approve a variation except where the Act so provides, it has an apparently unlimited discretion to *refuse* its approval where it is given jurisdiction under the Act.

Though it will be rare for the court to look beyond the financial advantages contained in the proposed arrangement, the unfettered discretion given by the Act to the courts can lead them to refuse a variation where there is a clear financial benefit. In *Re Weston's Settlements* [1969] 1 Ch 223, the

Court of Appeal refused to approve a scheme which would have removed the trusts to a tax haven (Jersey), where the family had moved three months previously, on the ground that the moral and social benefits of an English upbringing were not outweighed by the tax savings to be enjoyed by the infant beneficiaries. Harman LJ said that 'this is an essay in tax avoidance naked and unashamed', and Lord Denning MR noted (at p. 223) that:

> There are many things in life more worthwhile than money. One of these things is to be brought up in this our England, which is still 'the envy of less happier lands'. I do not believe it is for the benefit of children to be uprooted from England and transported to another country simply to avoid tax . . . Many a child has been ruined by being given too much. The avoidance of tax may be lawful but it is not yet a virtue.

Re Weston is perhaps atypical, and the court will not always refuse approval to the removal of a trust from the jurisdiction. It will depend on the circumstances. In *Re Windeatt's WT* [1969] 1 WLR 692, a similar scheme was approved by Pennycuick J, but there the family had already been in Jersey for 19 years and the children had been born there: there was no question of uprooting them. Similarly, in *Re Seale's Marriage Settlement* [1961] Ch 574, Buckley J approved a scheme removing the trusts to Canada, to which country again the family had moved many years previously, with no thought of tax avoidance, and had brought up the children as Canadians.

In reality, the use of the 1958 Act to export trusts is quite common, but *Re Weston* shows that all circumstances will be taken into account, and that the existence of a clear financial benefit will not necessarily be conclusive.

Another possibility, included for the sake of completeness, is that some beneficiaries will benefit at the expense of others. An example is *Re Remnant's ST* [1970] Ch 560, where Pennycuick J approved the deletion of a forfeiture clause in respect of children who became Roman Catholics. Some of the children were Protestant and others Roman Catholic, but the court deleted the clause on policy grounds, as being liable to cause serious dissension within the family, although this was clearly to the disadvantage of the Protestant children. The settlor's intentions were also not considered conclusive (indeed, they were overridden).

The courts may go further and approve schemes where there is only a positive disadvantage in material terms. In *Re CL* [1969] 1 Ch 587, the Court of Protection held that there was a benefit to an elderly mental patient in giving up, in return for no consideration, her life interests for the benefit of adopted daughters. The lady's needs were otherwise amply provided for, and the court, in approving the arrangement, was acting as she herself would have done, had she been able to appreciate her family responsibilities.

There are two likely areas upon which examiners might concentrate. One is where no clear financial benefit can be shown, or, if it can, the benefit is postponed into the far future. The second is where, although there might be a clear benefit, there is no certainty of any benefit at all, and indeed a risk of loss.

Non-financial benefits, and risks

The following question appeared on a recent exam paper:

> The trustees of a testamentary trust, whose investment clause is no wider than the provisions of the Trustee Investment Act 1961, seek a variation under the Variation of Trusts Act 1958. The testator, who died in 1965, was a well-known environmentalist, and the beneficiaries include infants and people who are mentally incapacitated. The variation sought is to allow the trustees to invest a large proportion of the trust capital in Ecological Enterprises Ltd, and Dam for the Future Ltd. Neither investment comes within the terms of the Trustee Investment Act 1961.
>
> In purely financial terms, Ecological Enterprises Ltd do not offer a more attractive rate of return, nor any greater security, than the present investments (authorised by the 1961 Act). The trustees wish to invest in Ecological Enterprises Ltd primarily on ideological (i.e., green) grounds, but would take the view that the investment would make the beneficiaries feel better, and would be in line with the testator's wishes.
>
> Dam for the Future Ltd plan to build a dam across the Bristol Channel to produce wave-powered electricity. They offer an unusually high rate of return, but because of the nature of the project the return is expected only in the very long term (say 30 years). In the short term the investment is expected to perform very badly. While it is likely that most of the infant beneficiaries will survive long enough to see a substantial return, the same cannot be said of those beneficiaries who are mentally incapacitated.
>
> Discuss.

The first point to notice about this question is that the variation sought will extend the trustees' powers of investment beyond those provided by the Trustee Investment Act 1961. Since the 1961 Act was a later provision than the Variation of Trusts Act, it might be thought that its provisions were intended to be conclusive on questions of investment, and that variations would not be permitted under the 1958 Act, to extend the trustees' powers of investment beyond those provided by the 1961 Act.

In *Trustees of the British Museum* v *Attorney-General* [1984] 1 WLR 418, however, Sir Robert Megarry V-C took the view that the powers conferred by the Trustee Investments Act 1961 were becoming outdated, and that the effects of inflation and the character of the trust may amount to special circumstances in which it would be proper to give approval under the 1958 Act. The arguments in that case were all of an economic nature, however, essentially that the trustees could make more money if their investment powers were extended. The decision was based on the changes of investment pattern, including the movement from fixed interest investments to investments in equities and property, that had occurred between 1961 and 1983. In the case, at least, of Ecological Enterprises Ltd, no similar arguments can be advanced here, and it is at least arguable that the principles in *Trustees of the British Museum* do not apply to that type of investment.

So far as Dam for the Future is concerned, arguments of a financial nature could be advanced. Even so, it does not follow that the principles in *Trustees of the British Museum* will necessarily, since Sir Robert Megarrry V-C's judgment is in quite restricted terms. At the time of the case, investing in equities was relatively risk-free, and there had been a more or less continuous bull market for some eight years. That is not the case today. Sir Robert Megarry V-C also said:

> The size of the fund may be very material. A fund that is very large may well justify a latitude of investment that would be denied to a more modest fund; for the spread of investment possible for a larger fund may justify the greater risks that wider powers will permit to be taken.

It is by no means clear, therefore, that a variation beyond the terms of the 1961 Act will necessarily apply here.

This problem also shows the advantage of reading the case fairly closely. Many textbooks do not analyse *Trustees of the British Museum* in much detail, and it would be very easy to fall into the trap of assuming that it covers the present situation, whereas the close reading of the judgment makes the limitations of the case clear.

The other issues in the problem have to some extent already been covered. So far as Ecological Enterprises Ltd is concerned, the variation offers no financial advantage, but may offer moral benefits. Obviously, you are invited to consider *Re Weston's Settlements* [1969] 1 Ch 223, discussed above, which was actually the reverse situation: there was a financial advantage, but a moral disadvantage. You might also mention *Re CL* [1969] 1 Ch 587, above, where in a different context financial benefits were not regarded as conclusive.

So far as Dam for the future is concerned, there may well be a financial benefit, but it is very risky. Sometimes, a proposed arrangement may involve some element of risk to the beneficiary for whom the court is asked to consent. An element of risk will not prevent the court from approving the arrangement, if the risk is one which an adult beneficiary would be prepared to take. Such a test was applied by Dankwerts J in *Re Cohen's WT* [1959] 1 WLR 865.

In *Re Robinson's ST* [1976] 1 WLR 806, the fund was held on trust for the plaintiff for her life, with remainders over to her children, one of whom was under 21 (the age of majority at the time). The plaintiff was 55 and expected to live for many years. The variation proposed was to divide up the fund, giving the plaintiff an immediate capital share of 52% (the actuarial capitalised value of her share), the children dividing the balance in equal shares. The children who got their share immediately, and those who were over 21 consented to the variation. The court was asked to approve variation on behalf of Nicola (who was 17).

Before the introduction of Capital Transfer Tax in 1975, division of the fund in this way, by giving the children their interests immediately rather than on the death of the life tenant, was almost certain to reduce liability to estate duty, because at that time there was no liability to estate duty on any advance made more than seven years before the death of the life tenant. The same is true today under inheritance tax. However, for a short period following the Finance Act 1975, which introduced Capital Transfer Tax, all *inter vivos* gifts were also taxable, albeit that liability was lower so long as the transfer was made more than three years before the death of the life tenant.

At the time of *Re Robinson's ST*, therefore, the division would not necessarily have favoured Nicola. The transfer would have been taxed immediately, so that the value of the fund would be reduced. On the other hand, Nicola would get her share immediately, and not have to wait for the death of her mother. Whether this would be to her benefit or not would depend entirely on how long her mother was likely to live. If she died immediately, Nicola's share would be less than she would have received under the unvaried trust, since tax would have been paid on it. It was calculated, however, that, given the mother's life expectancy, the deficiency would be made up in income on her share between the date of the variation and her mother's death.

Templeman J took the view that the court should require evidence that the infant would at least not be materially worse off as a result of the variation. He adopted as the test whether an adult benficiary would have been prepared to take the risk: a 'broad' view might be taken, but not a 'galloping, gambling view'. The arrangement was approved subject to a policy of insurance to protect the infant's interests.

A different type of case was *Re Holt's Settlement* [1969] 1 Ch 100. The trust provided for a life interest of personal property for Mrs Wilson, and then to her children at 21 in equal shares. The variation proposed was that Mrs Wilson should surrender the income of one-half of her life interest to the fund, but another effect of the proposed variation was to postpone the vesting of the children's interests until 30. The court was asked to approve the variation on behalf of Mrs Wilson's three children who were 10, 7, and 6.

The surrender of the income (the real purpose of which was to reduce Mrs Wilson's liability to surtax) was also clearly to the advantage of the children, since the value of the trust property would be increased. However, the postponement to 30 (on the grounds that it would be undesirable for Mrs Wilson's children to receive a large income from 21) was clearly to their disadvantage. Megarry J nevertheless approved the variation as a whole, on the same test adopted in *Re Robinson*.

Benefit must be to individuals, not just class as a whole

Another difficulty with the Dam for the Future Ltd investment in the problem question is that some of the beneficiaries who are mentally incapacitated would seem to stand only to lose from the investment, since they would not be expected to live long enough to benefit from the long-term return, and would only suffer from the likely poor short-term performance of the investment.

The 1958 Act requires, in general, that the court must be satisfied the the arrangement will be for the benefit of the persons for whom it is consenting. Stamp J took the view in *Re Cohen's ST* [1965] 1 WLR 1229 that the benefit must be to those persons considered as individuals, and not merely as members of a class. It follows that if only one member of the class can be envisaged who cannot possibly benefit from the proposed variation, even if the class as a whole will benefit, the court will refuse its consent. This was in fact the outcome in *Re Cohen's ST*, and would probably be fatal to the second investment in this problem.

Re Cohen's ST is a very interesting case in its own right, and the following recent exam question is based around it:

Under a settlement made in 1940, a large fund was left to Alison for her life, and then to her grandchildren living on her death. Alison was born in 1915, and has a number of grandchildren, some of whom are very young. Consider whether the court will approve the following ALTERNATIVE variations under the Variation of Trusts Act 1958.

ANSWER BOTH PARTS:

(i) Under the Capital Acceleration Act 1992, a heavy tax is imposed on all capital transfers made after 31 July 2005. A variation is sought substituting for Alison's death 31 July 2005 (or Alison's death, whichever is the earlier), as the date both for ascertaining the grandchildren to take, and for distribution of the fund.

AND

(ii) Under the Capital Stultification Act 1992, a heavy tax is imposed on all capital transfers made before 1 July 2005. A variation is sought postponing distribution of the fund until 1 August 2005 (or Alison's death, whichever is the later), the class being ascertained on Alison's death.

In both parts of the problem the proposed variation appears to offer a clear financial benefit (avoidance of a heavy tax). The problem in part (i) is this, however. Suppose Alison is still alive on 31 July 2005, and a grandchild is born after 31 July 2005, but before Alison's death. The chances of this happening must be fairly low, since by 2005 Alison will be 90 years old, and it may well be thought that the class of unborn grandchildren, as a whole, might be prepared to take the risk of Alison living that long, and having further grandchildren before she dies. Weighed against the substantial tax advantages of the proposed variation should Alison live to be 90, any reasonable unborn grandchild may well be prepared to take the risk.

The problem is that it is not permissible only to consider the position of the class as a whole. If an individual grandchild was born after 31 July 2005, but before Alison's death, then under the proposed variation, he or she would lose his or her entire interest. That individual would clearly not consent, since he or she would have no conceivable benefit, and that will be fatal to the proposed variation: indeed, *Cohen* itself was just such a case as this, and Stamp J refused his consent. It was not enough that the proposed variation would benefit the class as a whole, if it were possible to envisage a single individual who could not possibly benefit.

So far as the infants are concerned, the position is different (as it was in *Cohen* itself). They all stand to gain from the tax advantages of the proposed variation. They can only lose under the variation if grandchildren are born after 31 July 2005, but before Alison's death, since then their share of the fund will be reduced. Even then, a large number of grandchildren would probably have to be born at that time, in order to reduce their interest more than the imposition of the heavy tax on the unvaried trust.

The equation is the same for all of them, and each as reasonable individuals would probably consent.

The variation will fail overall, however, because of the possibility, admittedly remote, that there will be persons unborn who would stand only to lose from the variation.

It might be thought that the second part of the question is essentially similar, but it is not. The crucial difference here is that the class is ascertained on Alison's death, even though the date of distribution is postponed should Alison die before 2005. Even if Alison dies in 1993, the class of beneficiaries who will take will be the same, whether the trust is varied or not. It might be thought that a beneficiary who dies in that event, between 1993 and 2005, must lose out, but in fact he or she still keeps the interest, and it will be added to his or her estate. The only evaluation that each beneficiary has to make in such a case is whether the delay outweighs the tax advantages. That is to be decided simply on the principles of *Re Robinson's ST*, above.

It follows that the reasoning in *Cohen* applies only when the date of *vesting in interest* (or in other words the date on closing the class) is altered, and does not apply merely to alterations in *vesting in possession*.

In *Re Holt's Settlement* [1969] 1 Ch 100 (see above), the settlement was in essence that Mrs Wilson gave up part of her income from the fund (so increasing the size of the fund), but vesting of the children's interest in possession would be postponed. If a child was born the year after the variation, and his mother died very soon afterwards, that child could not possibly benefit. The benefit from Mrs Wilson surrendering part of her income under the trust would be minimal if Mrs Wilson died soon after the birth, whereas the postponement would operate entirely to his or her disadvantage. *Cohen* was distinguished, however, because here two chances had to occur: that of the unborn person being born next year, and secondly, that child having been born (and thus become a legal entity), his or her mother dying shortly afterwards. The first chance could be disregarded on *Cohen* principles, but not the second. Both were independently unlikely possibilities, so approval for the scheme was given. Even once the theoretical unborn child had been born, he or she would still have been well advised to agree to the variation, and accept the slight risk of his or her mother dying shortly afterwards.

TEN

STRANGERS TO THE TRUST AS CONSTRUCTIVE TRUSTEES

This chapter considers the liability, not of the trustees themselves, but of strangers who may nevertheless have some connection with the trust, or with the trust property.

There are two distinct situations. If the property still exists, or if it is traceable, the beneficiary may have a proprietary remedy against whoever has the property, whether or not that person is one of the original trustees. Space considerations do not permit detailed examination of tracing at common law, or tracing in equity, but it is important to appreciate that for either of those doctrines to operate it is necessary for the trust property still to be identifiable. It need not be *physically* identifiable, at any rate for the doctrine to operate in equity, so that if, for example, the trust property has been sold, it may still be possible to trace the *proceeds* of sale. There are also rules in equity for the tracing of trust money which has become mixed with other money.

The second possibility is that the property no longer exists in any identifiable form. Trust money may have been spent, for example, with nothing identifiable to show for it. If the trust property no longer exists, and is not traceable, there is still the possibility that a stranger could be liable as a constructive trustee.

There are a number of recent cases on this type of constructive trusteeship, and this chapter is devoted entirely to it. The cases are nearly all of a commercial nature, and another reason for including them is as an illustration of how trusts can operate in a commercial context: trusts are not just about family settlements and ownership of the matrimonial home!

Knowing receipt and knowing assistance

It is possible for a stranger to become liable as constructive trustee if he either assists a trustee (or other fiduciary) in breach of trust (or other fiduciary duty), regarding property under his control, or receives trust property with knowledge of breach of trust (or other fiduciary duty). The first type of case is categorised as 'knowing assistance', the second as 'knowing receipt'.

In spite of a number of recent decisions on 'knowing assistance' and 'knowing receipt', the law is by no means clear. Areas upon which there have been recent decisions, and where the law is unclear, are of course prime candidates for examination essay and problem questions.

Essay question

Essay questions will typically address the degree of knowledge required for imposition of a constructive trust on grounds of knowing receipt or knowing assistance. A possible question might be:

In *Baden, Delvaux and Lecuit* v *Société General pour Favoriser le Développement du Commerce et de l'Industrie en France SA* [1983] BCLC 325, Peter Gibson J suggested five possible categories of knowledge sufficient to found constructive trusteeship:

  (i)   actual knowledge;
  (ii) wilfully shutting one's eye to the obvious;
  (iii) wilfully and recklessly failing to make such inquiries as an honest and reasonable man would make;
  (iv) knowledge of circumstances which would indicate the facts to an honest and reasonable man; and
  (v)   knowledge of circumstances which would put an honest and reasonable man on inquiry.

To what extent, if at all, are any or all of these categories necessary to found liability for knowing assistance and knowing receipt?

This question invites you to discuss a categorisation which has been the starting point, upon which the later cases have nearly always been based. It is clear that categories (ii) to (v) all represent varieties of constructive notice. Only categories (i) to (iii) would normally suggest dishonesty, however, requiring either intention or something akin to criminal law recklessness. The test in categories (iv) and (v) is objective (i.e., akin to negligence), as opposed to the subjective test in (i) to (iii). Nevertheless, it is possible for someone to be dishonest even within (iv) and (v).

   Although the authorities are less than entirely clear, it now seems that liability for both knowing receipt and knowing assistance can be founded on the basis of any of the five categories. In the case of knowing assistance, however, there is an additional requirement for dishonesty (or lack of probity). This will usually be present in the case of the first three categories, but would not inevitably be present in categories (iv) and (v). In the two central cases of *Belmont Finance Corporation* v *Williams Furniture Ltd*

((No. 1) [1979] Ch 250, and (No. 2) [1980] 1 All ER 393), the Court of
Appeal was able, on the same facts, to consider both knowing assistance
and knowing receipt principles, so that a direct comparison can be drawn.

Facts of Belmont cases

The facts of these two cases are exceptionally complicated, but I have
attempted to simplify then for the purposes of the following discussion.

The litigation arose, in essence, from an arrangement to finance and
acquire a company (Belmont Finance Corporation). Williams Furniture
owned all the shares in City Industrial Finance Co., which in turn owned
all the shares in Belmont. All three companies had the same secretary (Mr
Foley). Belmont and City shared the same chairman (Mr James, who during
the negotiations also became chairman of Williams), and most of the same
directors.

Williams wanted to sell Belmont, because the company was making
insufficient profit. Grosscurth and two other individuals, who between them
owned all the shares in another (entirely independent) company, Maximum
Finance Ltd, wished to acquire Belmont, but needed finance. Grosscurth
therefore proposed to finance the deal by selling Maximum to Belmont.

The acquisition of Belmont by Grosscurth was made under a single
agreement, whereby Belmont agreed to purchase all the shares of Maximum
from Grosscurth and his fellow shareholders, at a price of £500,000. Under
the same agreement Grosscurth, having thus received £500,000 for his
Maximum shares, agreed to purchase all Belmont's shares from City (which
owned all the shares in Belmont, remember) for £489,000, retaining for
himself £11,000 of the £500,000.

Of course, because Maximum was, as a result of the agreement, now
a wholly-owned subsidiary of Belmont, Grosscurth in purchasing Belmont
from City was able to retain his interest in Maximum as well. Thus, the
end result of the acquisition agreement was simply that Grosscurth had
acquired Belmont. He still had Maximum, since that was now a Belmont
subsidiary. He was also £11,000 richer as a result of this transaction, than
he had been at the start.

Clearly this apparently extraordinary state of affairs requires explanation,
but the position becomes clearer when considered in the light of the finance
arrangement. Some form of finance was clearly necessary, since Belmont
had to find the £500,000 required for its purchase of Maximum.

The finance was achieved in three ways. First, under the same agreement,
City agreed to subscribe for 230,000 redeemable £1 Belmont preference
shares. This was effectively a way of making a secured loan to Belmont,
the money being repayable on the redemption of the shares. City therefore

presented a cheque to Belmont for £230,000. Obviously there was no difficulty in their doing this, since under the acquisition arrangement they had obtained £489,000 from Grosscurth. It was also agreed that Grosscurth would purchase the redeemable preference shares over a (lengthy) period, so that the redeemable preference shares (in effect) provided security for a cash advance from City to Grosscurth.

Secondly, Grosscurth agreed to subscribe for 70,000 £1 Belmont shares, presumably out of his own money. Thirdly, City and Williams agreed to lend Belmont £200,000 for 12 months on the security of Maximum, various undertakings being given by Grosscurth about Maximum's profitability. There was no particular problem finding this amount, since City were still ahead by £259,000, £489,000 having been received from Grosscurth, and only £230,000 having been used on the redeemable preference shares.

The net effect of the various aspects of what was a single agreement was that Belmont had secured the £500,000 necessary for the acquisition of Maximum (£230,000 by subscription from City, £70,000 by subscription from Grosscurth, £200,000 by loan from City and Williams). Grosscurth had obtained Belmont for £489,000, but he had only had to provide immediately £70,000 by subscription, and since Belmont had paid £500,000 for Maximum, he had made £11,000 on the cash transactions. Thus his immediate outlay was £59,000, the remaining £430,000 to be paid as follows: £200,000 to be paid by Belmont to City under the 12-month loan agreement, and £230,000 to be paid by Grosscurth in the long term by repurchasing the redeemable preference shares.

There was nothing wrong with this transaction in principle, except for the fact that no independent valuation of Maximum was obtained. Although the directors of Belmont and City thought that Maximum was worth £500,000, and indeed Belmont paid £500,000 for Maximum, in reality the company was worth only around £60,000. This had two legal consequences. First, because the purchase of Maximum was at a greatly inflated price, and not in Belmont's best commercial interests, the transaction was held unlawful under what was then the Companies Act 1948, s. 54. Secondly, and more importantly for the purposes of the present discussion, the transaction involved a breach of fiduciary duty by Belmont's directors.

Belmont, having in consequence lost a great deal of money on the deal, went into liquidation, and they embarked upon litigation against City and Williams. Two causes of action were alleged: first, that they were liable in common law (tortious) conspiracy, and secondly that they were liable as constructive trustees.

We are only directly interested in the trusts aspects of this litigation, of course, but the common-law liability is not entirely irrelevant, since it probably renders the discussion of the trusts issues in these cases technically *obiter*.

First Belmont case

The first case ([1979] Ch 250) was heard on the pleadings only, the full hearing being on the second case ([1980] 1 All ER 393). In the first hearing, the Court of Appeal held that on the pleadings, Belmont could pursue the claim against City and Williams for conspiracy, since James's knowledge could be imputed to City and Williams, and therefore Williams and City were aware of the facts. Given this decision, statements made on the constructive trust issue were technically *obiter dicta*. At this stage the case was pleaded as a knowing assistance case (in relation to the payment of the £500,000). It is also important to note that on the pleadings, fraud or dishonesty on the part of the directors of Belmont (and hence also the defendants) could not be established.

The Court of Appeal took the view that City and its directors were not liable (on the pleadings) for knowingly assisting in a fraudulent design. In particular, the court felt that constructive knowledge was not a sufficient basis for liability under that heading, Buckley LJ commenting (at p. 267):

> The knowledge of that design on the part of the parties sought to be made liable may be actual knowledge. If he wilfully shuts his eyes to dishonesty, or wilfully or recklessly fails to make such inquiries as an honest and reasonable man would make, he may be found to have involved himself in the fraudulent character of the design, or at any rate to be disentitled to rely on lack of actual knowledge of the design as a defence. But otherwise, as it seems to me, he should not be affected by constructive notice.

The views of Goff LJ were similar (at p. 275):

> Whilst wilfully shutting one's eyes to the obvious, or wilfully refraining from inquiry because it may be embarrassing is, I have no doubt, sufficient to make a person who participates in a fraudulent breach of trust without actually receiving the trust moneys, or moneys representing the same, liable as a constructive trustee, there remains the question whether constructive notice . . . will suffice.

He went on to say that in his opinion, it would not. The case clearly suggests, therefore, that at any rate in a knowing assistance case, constructive knowledge without dishonesty will not suffice.

Second Belmont case

The case then came back to the Court of Appeal on the second hearing, and the conspiracy claim was heard in full, where it succeeded. More important for present purposes is the constructive trust claim. The pleadings were amended, the receiver now suing City and its directors to recover the money *received* on its sale of Belmont shares. This could relate only to the £489,000 received by them, not the full £500,000 paid to Maximum. In other words, the second case was pleaded as knowing receipt, whereas the first had been pleaded (in respect of a slightly larger sum) as knowing assistance. The first case having failed, in the second the Court of Appeal held City *liable* as constructive trustees. Since the facts of the two cases, and the knowledge of the defendants, were (to all intents and purposes) identical, the case strongly suggests that the knowledge requirements for knowing assistance and knowing receipt are not the same.

The reasoning in the second case was that payment of the £500,000 for Maximum amounted to a breach of fiduciary duty by the directors of Belmont, because it was not in Belmont's commercial interests. Of that £500,000, £489,000 found its way into the hands of City. Since the knowledge of their directors could be imputed to City, City received the money knowing all the circumstances of the transaction (including the breach of trust by Belmont's directors). As in the first case, however, dishonesty could not be shown on the pleadings. Buckley LJ (quoting *Barnes* v *Addy* (1874) 9 Ch App 244) said (at p. 405b):

> If a stranger to a trust (a) receives and becomes chargeable with some part of the trust fund or (b) assists the trustees of a trust with knowledge of the facts in a dishonest design on the part of the trustees to misapply some part of a trust fund, he is liable as a constructive trustee.

Whereas dishonesty appears to be a requirement under part (b), there is nothing in this quote suggesting a need to show fraud or dishonesty under part (a). Indeed, no fraud or dishonesty was shown in *Belmont*. It appears, then, that whereas in the case of knowing assistance knowledge under one of the first three *Baden* heads is normally required, heads (iv) and (v) suffice for knowing receipt.

Cases subsequent to *Belmont* have cast little doubt on the requirements for knowing assistance, and although some doubt has been cast on the knowing receipt position, I would suggest that the weight of authority supports the conclusion drawn in the last paragraph.

Later knowing assistance cases

Belmont (No. 1) was followed by the Court of Appeal in *Lipkin Gorman v Karpnale Ltd* [1989] 1 WLR 1340. Cass, who was a partner in the plaintiff firm of solicitors, drew on the solicitors' client account at Lloyd's Bank, and gambled with the money at the Playboy Club (which later became Karpnale Ltd). Nearly £250,000 was lost. Lipkin Gorman sued the club for knowing receipt and the bank for knowing assistance.

Only the claim against the bank is of relevance to the present discussion. As in *Belmont (No.1)*, it was not open on the pleadings to claim dishonesty or lack of probity against the manager, so the case had to proceed on the basis that the bank should not have honoured the cheques drawn upon it. Claims based both on contract and on constructive trusteeship failed. The contractual claim failed because the cheques were drawn within the bank's mandate, signed by a person whose signature it was authorised and required to honour (Cass). The bank could only become liable if negligence were shown, and no negligence was proved.

So far as the knowing assistance claim was concerned, it was clear at any rate that there could not be any circumstances where an equitable claim would succeed where the contractual claim would not. Parker LJ said (at p. 1373D):

It is in my view clear that the bank could not have rendered itself liable as constructive trustee unless it was also liable for breach of contract and that if it was not liable for breach of contract it could not be liable as a constructive trustee. This is because, stated in broad terms, the bank's duty to pay cheques signed in accordance with its mandate is subject to the qualification that it must be performed without negligence and that (i) negligence may exist where there is no question of the circumstances giving rise to a finding of constructive trusteeship; (ii) if there is no negligence I cannot envisage, at least in this case, any facts which would found liability of the ground of constructive trusteeship.

It is not, however, clear from Parker LJ's judgement (with which on this issue Nicholls LJ agreed) exactly what are the requirements for a knowing assistance claim, since elsewhere (e.g., at p. 1378A) he seemed almost to equate the requirements for breach of contract with those for breach of trust. The later passage is not especially clear, however, and the passage quoted above suggests that more than mere negligence may be required to found constructive trusteeship (although the exact requirements are not laid down). May LJ's view was much clearer. After approving statements from *Belmont (No. 1)*, he continued (at p. 1355D):

In my opinion, therefore, there is at least strong persuasive authority for the proposition that nothing less than knowledge, as defined in one of the first three categories stated by Peter Gibson J in *Baden, Delvaux and Lecuit v Société General pour Favoriser le Développement du Commerce et de l'Industrie en France SA* [1983] BCLC 325, of an underlying dishonest design is sufficient to make a stranger a constructive trustee of the consequences of that design.

A different position again was taken by Fox LJ in *Agip (Africa) Ltd v Jackson, Financial Times*, 18 January 1991. He appeared to accept that dishonesty was a requirement for knowing assistance, but that subject to this requirement, any of the five *Baden* heads of knowledge would suffice. A similar view had been taken by Millett J in *Agip (Africa) Ltd v Jackson* [1989] 3 WLR 1367. Of knowing assistance he said (at p. 1389):

> It is not necessary that the party sought to be made liable as a constructive trustee should have received any part of the trust property, but the breach of trust must have been fraudulent. The basis of the stranger's liability is not receipt of trust property but participation in a fraud . . .
>
> In *Belmont Finance Corporation v Williams Furniture Ltd* [1979] Ch 250, the Court of Appeal insisted that to hold a stranger liable for 'knowing assistance' the breach of trust in question must be a fraudulent and dishonest one. In my judgment it necessarily follows that constructive notice of the fraud is not enough to make him liable. There is no sense in requiring dishonesty on the part of the principal while accepting negligence as sufficient for his assistant. Dishonest furtherance of the dishonest scheme of another is an understandable basis for liability; negligent but honest failure to appreciate that someone else's scheme is dishonest is not.

He nevertheless suggested caution regarding the five *Baden* categories set out above, continuing:

> I gratefully adopt the [*Baden*] classification but would warn against over refinement or a too ready assumption that categories (iv) or (v) are necessarily cases of constructive notice only. The true distinction is between honesty and dishonesty. It is essentially a jury question.

Although, because of the ambiguity of Parker LJ's judgment in *Lipkin Gorman*, the issue has not been conclusively decided, the balance of authority nevertheless suggests that whatever the requirements for knowing receipt, dishonesty or 'lack of probity' (a term used by May LJ in *Lipkin Gorman*, which requires more than mere negligence) is required to found a constructive trusteeship claim based on knowing assistance.

Later knowing receipt cases

Belmont (No.2) clearly suggests that dishonesty is not required, however, for a knowing receipt claim. It is usually assumed that something akin to constructive notice in land law is sufficient, but doubt was cast on this by *dicta* in *Re Montagu's ST* [1987] Ch 264, where Megarry V-C thought that while constructive notice might be appropriate for a *tracing* claim, where the actual money or property can still be identified, something more should be required before *constructive trusteeship* is imposed. He seemed inclined to the view that even for a knowing receipt claim only the first three heads of *Baden* knowledge would suffice. In *Agip (Africa)* Millett J expressed 'no opinion' on whether this was correct, but I would suggest that *Montagu* should be treated with caution for the following reasons:

(1)   Megarry V-C's view was unnecessary to the actual decision in the case, since he did not think that the Duke had the requisite knowledge under any of the five *Baden* heads. At p. 286B he said that:

> even if, contrary to my opinion, all of the five *Baden* types of knowledge are in point, instead of only the first three, I do not think that he had any such knowledge.

(2)   The distinction between constructive notice and the requisite knowledge for knowing receipt has been convincingly criticised as being wrong in principle, for example, by Harpum (1987) 50 MLR 217.

(3)   It is difficult to reconcile Megarry V-C's view with *Belmont (No. 2)*.

(4)   If, as Fox LJ thought in *Agip Africa*, all five *Baden* heads can (where appropriate) suffice for knowing assistance, it would be odd to require a *higher* standard of knowledge for knowing receipt.

It seems not unreasonable to conclude, therefore, that no element of dishonesty is required to found liability for knowing receipt, whatever is the position for knowing assistance.

Problem question

The following question appeared on a recent exam paper:

Bloggs wishes to buy a racehorse, 'Fillie', but does not wish to negotiate personally, since he is well-known in racing circles, and is worried that if he expresses an interest the price will rise. He therefore gives £20,000 to his friend, Cloggs, to be used for the express purpose of buying 'Fillie' from its owner, Foggs, any surplus remaining after the transaction has been completed to be returned to him.

Cloggs is an ardent motor-racing enthusiast, and is worried that if he keeps the £20,000 himself he will be tempted to blow it on tuning and other equipment for his 'Group A' Sierra Cosworth. At the next club meeting at Castle Combe (motor-racing) circuit, therefore, he asks Soggs, a long-standing business acquaintance (and fellow motor-racing enthusiast), to keep the money for him. He tells Soggs what the money is for, but in the noise of the paddock area Soggs misunderstands him, thinking instead that it is to be given to Phyllis, Bloggs' 20-year-old stepdaughter (had Soggs given any thought to the matter he would have realised the absurdity of this, since it is well-known that Bloggs hates his stepdaughter).

Soggs, in the belief that he is carrying out Cloggs's instructions, gives the money to Phyllis, who is surprised to receive it, given her relationship with her stepfather, but makes no further inquiries. She spends all the money, and her only assets are £5,000 which she wins on the premium bonds, subsequently to spending the £20,000 'gift'.

In the meantime 'Fillie' unexpectedly dies (this happens after Soggs receives the money from Cloggs, but before he gives it to Phyllis). Cloggs's Sierra Cosworth, his only asset, is totally destroyed in an accident. Soggs has substantial assets.

Advise Bloggs.

This question is deliberately phrased in such a way that the original property (the £20,000) is no longer in existence, or traceable (having been spent), and that there is no point in suing Cloggs, the original trustee (if there is a trust at all), since he has no assets. If Bloggs is to succeed, therefore, he must sue someone else, such as Soggs or Phyllis, and can only do this if they are liable as constructive trustees.

It might be possible to make out an argument that Soggs is a knowing assister, but Phyllis can clearly be liable only on the basis of knowing receipt. Her position is clearly intended to be comparable to that in *Montagu* (above), and the problem therefore invites detailed discussion of that case, and of the criticisms of it.

If Soggs is a knowing receiver, he could well be negligent in not taking appropriate steps to ascertain the true terms of the trust, but it would be difficult to argue that he is reckless, or dishonest. His position therefore requires consideration of the knowledge requirements for knowing receipt, which were considered in detail in answer to the essay question above.

It may be that Soggs is not a knowing receiver at all, however, since when considering liability for knowing receipt, Millett J said in *Agip Africa* (at p. 1388F): 'the recipient must have received the property for his own use and benefit.' Here, Soggs has agreed merely to transmit the money to someone else, so may be able to avoid liability on that ground. Millett J's views are directed specifically towards the liability of banks for money in customer's accounts, however, and may not necessarily be of any more general application.

This problem is a bad problem, in that three of the names are very similar, which can cause unnecessary confusion. Confusion of this type is by no means unusual in exam papers, however, and you will simply have to be very careful if you are confronted with a question of this type.

Most of the points in the problem can be answered by reference to the previous discussion. There is an additional point, however, which is whether there is a trust at all. No words of trust have been used, and if there is a trust, it can only be on the basis of a *Quistclose* trust (the leading authority being the House of Lords decision in *Barclays Bank Ltd* v *Quistclose Investments Ltd* [1970] AC 567). Before considering the application of *Quistclose* trusts to the problem, I shall consider *Quistclose* trusts in general, and shall then return to the problem. Note that this is done purely for ease of explanation. Do not, in the exam, write all you know about an area before applying it to the problem. Stick to what is directly relevant. Not all of the following section is directly relevant to the problem.

Quistclose trusts in general

The leading authority for the *Quistclose* variety of trust is the House of Lords decision in *Barclays Bank Ltd* v *Quistclose Investments Ltd* [1970] AC 567. The case revolved around Rolls Razor Ltd, who were in serious financial difficulties, and had an overdraft with Barclays Bank of some £484,000, against a permitted limit of £250,000. If Rolls Razor were to stay in business, it was essential for them to obtain a loan of around £210,000 in order to pay dividends which they had declared on their ordinary shares, and which in the absence of such a loan they were unable to pay. They succeeded in obtaining the loan from Quistclose Investments Ltd, who agreed to make the loan on the condition 'that it is used to pay the forthcoming dividend due on July 24, next'. The sum was paid into a special account with Barclays Bank, on the condition (agreed with the bank) that the account would 'only be used to meet the dividend due on July 24, 1964'.

Rolls Razor went into voluntary liquidation on 27 August, without having paid the dividend. Barclays wanted to count the money in the special account against Rolls Razor's overdraft, but the House of Lords held that Barclays held the money on trust for Quistclose, so that Quistclose was able to claim back the entire sum. Lord Wilberforce stated, at p. 580:

> The mutual intention of the respondents [Quistclose] and of Rolls Razor Ltd, and the essence of the bargain, was that the sum advanced should not become part of the assets of Rolls Razor Ltd, but should be used exclusively for payment of a particular class of creditors, namely, those entitled to the dividend. A necessary consequence of this, simply by process of interpretation, must be that, if for any reason, the dividend could not be paid, the money was to be returned to the respondents: the word 'only' or 'exclusively' can have no other meaning or effect.
>
> That arrangements of this character for the payment of a person's creditors by a third person, give rise to a relationship of a fiduciary character or trust, in favour, as a primary trust, of the creditors, and secondarily, if the primary trust fails, of the third person, has been recognised in a series of cases over some 150 years.

The effect of the decision, of course, was that the money loaned by Quistclose was secured from the consequences of Rolls Razor's bankruptcy, since it never became part of Rolls Razor's general assets.

The decision seems to depend on the fact that the money was to be used for a specific purpose, that that purpose was known to the recipient, and that the money was paid into a special account, which could be used for no other purpose. The last requirement, for a special account, may not be absolutely rigid, but at the very least the money must be earmarked for the particular purpose *and no other*, in order to negative the inference that the payments are to be included in the general assets of the company. In the absence of such a requirement, a prospective purchaser through a car import company, for example, who pays a deposit of £1,000 for the purpose of importing a car, would be able to reclaim that £1,000 in the event of the car import company going into liquidation before the car is obtained. The payment, after all, is made for a particular purpose, which is known to the recipient (the company), but except in the unlikely event that the company can use that money for *no purpose other* than obtaining the car, the prospective purchaser is not protected on *Quistclose* principles. The position is somewhat similar to cases where money has been paid to a company for the purpose of obtaining an allotment of shares, but no trust has been held to have been created. Commenting on those cases, Lord Wilberforce said (at p. 581):

I do not think it necessary to examine these cases in detail, nor to comment on them, for I am satisfied that they do not effect the principle on which this appeal should be decided. They are merely examples which show that, in the absence of some special arrangement creating a trust . . ., payments of this kind are made on the basis that they are to be included in the company's assets. They do not negative the proposition that a trust may exist where the mutual intention is that they should not.

The setting up of a special fund negates the inference that the payments are to be included in the company's assets, but so long as that inference is negated, it may be that a special fund is not absolutely necessary. In *Re EVTR* [1987] BCLC 646, for example, the appellant, Barber, who had just won £240,000 on premium bonds, agreed to assist a company for whom he had worked in purchasing new equipment. He accordingly deposited £60,000 with the solicitors to the company, and authorised them to release it 'for the sole purpose of buying new equipment'. The money was not paid into a special fund, but was paid out by the company in pursuit of the purpose. Before the new equipment was delivered EVTR went into receivership. The Court of Appeal held that Barber was entitled to recover his money (or at any rate, the balance of £48,536, after agreed deductions) on *Quistclose* principles. Dillon LJ also thought (at p. 649):

> in the light of *Quistclose*, that if the company had gone into liquidation, or the receivers had been appointed, and the scheme had become abortive before the £60,000 had been disbursed by the company, the appellant would have been entitled to recover his full £60,000, as between himself and the company, on the footing that it was impliedly held by the company on a resulting trust for him as the particular purpose of the loan had failed.

At this stage, however, the money would not have been held in a special account, but the inference that it was intended to be included as part of the general assets would have been negated by other factors. The existence of a special account does not appear, then, to be absolutely essential, so long as the inference that the payments are to be included in the company's assets is negated.

On the question of the bank's notice, in *Quistclose* the money was given to Rolls Razor and not to Barclays themselves on trust, so that the principles applicable to Barclays' liability as constructive trustees were (presumably) the same as those discussed in the section on knowing receipt, above. In *Quistclose* itself, Lord Wilberforce commented (at p. 582):

It is common ground, and I think right, that a mere request to put the money into a separate account is not sufficient to constitute notice. But [in this case] . . . there is no doubt that the bank was told that the money had been provided on loan by a third person and was to be used only for the purpose of paying the dividend. This was sufficient to give them notice that it was trust money and not assets of Rolls Razor Ltd: the fact, if it be so, that they were unaware of the lender's identity (though the respondent's name as drawer was on the cheque) is of no significance.

He went on to say that the bank were also aware that Rolls Razor could not themselves, without a loan from an outside source, provide the money to pay the dividend, and that the bank never contemplated that the money so provided could be used to reduce the existing overdraft.

For the purposes of *Quistclose*-type trusts, it does not seem to matter where the money comes from. In *Quistclose* itself it was a loan made voluntarily by a third party. *EVTR* also involved a voluntary disposition. In *Carreras Rothmans Ltd* v *Freeman Mathews Treasure Ltd* [1985] Ch 207, on the other hand, the money paid into the special account was money that Carreras Rothmans (CR) were contractually obliged to pay to Freeman Mathews Treasure (FMT) in any event. Applying *Quistclose*, however, Peter Gibson J held that the money in the special account was held on trust.

The plaintiff (cigarette manufacturers) engaged the defendant advertising agency. The defendant contracted as principal with production agencies and advertising media. The arrangement was that CR paid a monthly fee to FMT, which was used:

(a)   as payment in arrears for FMT's services, and
(b)   to enable FMT to pay debts incurred to agency and media creditors

The defendant (FMT) got into financial difficulties, but needed funds to pay its production agencies and advertising media, if it was to carry on acting for the plaintiff.

Carreras Rothmans also knew that if FMT went into liquidation still owing money to media creditors, the media creditors would have sufficient commercial power to compel CR to pay, and therefore (although they were not legally obliged to do so) they would in practice have to pay twice over. An agreement was therefore made between CR and FMT whereby the plaintiffs would pay a monthly sum into a special account at the defendant's bank, the money to be used 'only for the purposes of meeting the accounts of the media and production fees of third parties directly attributable to CR's involvement with the agency'. The first payment (of just under £600,000) was made at the end of July, covering debts incurred in June. Unlike the position in the cases discussed above, however, this was money which CR owed to FMT in any event.

The defendant went into liquidation before the debts were cleared. CR immediately found another advertising agency, and so that its advertising campaign would not be jeopardised, paid the debts of the media creditors, taking assignments of those debts. Of the money in the special account, Peter Gibson J held that it was held by FMT (and hence by the liquidator) on trust, since it had been paid for a specific purpose, and he made an order requiring the liquidator to carry out that purpose (i.e., payment to the third parties). He did not think (at pp. 221–2) it relevant that CR was under a contractual obligation to pay the money to FMT in any event, noting (at p. 222C–E) that:

> if the common intention is that property is transferred for a specific purpose and not so as to become the property of the transferee, the transferee cannot keep the property if for any reason that purpose cannot be fulfilled. I am left in no doubt that the provider of the moneys in the present case was the plaintiff. True it is that its own witnesses said that if the defendant had not agreed to the terms of the contract letter, the plaintiff would not have broken its contract but would have paid its debt to the defendant, but the fact remains that the plaintiff made its payment on the terms of that letter and the defendant received the moneys only for the stipulated purpose. That purpose was expressed to relate only to the moneys in the account. In my judgment therefore the plaintiff can be equated with the lender in the *Quistclose* case as having an enforceable right to compel the carrying out of the primary trust.

In both *Quistclose* and *EVTR*, the provider of the money was able to claim it back, the primary purpose of the trust having failed. In *Carreras Rothmans* the primary trust could still be carried out, and the order made was to that effect (presumably the court would have been reluctant in any event to order repayment to Carreras Rothmans themselves, given that this was money owed by CR under contract). Peter Gibson J even thought (at p. 223) that the third-party creditors might themselves have had enforceable rights, but at the end of the day it was CR, as provider of the money, who was able to apply for the order. It is also clear from *Quistclose* itself (at p. 581) that it is the provider of the money who can enforce the trust, that:

> the lender acquires an equitable right to see that [the money advanced]

is applied for the primary designated purpose . . . if the primary purpose cannot be carried out, the question arises if a secondary purpose (i.e., repayment to the lender) has been agreed, expressly or by implication: if it has, the remedies of equity may be invoked to give effect to it . . .

It is also the view of PJ Millett QC (as he then was), counsel for CR, that the provider of the moneys, and only he, can usually enforce a *Quistclose* trust: (1985) 101 LQR 269, at pp. 290-91

Quistclose trusts and the problem

It is obvious that not all the above discussion is relevant to the problem. The points raised in *Carreras Rothmans*, for example, do not arise, since Bloggs was not a debtor of Cloggs, nor was he under any prior obligation to pay any money to him. The money belonged beneficially to Bloggs, and was paid to Cloggs voluntarily. It was for a specific purpose, and the contingency of failure was also provided for. The transaction appears to be almost on all fours with *Quistclose* itself, except that the money was not put into a separate account. Nevertheless, it does not appear that the money was ever in fact mixed with Cloggs's general funds (is that relevant?), and my own reading of the facts is that it was probably never intended to be. I would suggest, therefore, that a *Quistclose* trust is probably established here.

Do not worry unduly, incidentally, if there are insufficient facts in a problem to enable you to decide an issue one way or the other. In this problem, for example, while it is *reasonably* clear that Bloggs never intended the money to be mixed in with Cloggs's general funds, it is not clear beyond doubt. This is probably deliberate, the examiner intending that you should discuss both possibilities.

BIBLIOGRAPHY

H.G. Hanbury and R.H. Maudsley, *Modern Equity*, 13th ed. by Jill E. Martin (London: Sweet & Maxwell, 1989).

B.W. Harvey, *Settlements of Land* (London: Sweet & Maxwell, 1973).

D.J. Hayton and O.R. Marshall, *Cases and Commentary on the Law of Trusts*, 9th ed. by D.J. Hayton (London: Sweet & Maxwell, 1991).

R.H. Maudsley, *The Modern Law of Perpetuities* (London: Butterworths, 1979).

R.H. Maudsley and E.H. Burn, *Maudsley and Burn's Trusts and Trustees: Cases and Materials*, 4th ed. by E.H. Burn (London: Butterworths, 1990).

A.J. Oakley, *Constructive Trusts*, 2nd ed. (London: Sweet & Maxwell, 1987).

P.H. Pettit, *Equity and the Law of Trusts*, 6th ed. (London: Butterworths, 1989).

P. Todd, *Textbook on Trusts* (London: Blackstone Press, 1991).

INDEX

TITLES IN THE SERIES